The Data-Driven School

The Guilford Practical Intervention in the Schools Series

Kenneth W. Merrell, Founding Editor
Sandra M. Chafouleas, Series Editor

www.guilford.com/practical

This series presents the most reader-friendly resources available in key areas of evidence-based practice in school settings. Practitioners will find trustworthy guides on effective behavioral, mental health, and academic interventions, and assessment and measurement approaches. Covering all aspects of planning, implementing, and evaluating high-quality services for students, books in the series are carefully crafted for everyday utility. Features include ready-to-use reproducibles, lay-flat binding to facilitate photocopying, appealing visual elements, and an oversized format. Recent titles have Web pages where purchasers can download and print the reproducible materials.

Recent Volumes

Evidence-Based Strategies for Effective Classroom Management
David M. Hulac and Amy M. Briesch

School-Based Observation: A Practical Guide to Assessing Student Behavior
Amy M. Briesch, Robert J. Volpe, and Randy G. Floyd

Helping Students Overcome Social Anxiety:
Skills for Academic and Social Success (SASS)
Carrie Masia Warner, Daniela Colognori, and Chelsea Lynch

Executive Skills in Children and Adolescents, Third Edition:
A Practical Guide to Assessment and Intervention
Peg Dawson and Richard Guare

Effective Universal Instruction:
An Action-Oriented Approach to Improving Tier 1
Kimberly Gibbons, Sarah Brown, and Bradley C. Niebling

Supporting Successful Interventions in Schools:
Tools to Plan, Evaluate, and Sustain Effective Implementation
Lisa M. Hagermoser Sanetti and Melissa A. Collier-Meek

High-Impact Assessment Reports for Children and Adolescents:
A Consumer-Responsive Approach
Robert Lichtenstein and Bruce Ecker

Conducting School-Based Functional Behavioral Assessments, Third Edition:
A Practitioner's Guide
Mark W. Steege, Jamie L. Pratt, Garry Wickerd, Richard Guare, and T. Steuart Watson

Evaluating Educational Interventions, Second Edition:
Single-Case Design for Measuring Response to Intervention
T. Chris Riley-Tillman, Matthew K. Burns, and Stephen P. Kilgus

The Data-Driven School: Collaborating to Improve Student Outcomes
Daniel M. Hyson, Joseph F. Kovaleski, Benjamin Silberglitt, and Jason A. Pedersen

Implementing Classwide PBIS: A Guide to Supporting Teachers
Diane Myers, Brandi Simonsen, and Jennifer Freeman

Social and Emotional Learning in the Classroom, Second Edition:
Promoting Mental Health and Academic Success
Barbara A. Gueldner, Laura L. Feuerborn, and Kenneth W. Merrell

The Data-Driven School

*Collaborating to Improve
Student Outcomes*

DANIEL M. HYSON
JOSEPH F. KOVALESKI
BENJAMIN SILBERGLITT
JASON A. PEDERSEN

THE GUILFORD PRESS
New York   London

Library of Congress Cataloging-in-Publication Data is available from the publisher.

ISBN: 978-1-4625-4306-9 (paperback)

The online Data Book PowerPoint template that accompanies this book was created by Dan Hyson
while he was employed at Hiawatha Valley Education District in Winona, MN. Hiawatha Valley
Education District is the sole owner of all rights, title, and interest in that template.

About the Authors

Daniel M. Hyson, PhD, NCSP, is Assistant Professor in the School Psychology Graduate Program at the University of Wisconsin–La Crosse. Previously, Dr. Hyson was a school psychologist in Minnesota public schools. He then served as Data Management Coordinator for Hiawatha Valley Education District, a consortium of 13 school districts in southeastern Minnesota. In that role, he consulted with teachers and administrators to help them access, interpret, and use data from academic and behavioral assessments to improve instruction for all students. Dr. Hyson's research interests include teacher–student relationships and their association with student engagement and achievement, and the school psychologist's role in systems-level consultation and data-driven decision making.

Joseph F. Kovaleski, DEd, NCSP, is Professor Emeritus of Educational and School Psychology at Indiana University of Pennsylvania, where he was Director of the Doctoral Program in School Psychology from 2003 to 2017. He now consults with school districts and state departments of education. Dr. Kovaleski directed Pennsylvania's Instructional Support Team Project and served as a university consultant for Pennsylvania's Multi-Tiered System of Support Initiative. He has published numerous articles and book chapters on response to intervention (RTI) and data-based decision making, and presents frequently at national and state conferences. He is coauthor (with Jason A. Pedersen) of a chapter on data-analysis teaming in *Best Practices in School Psychology, Sixth Edition*, and coauthor (with Amanda M. VanDerHeyden and Edward S. Shapiro) of *The RTI Approach to Evaluating Learning Disabilities*.

Benjamin Silberglitt, PhD, is Executive Director of Research, Outcomes, and Implementation at Intermediate District 287, a consortium of 11 school districts in the Twin Cities metropolitan area in Minnesota. He has founded, launched, and led the implementation of multiple education technology products since the early 2000s. Dr. Silberglitt is a cofounder of Cedar Labs, a universal data integration platform with statewide implementations in the

United States and Australia. He regularly consults with school districts and presents on the effective use of data to support decision making.

Jason A. Pedersen, PhD, NCSP, is a school psychologist in the Derry Township School District in Hershey, Pennsylvania. He has worked with school staff to develop a comprehensive K–12 curriculum to foster and promote resilience, and he previously spearheaded schoolwide positive behavior support, RTI, and multi-tiered systems of support (MTSS) initiatives. Dr. Pedersen is coauthor (with Joseph F. Kovaleski) of a chapter on data-analysis teaming in *Best Practices in School Psychology, Sixth Edition,* as well as several articles in peer-reviewed journals. He has given numerous presentations on MTSS and RTI at the local, state, and national levels, and has consulted with school districts in Pennsylvania, New York, New Jersey, and Texas.

Acknowledgments

We would like to express our appreciation to:

Jim Appleton, friend and colleague of Dan Hyson and Ben Silberglitt, for his integral involvement with earlier drafts of a related book proposal;

Stefanie Eggert, Amanda Yenter, Lauren Nixon, Joe Converse, Rachel Pfarr, and Kayla Scheevel, Dan's University of Wisconsin–La Crosse school psychology graduate students, for their essential contributions to a wide variety of elements of this book;

Natalie Graham and T. Chris Riley-Tillman, for their critical feedback, patience, and support during the long and winding journey to this book's completion; and

A range of coffee shops in Minnesota and Wisconsin, for providing Dan with homes away from his home or office as he tried to find places to write where he could be both relaxed and productive.

Contents

Introduction

Data geeks have a way of finding one another. Prior to joining forces on this project, this book's coauthors were working over a thousand miles apart addressing overlapping and complementary issues related to systems-level data-driven decision making, but knowing little about what each was doing.

Ben Silberglitt and Dan Hyson had been trained as school psychologists around the same time at the University of Minnesota, an institution long well-known for its training emphasis on the essential role of the school psychologist in data-driven decision making at the district, school, grade, and classroom levels. Both have also since worked in a similar systems-level data leader role within an educational cooperative serving multiple school districts and have extensive background in using and training others to use student management systems, single-function technology tools (e.g., AIMSweb, FastBridge Learning, Northwest Evaluation Association [NWEA], Star assessments), and data warehouses. Ben and Dan, in fact, wrote a chapter in the sixth edition of *Best Practices in School Psychology* on the topic of best practices in using technology for data-driven decision making (Silberglitt & Hyson, 2014).

Starting in 2008, along with their colleague Jim Appleton, Ben and Dan began copresenting a series of workshops for school psychologists at the state and national levels focused on creating and building what they at that time referred to as a "data-driven culture," but what in this book we now refer to as a "data-driven school." In response to the interest attendees at their workshops expressed in maintaining ongoing communication with one another and with the presenters, and exchanging ideas and resources, Ben and Dan created a National Association of School Psychologists (NASP) interest group and online community for school psychologists playing systems-level data-driven decision-making roles.

Finally, Ben, Dan, and Jim concluded that to more effectively support the data-driven decision-making needs of a greater number of school psychologists, as well as other school data leaders, they needed to collaborate on a book. They were particularly interested in having the book provide readers with practical resources, both in print form and/or through an associated CD or website, and target readers with a range of experience serving in systems-level data-driven decision-making roles, including both those new to the role and those with more extensive interest or experience. They proposed this idea to a publisher in 2011, but despite initial interest, it never came to fruition.

Meanwhile, over a thousand miles away in Pennsylvania, Joe Kovaleski and Jason Pedersen had been trained (years apart) in the Penn State School Psychology Program and began piloting data-analysis teams while working together in a school district in central Pennsylvania. Prior to that, Joe had spent the 1990s directing the Instructional Support Team Project for the Pennsylvania Department of Education, and had written and presented extensively on team-based collaboration in the schools. When universal screening was developed later in that decade, Joe and Jason made the link between more available and timely assessment data and the team collaboration process. Their work together led to chapters on data-analysis teaming in the two most recent editions of *Best Practices in School Psychology* (2008 and 2014). In addition, both were active consultants to the rollout of the multi-tiered system of support (MTSS) project in Pennsylvania, as well as to school systems in other states.

These two worlds of data geeks began to collide in 2012 when Joe presented a virtual training on data-analysis teaming to the Minnesota Department of Education (MDE) response to intervention (RTI) community of practice (COP), of which Dan was a member. The COP had been interested in learning more about earlier versions of the data-analysis teaming recording forms and processes described in Chapters 6 and 7 of this book. Having been introduced through this training, Dan, Joe, Jason, and two other colleagues decided to propose and subsequently present a symposium at the NASP annual convention in February 2013 in Seattle, Washington (Hyson, Pederson, Richardson, McNamara, & Kovaleski, 2013), addressing their varying perspectives on and experiences with the school psychologist's role in data-analysis teaming.

Following the symposium, Joe approached Dan to ask whether he would be interested in joining Joe and Jason in pursuing a book proposal. As they discussed the proposal, they realized that it appeared to nicely complement the goals of the book that Ben, Dan, and Jim had been working on. Dan, Joe, Jason, and Ben therefore decided to combine the book ideas into one proposal. It was this combined proposal that eventually led to what you will read in this book. Due to other commitments, Jim was unable to continue to be involved in the project. Ben and Dan, however, owe an immeasurable debt of gratitude to Jim for his significant contributions to the workshops, interest group, and online community, and to the initial planning for the previous version of this book proposal. Without his input, this book would not have been possible.

In developing this book, we have drawn on our individual and collective experiences and work in developing data-driven schools. We represent practitioners, systems-level data leaders and trainers, and have worked across a broad range of school districts—large and small; rural, suburban, and urban; with various student demographics; both in consortia and individual districts. Through our work, we have gained experience with many aspects of the use of data by school districts, including training teachers, school psychologists, other related services personnel, school and district administrators, and school boards; analyzing data and presenting results to stakeholders to guide decisions at all levels, from the system to the individual student; and managing and streamlining the use of data.

When we use the term *data leader* here and throughout this book, we are referring to individuals, like us in our current or former roles, who value and utilize data. Data leaders include central-office administrators, school principals, department heads, specialists, lead teachers, and anyone else in a school system who uses data to inform decision making. We see these data leaders as not needing to be experts in organizing, analyzing, and sharing individual student, classroom, grade-level, schoolwide, and districtwide academic and behavioral data. They should, however, have the potential to develop and be interested in developing skills in these areas, as well as, where appropriate, using technology and facilitating training and collaborative discussions with and among staff regarding accessing these data themselves and interpreting and using the data to improve student outcomes. When we use this term, we do not (necessarily) mean institutional research staff. While institutional research staff may serve as data leaders in the ways highlighted above, they more traditionally serve instead as experts in sophisticated data analyses and/or in the use of technology to organize, analyze, and share data. These individuals tend to spend most of their time in an office creating data reports in isolation and then distributing them to staff, rather than facilitating collaborative discussions among staff about the data and building the capacity of staff to access, interpret, and use the data themselves.

While we have each served in a variety of functions, we have noticed that our roles have shared a common thread—providing leadership to districts to promote the effective and appropriate use of data. It has been our experience that the schools we have worked with are too often "data rich, information poor" (DRIP; Goodwin, 1996; Slotnik & Orland, 2010), gathering a great deal of student performance data, but not consistently using it to make instructional decisions. We are each regularly asked by educators and parents with whom we consult, "Are we testing kids too much?" Our typical response is "No, not if educators can be trained to interpret the data and are provided with the time and resources to use it to make decisions." If educators are trained and provided with the time and resources to interpret and use the data they are gathering, then we would argue that the time used for testing is worth it, because it will allow the educators to more efficiently and effectively identify district, school, grade, classroom, and individual student needs and interventions to address them. The school districts with which we have worked have frequently discussed limiting the number of times they administer or discontinuing administration of the computerized adaptive tests they are currently administering as screening tools two to three times per year. They often defend their proposed decisions by pointing out that their teachers are not using the results and that test administration takes too long and ties up their computer labs. Before they follow through on this decision, however, we caution the districts to ask themselves two questions:

1. Have teachers been trained and provided with the time and resources to interpret and use the data being gathered?
2. If they were to limit the number of times they administer or discontinue administration of the tests under consideration, what alternative information would they use to make decisions?

If the district has not adequately trained teachers or provided them with the time and resources to interpret and use the data, we would argue that they need to do this first and give the data a chance to make a difference in instruction and student outcomes before making a decision to limit or discontinue administration of the assessment—that is, unless the answer to the second question above is that the district has other reliable and valid measures that they are already administering and using to make the same decisions, discontinuing an assessment may not be warranted.

Other districts we have worked with have demonstrated similar challenges in effectively using the progress monitoring data they are gathering. We are not in support of gathering progress monitoring data only for the sake of gathering it without using it to make instructional decisions. We have worked with schools that gather months and months of weekly progress monitoring data on students, but only very rarely look at it to make decisions about adjusting instruction. We believe that if progress monitoring data are to be useful, schools must make the time and provide the resources to teachers to examine the data and make and document adjustments to instruction.

Our aim in this book is to help practitioners make decisions about the use of assessment data in their schools. We believe that our unique perspectives and complementary skill sets have allowed us to create a book that is practical, with specific ideas and strategies that we ourselves have used successfully in schools; broad based, with a range of tools that will support readers with a similarly wide range of skills; and timely, with a focus on topics and issues that are facing schools today. We know that educators are busy and at times need data leaders to simply provide them with answers to their questions. At the same time, however, we also recognize from experience that the expert model is not sustainable over the long term. Instead, we intend through this book to build the capacity of teachers, school psychologists, and administrators to engage in effective systems-level data-driven decision making themselves.

HOW THIS BOOK IS DIFFERENT

We believe that this book is different from others you may have read regarding systems-level data-driven decision making for several important reasons. First, we bring to the project unique and varied backgrounds. We have direct service experience, having served as teachers, school psychology practitioners, and administrators within schools. In addition, we have also been data leaders at the school, district, and educational cooperative levels.

Second, we believe that this book sets itself apart from other similar volumes in its strong emphasis on practical district-, school-, grade-, and classroom-level examples to illustrate concepts. At the beginning of each chapter, you will find a "Roadmap" section that provides a concise overview to guide you through the chapter. At the end of each chapter, there is a "Key Issues" section that gives a summary of key issues for educators stemming from the material shared in the chapter. Case studies are embedded throughout the book as well, offering more detailed examples of applications of concepts discussed in the chapter, drawn from our practical experiences. Reproducible forms and activities are included in Chapters 6 and 7 and Appendices 1 and 3. Purchasers of the book can download and print the reproducible materials and access online-only data spreadsheets and PowerPoint templates for data presentations (see the box at the end of the table of contents).

The third critical way in which this book is different involves the comprehensiveness of its approach, addressing the critical importance within a data-driven school or district of:

1. Systems-level problem solving,
2. Data-analysis teaming,
3. Technology, and
4. Relationships at all levels of the school community.

Other books cover one or two of these areas, but few, if any, address all four in an integrated volume. The role of relationships is particularly unique to this text. We repeatedly argue in this book that a data-driven school or district cannot be created or maintained by one data leader. Effective data leaders are able to successfully cultivate followers and facilitate buy-in from a range of stakeholders through their combination of emotional–social intelligence and leadership skills (Goleman, 2011; Svobodny, 2013). Staff in data-driven schools are also provided with the time and resources to engage in focused collaboration with their colleagues during the school day. Finally, once staff identify district-, school-, grade-, classroom-, or student-level needs and interventions to address those needs, the interventions must be delivered within the context of a trusting and responsive teacher–student relationship. Students are much more likely to respond to and benefit from interventions implemented by adults they trust and believe care about them.

The book takes an applied, step-by-step approach to framing the issues, providing specific activities and ideas that readers can use to immediately begin work on building a data-driven school. Because the book is also intended as a teaching tool for graduate programs, we include case studies from districts, schools, and classrooms we have worked with as exemplars of successful and unsuccessful practice. We also include suggestions and case examples on how and when to use tools, such as Microsoft Excel and Microsoft Access, as well as statistical analysis software, such as SPSS and SAS, to solve various data-analysis and data management problems.

Technology is an important aspect of building a data-driven school. Technology has served each of us in our efforts, especially when working with districts in a consortium across a wide geographic area. Through our practice, we have developed skills with technology tools that support communication and online learning, such as wikis, blogs, RSS feeds, learning management systems, and so on.

TARGET AUDIENCE

The primary expected audiences for this book are school- and district-level data leaders, which may include school psychologists, teachers, principals, and central-office administrators, as well as students training to work in any of these roles. School psychologists in particular are often well trained and eager to use the data analysis and consultation skills needed to be effective data leaders in facilitating the systems-level problem-solving and data-analysis teams described within this book. From our experience, however, they are only inconsistently provided with these opportunities within schools. We advocate for their enhanced involvement.

Secondary audiences include other school or central-office administrators with whom those data leaders work, since their support is critical to data leaders being able to effectively serve in their data leader roles. As these administrators increasingly recognize the connection between effective data-driven decision making and improved student performance, more and more of them are taking on instructional leadership roles within their schools and districts. We advocate for their active leadership in this area.

Prospective data leaders with some background knowledge and skill—or at least an interest in and opportunity to become more involved—in systems-level data-driven decision making will likely benefit most from this book. However, we aim to provide a continuum of resources that could meet the needs of novice, advanced, and expert readers.

We believe the audience for a book like this is already substantial and is actively growing. School districts today (especially those implementing initiatives such as MTSS, positive behavioral interventions and supports [PBIS], and/or professional learning communities [PLCs]) should, and often do, have multiple levels of school psychologists, teachers, administrators, and others serving as data leaders at the district, school, grade, and/or content-area levels. In effective schools, all educators, including school psychologists, teachers, and administrators, are committed to and responsible for the learning of all students, not just the students they directly serve on their caseloads, in their classrooms, or in their administrative roles. This book aims to help current and potential future data leaders to work with their administrators and other staff to meet this expectation.

ORGANIZATION OF THE BOOK

Chapter 1 of this book provides a context for understanding the importance of data-driven schools, as well as previewing the overarching systems-level problem-solving framework and key tenets that organize the rest of the book. Chapters 2–4 describe the framework in detail, showing how the problem-solving model most typically used to address the needs of individual students can be applied at the classroom, grade, school, or district level and serve as the engine for decision making within data-driven schools. This framework provides the foundation for discussions of specific tools and processes to be used in data-driven problem solving across these levels throughout the rest of the book. As we describe each step in the systems-level problem-solving process framework, we also review the multiple unique purposes of comprehensive assessment data within the model. Chapters 5–7 describe specific tools and processes that can serve as a roadmap and be used by data leaders to facilitate data-analysis teaming to address both the academic and behavioral needs of students within data-driven classrooms, grades, schools, or districts. Finally, Chapters 8 and 9 provide guidance for data-driven schools in building their capacity for data-driven problem solving across contexts through effectively using their technology resources, and identifying and fostering the growth of data leaders and initiating and sustaining relationships among administrators, staff, students, and community members connected with a data-driven school.

PART I

THE ENGINE FOR A DATA-DRIVEN SCHOOL
Systems-Level Problem Solving

CHAPTER 1

The Rationale and Context for a Data-Driven School

ROADMAP

1. A story of systems-level problem solving and relationships in a data-driven school
2. The need for data-driven schools
3. Key tenets of a data-driven school
    a. Strong leadership with buy-in from key stakeholders
    b. A comprehensive assessment system
        i. *Activity:* Identifying Gaps in Your Comprehensive Assessment System (Appendix 1)
    c. Easy access to appropriate data for all staff
    d. The time and resources for all staff to examine these data
    e. Clear connections between data and potential interventions at the district, school, and classroom levels
4. The data-driven school and MTSS

The following story, based on our experiences as data leaders, highlights the importance of systems-level problem solving and relationships in building a data-driven school.

Midway through the school year, third-grade teachers reported that office discipline referrals (ODRs) involving their students were significantly higher that year than would have been expected based on trends from past years and ODRs for other grades that year. After this problem was identified, it was brought to the school building leadership team for further discussion and analysis. The team included the principal, the assistant principal, general education teachers, special education teachers, and other related services personnel, such as the school social worker, school nurse, and school psychologist. The team agreed that the most important first step was to review the ODR data to determine when the referrals were most often occurring and who was involved. They found that the incidents leading to the referrals most frequently occurred on the playground and that seven third-grade boys accounted for a significant percentage of the referrals.

To further analyze the problem, the team decided to interview the seven target students and their parents to find out more about the students. They discovered that all seven students lived in the same low-income housing project 1 mile from the school. Furthermore, the students and their parents told the team that, while the housing project did have a playground, the seven boys did not use the playground because they and their parents did not see it as safe. The team then observed the seven students on the playground at school and saw that they did not play during recess, but instead walked around the outside of the playground picking fights with other children. Based on this analysis of the problem, the team hypothesized that the problem seemed to occur because the seven students lacked the skills to engage in cooperative play at recess and/or needed more practice to effectively demonstrate the skills.

To address this problem, the team developed and implemented a two-part plan. First, they worked with the school's physical education teachers to identify and teach cooperative games to all third-grade students, including but not limited to the seven target students, during their regular physical education classes. Once the students had learned the cooperative games, members of the leadership team went out on the playground during the third-grade recess time and helped all third-grade students play the games. As the plan was implemented, the team continued to gather data on ODRs for all third-grade students, including the seven target students.

To evaluate the effectiveness of the plan, the team first examined changes in third-grade ODR data. They found that the percentage of referrals coming from third-grade students had declined significantly, including specifically a marked decline among the seven target students. It is important to note as well that the target students showed improved relationships with their teachers and increased student achievement despite the fact that neither of those were outcomes that had been a focus of the intervention plan.

Most educators are familiar with the steps involved in problem solving regarding individual student academic and behavior problems, as illustrated in Figure 1.1 (Batsche & Knoff, 1995; Knoff, 2002), but fewer of them have explicitly used the problem-solving model to address problems at the classroom, school, or district level.

The story above shows how the problem-solving model can be used to address a schoolwide problem. It particularly highlights the importance of the problem analysis step of this systems-level problem-solving model. By carefully analyzing the problem and answering the question "Why is the problem occurring?", the leadership team was able to narrow the focus of the problem to the playground and to seven target students. The team was also able to uncover the fact that the target students might not have the skills—or ability to consistently demonstrate the skills—necessary to behave appropriately on the playground.

Relationships were also critical to the story. Administrator–staff relationships were critical in forming the school building leadership team and ensuring its effectiveness. Staff–staff relationships were critical in allowing the team to feel comfortable sharing data and

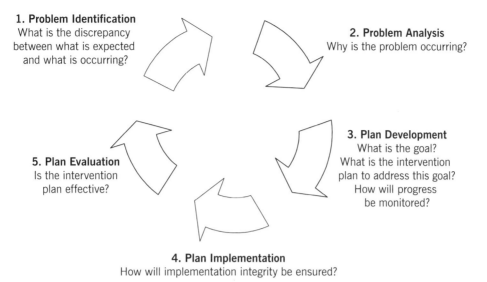

FIGURE 1.1. Problem-solving model. Reprinted with permission from St. Croix River Education District, Rush City, Minnesota.

collaborating with one another. Staff–student relationships were critical in helping the target students not only decrease their ODRs but also improve their achievement following the intervention. And staff–family relationships were critical in making the parents of the target students feel comfortable enough to share information about their children.

This story exemplifies the goal of this book. We believe that schools can solve many problems, both academic and behavioral, for both individual students and groups of students, by collecting meaningful and useful data, and having school teams use the problem-solving process to analyze the data and create workable plans to address the problem. Each step of the systems-level problem-solving model illustrated in the story is discussed in greater detail in Chapters 2–4. The importance of relationships and making connections at all levels within the school community in building a data-driven school, as demonstrated in the story, is the focus of Chapter 9.

The problem-solving model (Batsche & Knoff, 1995; Knoff, 2002) is a useful framework for guiding the process of using data to continually inform decision making. What we strive to present in this book is the idea that this same model is effective at all levels of the organization. At the district and school levels, the types of data may be slightly different, or they may be aggregations of data from those used at the individual level, but the questions to be asked and the decision-making process to walk through can be parallel to those used at the classroom and individual levels. In Table 1.1, we present the different types of data that might be accessed, the roles involved, and the processes that lead to data-based decision making at the district, school, grade, classroom, and individual levels, across both academic and behavioral data.

In order to help connect Table 1.1 to the problem-solving model and cue the reader to what level of the organization we are discussing, throughout the book we provide a visual of the problem-solving model with different levels of the organization at its center. See Figures 1.2 and 1.3 (on p. 14) for examples.

TABLE 1.1. A Consistent Data-Based Decision-Making Process at All Levels of the Organization, with Different Roles, Processes, and Data Used to Implement the Same Problem-Solving Model

Who's involved	What happens	Data used
	District-level planning	
District leadership teams • District leaders • Principals • Teacher representatives • Specialist representatives	Planning for strategic direction • Identify districtwide areas of need and resource focus (i.e., specific academic/behavioral areas) • Identify schools needing additional support and resources • Identify performance inequities through data disaggregation • Evaluate effectiveness of districtwide core curricula and supplemental intervention programs	Key performance indicator data • State assessments • Academic screening • Behavior screening and referrals • Student engagement assessments • Fidelity of implementation data • Resource allocation equity data
	School-level planning	
School improvement teams • District leader representative • Principal • Teacher representatives • Specialist representatives	Developing and implementing school improvement plans • Tier 1 priorities for focus • Resource allocation needs • Goal-setting and action steps for implementation • Focus of PLCs/data teams Evaluating fidelity of implementation of core curricula and supplemental intervention programs Planning for schoolwide PBIS program • School rules • Token economy • Reinforcement of positive behavior Evaluating fidelity of implementation of PBIS program	Key performance indicator data • Academic screening • Behavior screening and referrals • Student engagement assessments • Fidelity of implementation data • Resource allocation equity data School improvement data • Goal attainment • Fidelity of planned action steps
	Grade-level, class-level, and student-level planning	
	Tier 1	
Grade-level teams • Principal • Teachers • Specialists	Planning for core instruction • Whole-class instruction • Small-group differentiation	• Universal screening (benchmark testing) results • State test results
Grade-level teams • Principal • Teachers • Specialists	Implementing schoolwide PBIS program • Fidelity • Evaluation of impact and where additional supports may be needed	• ODRs • Behavior screeners • Classroom-level data

(continued)

TABLE 1.1. *(continued)*

Who's involved	What happens	Data used
	Tier 2	
Grade-level teams • Principal • Teachers • Specialists	Planning for supplemental academic interventions • Identification of deficient students • Assignment of students to intervention groups • Identification of supplemental interventions Evaluation of efficacy of supplemental academic interventions • Evaluation of fidelity of interventions • Evaluation of students' response to intervention	• Universal screening (benchmark testing) results • Progress monitoring data • Intervention fidelity data
Grade-level teams • Principal • Teachers • Specialists	Planning for supportive behavioral and emotional interventions • Identification of students needing support • Assignment of students to support groups • Identification of supplemental individual interventions Evaluation of efficacy of behavioral and emotional interventions • Evaluation of fidelity of interventions • Evaluation of students' response to intervention	• ODRs • Behavior screeners • Classroom-level data • Intervention fidelity data
	Tier 3	
Grade-level teams • Principal • Teachers • Specialists	Planning for intensive academic interventions • Identification of students making insufficient progress in supplemental interventions • Identification of intensive interventions Evaluation of efficacy of intensive academic interventions • Evaluation of fidelity of interventions • Evaluation of students' response to intervention	• Drill-down assessment data • Progress monitoring data • Intervention fidelity data
Grade-level teams • Principal • Teachers • Specialists	Planning for intensive behavioral and emotional interventions • Identification of students making insufficient progress in supportive interventions • Identification of individualized interventions Evaluation of efficacy of behavioral and emotional interventions • Evaluation of fidelity of interventions • Evaluation of students' response to intervention	• Data from functional behavioral assessments • Progress monitoring data • Intervention fidelity data

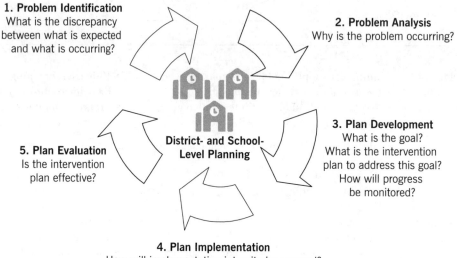

1. Problem Identification
What is the discrepancy between what is expected and what is occurring?

2. Problem Analysis
Why is the problem occurring?

3. Plan Development
What is the goal? What is the intervention plan to address this goal? How will progress be monitored?

District- and School-Level Planning

5. Plan Evaluation
Is the intervention plan effective?

4. Plan Implementation
How will implementation integrity be ensured?

FIGURE 1.2. Using the problem-solving model for district- and school-level planning.

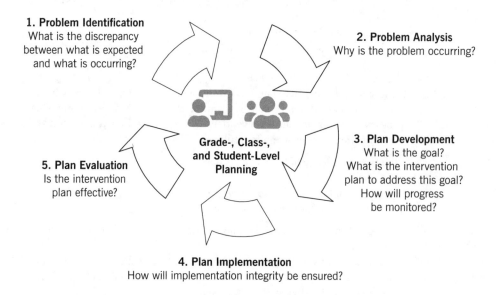

1. Problem Identification
What is the discrepancy between what is expected and what is occurring?

2. Problem Analysis
Why is the problem occurring?

3. Plan Development
What is the goal? What is the intervention plan to address this goal? How will progress be monitored?

Grade-, Class-, and Student-Level Planning

5. Plan Evaluation
Is the intervention plan effective?

4. Plan Implementation
How will implementation integrity be ensured?

FIGURE 1.3. Using the problem-solving model for grade-, class-, and student-level planning.

THE NEED FOR DATA-DRIVEN SCHOOLS

Federal legislative, policy, and societal changes since the turn of the 21st century have contributed to increased attention on the importance of building a data-driven school like the one described in the opening anecdote. For example, the No Child Left Behind Act (NCLB; 2001), as well as the most recent reauthorization of the Elementary and Secondary Education Act (ESEA), renamed the Every Student Succeeds Act (ESSA; 2015), have highlighted the importance of schools assessing and meeting the needs of all students, including those from special population subgroups, such as minority students and students receiving free/reduced-price lunch and special education services. The Individuals with Disabilities Education Improvement Act of 2004 (IDEIA; 2004) stressed the need to implement and use data to monitor the response of at-risk students to research-based interventions. Data-driven personnel evaluation models across the country have added a focus in recent years on assessing the impact that individual teachers have on the academic growth and school engagement that their students demonstrate.

All of this has occurred within the context of increased discussion of "big data" and the emerging field of "data science" (Davenport & Patil, 2012). To this point, these discussions have taken place primarily within the business realm. It is therefore not surprising that while the job description and proposed training for data scientists includes an emphasis on technical and statistical expertise and the ability to clearly communicate results to others, it does not appear to address the importance of ongoing systems consultation and problem solving. The data scientist is portrayed as an expert. While we, of course, agree that leaders within data-driven schools need to already have, or be able to develop, expertise in data analysis, we also believe it is equally important, if not more important, that they have expertise in collaborating with other educators to build the skills of these educators in data analysis and help them connect data to changes in instruction and more positive outcomes for students. We see the "data scientist" within schools (referred to in this book as a "data leader") not as self-sufficient but as the facilitator of and catalyst for the creation of a data-driven school.

This book is intended as a guide for these leaders in understanding the systems-level problem-solving process that can serve as the engine of a data-driven school, the data-analysis teaming process that can provide the school with a roadmap for moving forward, and the technology tools and relationships that can help foster future data leaders and build the capacity for creating such a school.

While the need for data-driven schools has become more of a focus in recent years due to the factors described above, it is by no means a new concept. Tiered problem solving and data-driven decision making within schools has a long history in education, dating back at least to the 1970s. Neither will the need for data-driven schools disappear as legislation, policy, or society changes, especially if data-driven schools are presented not as a new initiative with a potentially controversial name and/or associated baggage but as an integrated "way of doing business." We have all had this experience with systems-change efforts in schools in which we have worked. These schools have been successful in fostering effective focused collaboration among staff because they avoided "overfocusing" on the name of the framework involved (e.g., PLCs, instructional support teams) and instead stressed the key tenets of the framework as critical elements of the way the school would be doing business from now on.

KEY TENETS OF A DATA-DRIVEN SCHOOL

In that spirit, we next briefly review the key tenets of a data-driven school that serve as the overarching framework for this book—namely: (1) strong leadership with buy-in from key stakeholders, (2) a comprehensive assessment system, (3) easy access to appropriate data for all staff, (4) the time and resources for all staff to examine these data, and (5) clear connections between data and potential interventions at the district, school, and classroom levels. We believe that following these key tenets is critical in building and sustaining a school culture that embraces and utilizes—rather than pushes out or discredits—data as part of the school's efforts to improve student outcomes. When schools push out and discredit data, it has been our experience that this occurs most often because of a lack of understanding of the data, insufficient belief in the value of the data (e.g., "What you are measuring doesn't matter to me or my students"), and/or fear about how the data will be used (e.g., to evaluate individual teacher performance and determine that teachers "are not doing their job"). To combat these instincts and create a truly data-driven culture within schools, schools must work to develop an atmosphere in which staff trust that (1) they will be provided with the training and support to access and interpret the data they need, (2) while data will be considered, so will teacher observations and professional expertise, (3) all staff "own" all students, and (4) data will be used to identify needs and provide support to staff and students, not to evaluate individual teachers.

Strong Leadership with Buy-In from Key Stakeholders

Administrative support is critical because school and district leaders, like principals and superintendents, are the key decision makers in school districts—they also hold the purse strings. Administrators make the final decisions about the allocation of financial and human capital resources that are essential to the success of initiatives within a data-driven school. That being said, they do not need to be the ones who initiate the transition to a data-driven school. That impetus can come from other data leaders within the school—including general or special education teachers or related services personnel (e.g., school psychologists). If the movement toward creating a data-driven school is to gather momentum and ultimately garner success, however, administrators must be brought on board.

Not only must the initiator of the data-driven movement—if not an administrator—have the support of administration but this initiator also must be able to cultivate the additional buy-in of other key stakeholders. In 2010, Derek Sivers, an American entrepreneur best known for being the founder and former president of CD Baby, an online CD store for independent musicians, delivered a TED Talk entitled "How to Start a Movement" (*www. ted.com/talks/derek_sivers_how_to_start_a_movement*), during which he showed a video depicting a young man dancing awkwardly, but enthusiastically, in a park to music being blasted from a stereo boom box. As Sivers described the potential connection between this video and effective leadership strategies, one by one other young people in the park began joining the initial dancer. One of the key messages demonstrated in this video and explained by Sivers is the importance of "first followers." Sivers stresses that these first followers—in this case, the first people to join the initial dancer—transform the "lone nut" into a "movement."

Not all followers are created equal in a potential data-driven school, however. Malcolm Gladwell (2000), in the popular book *The Tipping Point*, highlights this in a unique and memorable way by describing the essential roles of "connectors," "mavens," and "salespeople" in facilitating systems change. *Connectors* know a lot of people. If they get inspired by a systems change, that inspiration is likely to spread quickly given their numerous connections to others within the system. *Mavens* are not only knowledgeable but are eager to talk to others about what they know. If they begin to learn about a change effort, they will share what they are learning with others, helping to educate the system on the key components of the initiative. Finally, Gladwell highlights the need for *salespeople* as well, people who have the skills to persuade others when they are unconvinced of what they are hearing from connectors or mavens.

We have seen firsthand the importance of paying attention to these special roles of potential stakeholders when an elementary school at which one of us (Hyson) worked was adopting the PLC school reform model. The school's principal at the time recognized that any proposed school reform effort was in danger of being rejected by the school's veteran staff, since they had already been through many other unsuccessful reform efforts over the years. As a result, he intentionally invited a fifth-grade teacher with over 20 years of experience who was well-known and respected by other veteran staff in the building to be a part of the select team of staff that would be involved in intensive initial training in the model, including traveling to Lincolnshire, Illinois, to visit Adlai E. Stevenson High School, where PLC innovator Richard DuFour had been principal and superintendent. If this teacher bought into the potential benefit of PLCs, because she was a key connector, the movement would be much more likely to gain increased momentum among others in the school.

Similarly, we realized through our experience as data coaches with large school districts or cooperatives that a "lone nut" approach to helping schools transform into data-driven schools had little chance of being successful. Instead, we found it more effective to identify cohorts of educators within the schools most likely to take on leadership roles in this effort (i.e., principals, school psychologists, and district assessment coordinators/research and evaluation directors) and conduct a series of face-to-face and virtual communications with these cohorts to cultivate their commitment to and understanding of the key components of the process. These cohorts of individuals were well connected like the fifth-grade teacher in the previous example. Just as important, they were also more likely because of their data-driven roles within their schools to be willing and able to have conversations with others about what they were learning through these face-to-face and virtual communications, thus serving as mavens within Gladwell's (2000) framework as well.

A Comprehensive Assessment System

Another key tenet of a data-driven school that is discussed throughout this book is a comprehensive assessment system. This system must include assessment data for multiple unique purposes:

1. *Screening,* in which all students in a school are assessed using a benchmark formative assessment tool linked to the outcome(s) that the school is working toward (e.g., general outcome measures [GOMs], computer adaptive tests, or common classroom tests of learning standards identified by grade level or content area) to determine whether general education instruction is meeting the needs of all students and to identify which students may need supplemental support to be successful.
2. *Diagnostic,* in which data are used to identify which specific skill or behavior deficits may be getting in the way for students not meeting standards.
3. *Progress monitoring,* in which the growth of students not meeting standards is

tracked using GOMs or skill-specific mastery monitoring tools to see whether they are closing the gap toward standards.

4. *Outcomes,* in which data are used to assess the degree to which students have learned what they have been taught during a predetermined period (e.g., annual state accountability tests, classroom unit tests).

It should be noted that when we use the term *diagnostic* above, we mean the process of conducting a fine-grained analysis of the student's academic or behavioral skills, which is essential to designing interventions that effectively target the student's deficiencies. The term *diagnostic* here does not mean the process of either determining a student's disability category (e.g., specific learning disability [SLD]) or analyzing a student's basic psychological processes (e.g., visual–motor functioning, auditory processing), because these types of assessment have not been empirically validated for the purpose of identifying effective interventions (Burns, 2016). Our approach here favors approaches based on a skills-by-treatment interaction rather than an aptitude-by-treatment interaction.

In a series of interviews conducted with school psychologists across Minnesota, Hyson (2006, 2007a, 2007b) confirmed that this comprehensive assessment system was seen by most interviewees as being a critical building block of a data-driven school. There is a difference, however, between seeing a comprehensive assessment system as a critical building block and implementing it with reliability and validity.

Ensuring the reliability of a comprehensive assessment system is particularly important because assessments must be administered with fidelity if results from those assessments are to be used to make instructional decisions within a data-driven school. Efforts to safeguard the reliability of the system must start with providing sufficient training to those administering or proctoring assessments within the system, as well as to those completing any necessary data entry tasks associated with the assessments. This training should include periodic initial trainings for new staff or staff changing roles, as well as refresher trainings and fidelity checks to guard against drift following an initial training.

Administrators' support is critical to the success of these efforts. Not only must principals and superintendents provide sufficient time for these trainings to occur but if the assessments involve technology, they must also commit to providing the infrastructure and support within the school or district necessary to limit challenges associated with the technology requirements and ensure an efficient and effective response to challenges if they do occur. Finally, within a comprehensive assessment system, assessments should only be used for the purposes for which they are reliable. For example, when differences among individual progress monitoring data points or outcome assessment test strands are being analyzed, data leaders within data-driven schools should remain aware of the error associated with these scores and be careful not to overinterpret small differences. Chapter 9 highlights the need for data leaders to possess and/or develop the data literacy skills necessary for taking a leadership role in these efforts.

The assessments used within a school's comprehensive assessment system must demonstrate adequate validity as well. One of the most critical forms of validity to evaluate within a comprehensive assessment system is criterion validity or the degree to which scores from one assessment are associated with scores on another assessment (typically this other assessment is seen as the "gold-standard" criterion and/or measures some critical outcome). For example, data-driven school personnel should ask themselves: "Are the screening assessments we're using related to the outcomes that our school views as important (e.g., state accountability test results)?" Chapter 2 discusses this issue in greater detail within the context of explaining the process for setting and using targets predicting from screening assessments to outcome assessments. As outlined in Chapter 2, data leaders and practitioners find most useful those screening assessments that research demonstrates to be highly correlated with these outcomes (e.g., reading curriculum-based measures [CBMs]; computerized adaptive tests, such as the NWEA Measures of Academic Progress [MAP] test).

Guaranteeing the "face validity" or acceptability of assessments within a comprehensive assessment system is equally essential. Staff and students must believe that assessments within a school's comprehensive assessment system are valid and can and will be used to help teachers teach and students learn. If students believe assessments are face valid, they will more consistently put forth their best efforts, making it more likely that the results will reflect their true ability or achievement. If teachers believe assessments are face valid, they will be more likely to communicate that belief consciously or subconsciously to their students, and if they are involved in assessment administration, they will be more likely to administer the assessment with fidelity, making it more likely again that results will reflect students' true ability or achievement. Convincing teachers of the face validity of reading CBMs is particularly challenging from our experience. One-minute measures of reading fluency are often used to screen or monitor student growth in reading. These CBMs are not meant to comprehensively measure reading achievement but instead to provide a quick and easy marker of student risk and/or progress. Teachers taught that assessments should directly measure what they teach may have difficulty seeing these assessments as face valid without the support and guidance of a data leader.

In our consultations with school districts concerning this building block, we have found the "Identifying Gaps in Your Comprehensive Assessment System" activity (Appendix 1) to be beneficial in helping consultees to identify—and address—potential gaps within their assessment systems.

Prior to the activity, it is critical to overview the four purposes of data within a comprehensive assessment system listed above to ensure that those completing the activity share the same operational definitions of the terms used. The facilitator then shares a copy of the activity handout with each participant. Each participant or small group is asked to start by writing in each of the four quadrants within the table the names of assessment tools that the school *administers* to address that purpose within a comprehensive assessment system, whether it be screening, diagnosis, progress monitoring, or outcomes-related decisions. It is critical to clarify for participants that one assessment administered in the school may be listed in more than one quadrant if it is used for multiple purposes. For example, the annual state accountability test might be used for both diagnosis of specific skill strengths and weaknesses and for outcomes-related decisions about whether students met the standards.

As a follow-up, participants are also asked to circle the names of assessments that are actually being *used* to make instructional decisions. This part of the activity can be enlightening, as it can uncover those assessments that are being given, but the results of which sit in a cabinet or on a server without having any impact on changing the way in which teachers teach the students who took the assessments. However, it is important to caution participants against assuming that those assessments that are being administered but not used should simply be eliminated. If the results are not being used because staff have yet to be trained and/or provided with the time and resources to examine the results, we recommend that those steps be taken before considering eliminating the assessment. If, on the other hand, staff have been trained in using the results and provided with the time and resources to examine and connect the results with instructional decisions, and the school has determined that the results cannot be effectively used to change instruction, then it may be appropriate to stop giving the assessment.

Easy Access to Appropriate Data for All Staff

In addition to having strong leadership and buy-in and a comprehensive assessment system, a third key tenet of a data-driven school is that all appropriate school staff must have easy access to data gathered through this comprehensive assessment system. Technology tools used to access the data need to be user-friendly and require just a few clicks for the everyday consumer to get to the most important and frequently used reports. The school cannot be reliant on one or even a few data experts to create and interpret these reports. While this book certainly promotes the importance of data leaders, they must, in essence, be continuously working themselves out of a job by building the capacity of all staff to create and interpret reports themselves. For this to happen, however, the data included in reports have to be relevant to the questions that are important to teachers and administrators. If not, staff will not access them, and they will not serve their ultimate purpose of spurring change in classroom instruction. Finally, technology tools should ideally provide users with an integrated "one-stop-shopping" experience, including data addressing all four purposes of assessment within a comprehensive assessment system in one place. Teachers and administrators are busy people. The more websites they need to go to and the more passwords they need to remember, the less likely they will be to come back. All of these issues must be balanced against the critical importance of maintaining data privacy and confidentiality. The Family Educational Rights and Privacy Act (FERPA; 1974) requires that only individuals with a "legitimate educational interest" in a student should have access to the student's performance data. As schools move from the traditional educational model in which individual teachers work in isolation with their classrooms of students to models in which teams of staff engage in focused collaboration across classrooms, grade levels, and content areas, administrators and data leaders need to engage staff in ongoing conversations about what these changes mean for continued appropriate access to student data. The use of technology tools for data management is discussed in detail in Chapter 8.

The Time and Resources for All Staff to Examine the Data

To communicate the integral importance of this focused collaboration and to avoid the previously described DRIP school culture, school staff must be provided with the time and resources necessary to examine the comprehensive assessment system data they access. This is the fourth key tenet of a data-driven school. PLC proponents consistently argue that a non-negotiable step in providing this time and these resources to staff is that the time be provided *within the school day*. Inviting teachers to meet with their colleagues to access, interpret, and use data to drive instruction solely before or after school communicates the message that this activity is an add-on. Scheduling these meetings during the workday, on the other hand, says that focused collaboration is an integral part of teachers' jobs and just as important as student contact.

Time during these meetings needs to be spent not on everyday logistical items but on systems-level data-driven decision making, including such tasks as:

1. Evaluating the effectiveness of instruction and identifying and assessing the impact of interventions designed to provide supplemental support;
2. Identifying students in need of this supplemental support; and
3. Monitoring the progress of these students in response to the support.

While staff should not be dependent on a single or small number of data leaders to produce and interpret reports for them, these data leaders should serve other important functions, including facilitating data-driven discussions, providing face-to-face and virtual training, and helping individual staff, teams, and schools or districts set and monitor their progress toward appropriate data-driven goals. More detailed discussion of data-analysis teaming at the district and school levels with respect to academic and behavioral issues can be found in Part II.

Clear Connections between Data and Potential Interventions at the District, School, and Classroom Levels

Finally, the fifth key tenet of a data-driven school is that administrators and data leaders clearly articulate the connections between data and potential interventions at the district, school, and classroom levels. Avoiding a DRIP culture involves not only providing time and resources for staff to access and interpret data but also for connecting those data with instruction and intervention.

In a data-driven school, in addition to providing staff with easy access to data, it is also critical to provide them with easy access to information about research-based interventions to address student needs identified through the data. Chapter 4 provides readers with recommendations regarding online clearinghouses, as well as frameworks, for identifying and monitoring the impact of data-driven interventions. In examining the data and attempting to use the data to identify interventions, data leaders and staff must remain aware of the potential limitations of the data. Assessments must be both reliable and valid for the purpose for which they are designed for data leaders to be confident in using them to identify data-driven interventions. To do so, data leaders must have, or be able to develop, assessment and intervention literacy skills. Chapter 9 of this book further addresses this need.

THE DATA-DRIVEN SCHOOL AND MTSS

Throughout this text, we conceptualize that the key features of a data-driven school are best implemented within an MTSS structure. Previously or synonymously identified as RTI models, MTSS has been widely promulgated as a quintessential data-driven, research-based structure for schools. While other sources provide more extensive treatments of

MTSS (Batsche et al., 2005; Brown-Chidsey & Steege, 2010; Burns & Gibbons, 2012), a brief summary follows.

An MTSS typically consists of three tiers of increasingly specific assessments and increasingly intensive interventions, and is intended to help school personnel meet both the academic and behavioral–emotional needs of all students. An MTSS is typically depicted graphically as a triangle (see Figure 1.4), with the width of the triangle indicating the number of students and the height indicating the increasing intensity of the supports provided. In Tier 1 of the MTSS, all students receive core instruction and classroom management that is based on research-based practices that have been shown to produce high levels of proficiency and low levels of discipline problems. Universal screening, as described previously, is conducted three times per year, and data-analysis teams meet on this schedule to review the results and to plan and evaluate core instruction and management tactics. These deliberations support the use of research-based practices, as well as the differentiation of instruction for learners who display a wide range of academic skills.

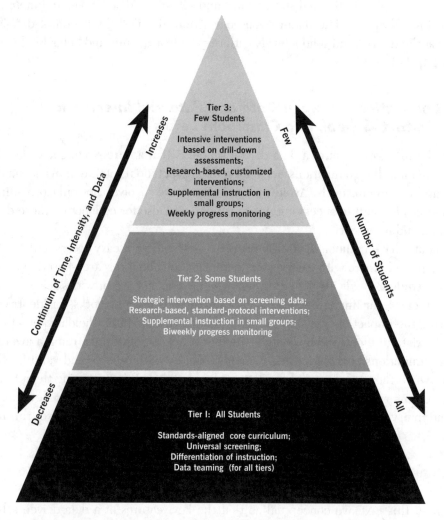

FIGURE 1.4. Graphic depiction of MTSS. Reprinted with permission from Kovaleski, VanDerHeyden, and Shapiro (2013). Copyright © 2013 The Guilford Press.

In Tier 2 of the MTSS, students who do not attain benchmark performance on the universal screeners and who are not projected to attain benchmark by the next administration are provided with group-based supplemental interventions during additional periods of the school day (while they are maintained in the core instructional program). Schools typically use "standard-protocol" intervention programs and group students according to common needs. Standard-protocol interventions are typically commercially available intervention packages that are based on research trials that have proven the effectiveness of the procedures to improve student performance. The concept here is that if these interventions are closely matched to students' assessed needs (through universal screening) and if the interventions are delivered with a high degree of fidelity (i.e., according to the procedures prescribed in the intervention directions), the majority of students receiving the intervention should make desired gains. The amount of progress made by students in Tier 2 is determined by analysis of progress monitoring data. For students in Tier 2, progress is typically monitored every other week. Examples of interventions used in Tier 2 are included in the extensive case studies described in Chapters 6 and 7.

Students who fail to make adequate progress during Tier 2 interventions are provided with additional and more intensive supports in Tier 3. In this tier, diagnostic (later also referred to as "drill-down") assessments are used to pinpoint specific skill deficiencies and to plan for more incisive interventions. Like Tier 2, students receiving Tier 3 interventions continue to participate fully in Tier 1 core instruction, and standard-protocol interventions typically serve as the base interventions for the identified students. However, in Tier 3, interventions are more precisely customized to match students' needs based on the assessment data. Although not legally a special education service, interventions at this point begin to approximate many of the hallmarks that have historically been associated with special education, including decreased teacher–student ratio, the amount of time allocated to the intervention outside of core instruction (both in amount of time per day and days per week), the level of explicitness of the instruction, and the number of opportunities for the student to respond. In addition, because students in this tier often display both academic deficiencies and behavior concerns, assessment and intervention in both domains frequently occurs. Students' progress in this tier is typically monitored weekly, although, as we discuss later in the book, how frequently progress is monitored should also be dependent on other factors, including the sensitivity of the progress monitoring tool to change.

It is anticipated that full implementation of an MTSS will result in high percentages of students demonstrating academic proficiency and appropriate behavior. Authors in this area frequently note that Tier 1 should be effective in and of itself for 80% of students, with 15% of students needing Tier 2 support and 5% needing Tier 3 services (Batsche et al., 2005). It is also expected that, as increasingly intensive interventions are provided in Tiers 2 and 3, students will accelerate their progress, with more students receiving Tier 2 interventions "returning" to Tier 1 and students in Tier 3 moving to Tier 2 (Shapiro & Clemens, 2009). It is also understood that students who fail to make acceptable progress through three tiers of intervention should be referred for a full and individual evaluation for eligibility for special education. Kovaleski, VanDerHeyden, and Shapiro (2013) provide detailed procedures on how data derived from students' response to intervention, as demonstrated through the tiers, can be used to inform the special education evaluation process.

KEY ISSUES

■ The five-step problem-solving model can be used not only to address individual student problems but also schoolwide problems, like the one illustrated in the playground story.

■ Administrator–staff, staff–student, and staff–family relationships are critical to effective use of the problem-solving model at the schoolwide level.

■ While administrators do not need to initiate the transition to a data-driven school, their support is critical, since they are the key decision makers within schools.

■ Leaders must also be able to recruit first followers, including those who can explain, make connections with, and sell the initiative to others.

■ A comprehensive assessment system—including assessment data that address screening, diagnosis, progress monitoring, and outcomes-related decisions—is also a key component of a data-driven school. Completing the "Identifying Gaps in Your Comprehensive Assessment System" activity (Appendix 1) can help schools identify and address their assessment-related needs.

■ Data-driven schools must not rely on individual data experts to provide data to staff, but instead ensure that all staff have independent access to the appropriate assessment data and the time and resources to help them interpret the data and make instructional decisions.

■ Staff in data-driven schools must also have easy access to information about research-based interventions to address the student needs they identify so as to avoid a DRIP culture.

■ These key tenets of a data-driven school are best implemented within an MTSS.

CHAPTER 2

Systems-Level Problem Identification

THE PROBLEM-SOLVING MODEL AND SYSTEMS-LEVEL APPLICATION

As previously described, the problem-solving model presents a step-by-step framework for governing the decision-making process. The "problem-solving model" is so named because it has its roots in team-oriented strategies to solve problem behaviors or poor academic performance exhibited by individual students (Bergan, 1977; Deno & Mirkin, 1977). However, as was presented in the Chapter 1 example of the analysis of behavior issues in a suburban elementary school, the use of this model can evolve to a much broader range of applications, including systems-level data-driven decision making. Just as teams strategize on how to improve performance for individual students, the problem-solving model can be used to develop data-driven strategies for improving the performance of the overall system. System is defined as any organizational grouping within or across the entire education organization, and can range in level from the classroom to the grade level, content area, school, district, grouping of districts, state, and even nation. Applying the problem-solving model to develop and inform data-based improvement strategies at the systems level has the same underlying goals as when the model is applied at the individual level: to measure the effectiveness of these strategies and to make adjustments as indicated by the data (see Howe, Scierka, Gibbons, & Silberglitt, 2003, for an example). Application of the problem-solving model at the systems level is the focus of the first section of this book, focusing primarily on systems analysis at the district and school level (see Figure 1.2).

Let's take the first step in our systems-level problem-solving model, known as *problem identification*. In order to understand systems improvement, we first must establish what we are setting out to improve. Problem identification asks us to operationalize what we will improve, in observable and measurable terms. This operational step is performed by asking a single question: "What is the difference between what is expected and what is occurring?"

ESTABLISHING WHAT IS EXPECTED

In that key question that drives the problem identification step, there is an important unstated assumption; actually, two. In order to establish a difference between what is expected and what is occurring, the first assumption is that one can measure what is occurring, and the second is that one knows what should be expected. So, despite the phrasing as a single question, there are in fact two separate questions that need to be answered: "What is occurring?" and "What is expected?" Once these have been answered, we can then go on to determine the difference between the two.

We presented these assumptions in logical order—first you know where you are, then you know where you are going. This concept applies to many aspects of personal and professional life. At the organization level, it is often a key to developing an organization's strategic plan. However, there is some debate about which question actually needs to come first. Do we need to know where we are in order to know where we are going? Probably not. In fact, we won't need to know where we are until we begin to plot a course to help us get to where we are going. More important, in fact, is that we know where we want to go. The process of planning is far more effective when we first establish our goal, and then work backward from there (Wiggins & McTighe, 2007). It also ensures that we focus on the goal—lack of "constancy of purpose" is one of organizational management's "five deadly diseases" (A simple Google search on this well-known theory can provide the reader with additional information.). So it is the question of where we are headed—"What is expected?"—that we must tackle first.

Understanding what is expected brings to mind a great quote, often attributed to Yogi Berra: "If you don't know where you are going, you'll end up someplace else." Establishing expectations may in fact be the single most important step in applying the problem-solving model to the systems level. Without a solid understanding of expectations, the remaining steps in the process will all have been built on a shaky foundation. Fortunately, we have strategies to help us determine expectations and to define them in observable and measurable terms.

In many cases, expectations of performance will have been set a priori, often based on prior research or on expert judgment. An example from the assessment world: state-mandated assessments have target or cutoff scores, above which a student is determined to be meeting grade-level standards. NCLB (2001) institutionalized the development and delivery of such state-mandated assessments across all 50 states. More recently, consortia have developed (Partnership for Assessment of Readiness for College and Careers [PARCC] and Smarter Balanced Assessment Consortium [SBAC]; United States Department of Education, 2010) to establish greater commonality of both the assessments themselves and the grade-level standards across states. Even more recently, ESSA (2015) provided greater flexibility to states in setting standards, and encouraged the use of multiple measures to set student performance targets, while retaining the important concept of establishing performance criteria and holding systems accountable to meeting them. In these examples, the expectation has been set via the expert committees and processes states have implemented to establish grade-level standards.

In another example from the dropout prevention literature, the expectation seems clear from the outset: Students will successfully graduate from high school (i.e., not drop out). In both the state assessment example and the dropout example, the expectation that has been established is a summative outcome. At the culmination of the journey through K–12, we want students to graduate. At the culmination of the school year, we want students to meet grade-level standards.

Using observable and measurable expectations to drive change cannot only be limited to a focus on summative outcomes. While establishing these outcomes is important, the outcomes tend to be relatively easy to set and they don't represent true leadership. Some have questioned whether those establishing NCLB did in fact take the approach of setting a summative outcome—"No child will be left behind"—without sufficient focus on the details of how to get it done, but that is an argument for a different book. Leading with data involves setting both summative and formative outcomes, understanding the end goal, but then drilling in and checking whether we are on track to meet that goal, so that we can make course corrections along the way. And setting the formative outcomes so that we can make course corrections is a guiding principle of the problem-solving model.

TARGET SETTING USING BACKWARD PLANNING

A straightforward, data-based method for setting formative outcomes is known as backward planning (Wiggins & McTighe, 2007). In backward planning, we look first at the summative outcome that is the end goal, and then walk backward from there, toward where we are now. In education, this approach typically involves moving backward through time, since summative outcomes are set at the end of a K–12 career, a school year, and so forth. If the end goal is to graduate in grade 12, our formative outcomes can tell us how many credits, what level of attendance, what performance on test scores, and so on are needed in grade 11, grade 10, and so forth, moving backward from the goal.

In the case of state-mandated assessments, the end goal is to reach the grade-level standard. Consider that the first state-mandated assessment in many states occurs at the end of third grade. Consider also that research suggests that third grade is a pivotal point in children's literacy development; if a child is not a skilled reader by third grade, their[1]

---

[1] A note on language: In the book, we have given careful thought to pronoun use. In situations like this one in which pronoun use was needed and the gender identity of the person being referenced is unknown, we used "they/them/their" to indicate a gender-neutral pronoun.

chances of becoming a successful reader into adulthood diminish significantly (Annie E. Casey Foundation, 2007). Given these facts, we realize that we cannot afford to simply use the state assessment at the end of third grade as our measurement of whether we are meeting expectations. If we were to do that, by the time we learned we weren't on track, we would be too late. In the absence of an a priori model (such as those used to set grade-level standards on state assessments) to determine expectations at second grade, first grade, and earlier, we need to consider how we might set formative outcomes leading up to what is essentially a summative outcome: meeting grade-level standards in third grade. Similarly, if we are myopically focused on how the organization as a whole (i.e., the district) performs on the summative assessment, we lose some critical information that can help guide us, in terms of what course corrections may be needed. By taking the systems-level approach down to the school, content area, grade level, and even classroom or small-group level, we can get valuable information to guide what will be a multitude of educational decisions that are made long before that first summative assessment is completed and analyzed.

Fortunately, many local school districts have made the decision that formative assessments are necessary to determine whether or not students are on track to success on this important outcome. While there are a number of formative assessment tools available, there is a single type of formative assessment that stands out from others as a tool well suited to a backward planning approach. GOM provides the capability to repeatedly measure students' growth over time, via an efficient and easy-to-understand methodology (Deno, 1985). Because GOM assesses in a way that is indicative of performance in a broad domain, such as reading, without attempting to measure the entire domain, it provides the ability to predict overall outcomes without onerous assessment plans that detract from critical instructional time. Additionally, because GOM assesses at a consistent level of difficulty across the school year, it is uniquely suited to measure growth in a way that facilitates a backward planning approach (Silberglitt & Hintze, 2005). Assessment of oral reading fluency (ORF) through curriculum-based measurement, for example, consists of a series of brief, 1-minute samples of students' reading fluency, yet it is highly predictive of performance on broad assessments of overall reading comprehension (Reschly, Busch, Deno, & Long, 2009). The brevity of these assessments allows them to be given repeatedly across the school year, while the consistent difficulty level and the predictive capability allow us to establish specific target scores at each assessment that determine whether a student is on track to success in reading.

GOMs, such as ORF assessment, are typically given using two separate but connected implementation strategies: progress monitoring and benchmarking. Progress monitoring is typically conducted monthly, biweekly, or even weekly for individual students who may need additional attention (Howe et al., 2003). A student's sequence of scores on a GOM can be graphed longitudinally, and target scores are useful here as they represent the end-year goal. Growth toward that goal is tracked ideographically across the year. Benchmarking is typically administered three times per year (i.e., fall, winter, and spring) to all students in a grade, school, or district. Benchmarking is also useful at the individual student level, as a sort of child find. However, it provides great value for problem identification at the systems level as well, when a coordinated set of target scores is applied.

The methodology (see the case example in Appendix 2 for a description of the methodology of target setting) presents a consistent statistical process for linking performance at each benchmark period across multiple grade levels to a common outcome. In the example we have been unfolding, target scores would be set such that ORF benchmarking in fall, winter, and spring of first, second, and third grade are all statistically linked to the same outcome, in this case, third-grade spring performance on the state-mandated reading assessment. Because both the outcome and the statistical process are consistent (over what amounts to a total of nine different benchmark periods across three grade levels), the target scores that are established have a special meaning, which enables us to conduct some incredibly powerful data analyses.

Consider the example set of target scores on ORF benchmarks in Figure 2.1, developed for a consortium of districts in rural Minnesota (Silberglitt, 2008b; see the online supplement for a copy of this unpublished manuscript). Looking across a row, you see that the target scores grow across the school year. For example, in second grade the fall target is 43, the winter target is 72, and the spring target is 90. Again, the target scores are all devised using the same statistical process and are linked to the same outcome. This means that, for an individual student, if the fall score falls below 43 but the spring score is above 90, we can say with confidence that the student's status moved from not on track to on track to meet grade-level standards. Had these targets instead been developed based on local or national norms, or on guesswork, we could not make this statement because we could not be confident that the targets had the same meaning across time.

Also notice the column labeled "Growth Rate/Week." Again, this consistency of target setting provides a roadmap for growth across the school year. In second grade, for example, students must grow at a rate of 1.31 words/minute/week in order to *maintain* their current status relative to grade-level standards. Essentially, we now have a statistically reliable definition for "a year's growth in a year's time." This metric has tremendous implications at the individual level, including establishing criteria for responsiveness to intervention in an MTSS model.

But this section of this book is about taking data leadership to the systems level, and these same two principles leveraged to evaluate individual students in the examples above can also be applied with great power to analysis of performance of the system. For individuals, we have a means for establishing movement from not on track to on track (and vice versa) across the school year. This same approach can help us understand the effectiveness of the system, by examining the number and percentage of students who are on track, as well as how those percentages change across the year. If 68% of our second graders are at or above an ORF score of 43 in the fall, what percentage are at or above 72 in the winter,

Grade	Fall	Winter	Spring	Growth Rate/Week
1		22	52	1.67
2	43	72	90	1.31
3	70	91	109	1.08

FIGURE 2.1. Example set of target scores on ORF benchmarks.

or 90 in the spring? Does this percentage increase? And which students move up or down relative to targets?

Also at the group level we now have a standard for the amount of growth a student should achieve in a year's time at a given grade level. What percentage of students reaches that standard? Which students are exceeding that standard? Which programs and interventions did they receive? (See Gibbons & Silberglitt, 2008; Shapiro & Clemens, 2009; Silberglitt, 2008a, for further discussion of the concepts of using target scores at the systems level.) We revisit some of these concepts as we walk through the remaining steps of the problem-solving model in more detail in the chapters to come. But, you now have a taste of both the importance and power of the target-setting framework.

Backward planning gives us an answer to "What is expected?" in the question "What is the difference between what is expected and what is occurring?" Furthermore, we have the capability to identify problems when they first arise, rather than waiting until an assessment is given at third grade to find out there *is* a problem, at which point it may be too late. This same approach can be extended to kindergarten and even early childhood assessments, to provide the capacity to recognize problems (and make course corrections) even earlier. Kindergarten GOMs, such as letter–sound fluency (LSF; Daly, Wright, Kelly, & Martens, 1997); early childhood GOMs, such as the individual growth and development indicators (IGDIs; McConnell, 2000); and the preschool numeracy indicators (PNIs; Floyd, Hojnoski, & Key, 2006) share the characteristics of ORF, described earlier.

Similarly, the backward planning approach can be extended to other assessments with some similar characteristics, even though these assessments may not fit in the realm of GOM. To name just a few examples, computer-adaptive assessments, such as the MAP (*www.nwea.org*; Kingsbury & Houser, 1997), the Performance Series (*www.scantron.com*; Scantron Corporation, 2004), the Star assessments (*www.renaissance.com*; Renaissance Learning, 2015), and the aMath and aReading assessments (*www.fastbridge.org*; FastBridge Learning, 2015) have a property known as a vertically equated scale. This means that a score increase from 125 to 130, for example, has the same meaning, regardless of a child's grade level or when the child was assessed. Essentially, the child grew 5 points, whether this growth took 2 months or 2 years, and regardless of whether the child is a second grader or an eighth grader. This is a much different approach to reporting performance than is seen on more traditional standardized assessments, where scale scores are often given relative to age or grade-level norms, and changes in scale scores across time can be difficult to interpret and confusing to communicate to a lay audience.

The advantage of the vertically equated scale is that backward planning is also well suited to its interpretation, since one can establish exactly what score represents "on track" at spring of second grade, fall of third grade, and so forth. This generates a set of target scores (and growth rates) similar to the ORF example shown above. As a side note, one difference is that in a vertically equated scale, you are not likely to see significant drops in target scores from spring to the ensuing fall, as you do in ORF targets. This is because ORF is typically administered using grade-level specific reading probes, so there is a jump in difficulty level (and a corresponding drop in score) from one grade level to the next. With a vertically equated scale, scores do not naturally drop from one grade level to another (except for typical losses that may be seen due to lack of instruction over the summer).

SETTING TARGETS ON OTHER KEY VARIABLES

Understanding what is expected is certainly not limited to assessment data; the breadth of data available to schools to help to identify problems is vast. Let's return to the dropout example from earlier in the chapter. In that example, the summative outcome was again clearly defined: whether or not a student successfully graduated from high school. However, similar to our example of the third-grade reading assessment, educators are not in a position to wait until the summative measurement is completed to decide whether or not a problem exists. What we need is a form of backward planning relative to dropout—that is, what indicators might there be that would allow us to predict whether students are on track to graduate?

Fortunately, the literature on dropout provides research on a variety of indicators of school completion, many of which are based on data that are already typically collected by the school. Attendance, behavior, grades, standardized test performance, and credit completion are all simple, observable indicators that can be statistically linked to dropout (Alexander, Entwisle, & Horsey, 1997; Allensworth & Easton, 2007; Balfanz, Legters, West, & Weber, 2007). Research can guide us in answering questions about where to set expectations, such as

- How many absences indicate a student may be at risk for dropping out?
- How many behavioral incidents?
- How many credits behind is too many?
- When are a student's test scores low enough that we become concerned about the potential for dropout?

More broadly, the instance of dropping out has been found to be the result of student disengagement from school over a period of time (Finn, 1989; Fredricks, Blumenfeld, & Paris, 2004). Also, early on, students display academic, behavioral, cognitive, and affective signs of their disengagement, and these can be used to estimate student risk for later failure to graduate. The indicators above would be considered useful proxies for academic and behavioral engagement. Yet, cognitive and affective measures of student engagement can also be used to understand the levels of engagement of individual students and across the classroom, grade level, content area, school, or district and may provide either earlier or additional information (Appleton, 2012; Christenson et al., 2008). While cognitive and affective engagement data may not already be a part of the typical data collection process in a school, gathering these data can yield a significant increase in the capacity of the organization to identify students who are at risk for dropping out (Fredricks et al., 2004). Further, these types of engagement measures are becoming more frequently discussed, researched, and made available (see Appleton, Christenson, & Furlong, 2008, for summaries of engagement and measures).

This dropout example gives rise to a couple of considerations. First, it is important to be careful in selecting your outcome. For instance, here we selected graduation; yet, does graduation ensure postsecondary success? Does the meaning of graduation differ by school or district? Perhaps graduation with a specific minimum SAT or ACT score (see Von Secker, 2009) or using postsecondary results as the outcome variable would be more appropriate (see National Student Clearinghouse, 2011). Regardless, a thorough mapping of the path to a desired outcome will never be wasted and specific pathways can be targeted within the larger map. Second, there are many cases where research is not definitive as to specific levels of performance needed to predict a successful outcome. Perhaps the outcome itself is not well studied, or perhaps the indicator being used to predict the outcome is not well researched, or perhaps the organization is simply concerned with the generalizability of other available research to its specific population. In setting these performance expectations, we are determining the "Where are we going?" part of the question. Where we want to go in the long run is successful graduation, but where we want to go in the short run is an engaged student body with strong attendance, low levels of behavior incidents, great test scores, and on track with their credit completion. By identifying where we want to go in the near term and establishing a set of measures to track systems-level performance, we can begin to also take a look at where we are, and then establish what the measurable difference is between the two. For a more detailed discussion on the actual statistical process of establishing target scores toward any outcome, again see Appendix 2.

UNDERSTANDING WHAT IS OCCURRING

Recall that the key question from problem identification is, "What is the difference between what is expected and what is occurring?" Now that we have a better understanding of what is expected (where we are going), we are ready to look at where we are, in order to properly map how to get there. Understanding what is occurring brings yet another great Yogi Berra quote to mind: "We're lost, but we're making good time." Deciding on summative outcomes and then backward planning from there creates an educational roadmap to success. This process allowed us to answer the question "What is expected?" in measurable terms that can be assessed now, rather than waiting to see whether the hoped-for outcomes are realized, several years into the future. This is why in the problem identification step, we first answer the question "What is expected?" Answering this question gives us a reference point for answering "What is occurring?" So, by measuring what is occurring, we learn not only where we are but how far we are from where we'd like to be.

Different Approaches to Communicating Data

In the assessment world, there is a dichotomy in how data are communicated that can be considered in the context of the problem identification step and the "What is occurring?" question. Norm-referenced assessment tells us where a student is relative to some comparable group of students, whether they be same-age/grade peers across the world, nation, state, or just that student's local school. Criterion-referenced assessment tells us where a student is relative to some benchmark or criterion. In both examples, data are communicated relative to some reference point, but the reference point is very different: the average score of a comparable group versus the preestablished benchmark level of performance. It is the "What is expected?" that changes.

Consider the following statement: Josie, a fourth grader, scored a 28 on the Hyson–Kovaleski–Silberglitt–Pederson (HKSP) test. The first question one might ask is "Is that a good score?" The way that question is answered depends on your approach to communicating data. In a norm-referenced approach, one might provide the average score for fourth graders (a score of 26). In a criterion-referenced approach, one might provide a benchmark, such as the grade-level standard (let's say this is a score of 23). Now that we know Josie is exceeding expectations, the next question might be "Is that a big difference?" In a norm-referenced approach, we look at the number of standard deviations from the mean (perhaps the standard deviation is 2, which puts Josie 1 standard deviation above the mean and in the 84th percentile). In a criterion-referenced approach, we design multiple levels of criteria. So, there may also be a cutoff score for the category "well below standard" (maybe a score of 19), and a cutoff for the category "well above standard" (let's say this is a cutoff of 27, which puts Josie in the "well above standard" category).

Interestingly, the very terms *norm-referenced assessment* and *criterion-referenced assessment* are a bit of a misnomer. It is not the assessment itself that possesses either of these characteristics, but rather how the user of the assessment decides to communicate the data. Many assessments can, in fact, take on both forms. For example, ORF scores can be presented in terms of below/above target, or Tiers 1–3 in an MTSS framework, or they could instead be presented in terms of percentile rank relative to local norms. (We have not yet seen a *national* norm for ORF where assessment integrity was carefully monitored across data collection sites, but that is a separate discussion.)

For the purposes of problem identification at the systems level, and the approach we have taken using backward planning, communicating data using a criterion-referenced approach is simply better suited to the task. There is certainly a time and a place for norm-referenced approaches, and we don't want to suggest that those are never valid, but criterion-referenced approaches provide the ability to communicate data about groups of students in ways that would be difficult to interpret in a norm-referenced environment. One major reason for this is the concept of "on track" indicates that a course has been set from one point to another—in this case, growth toward a desired outcome. Measuring growth using a norm-referenced communication approach is exceedingly difficult to interpret, since percentile rank is not an equal-interval scale, and the norm group itself may not grow at the desired rate to remain on track. So, even if we knew that a student who scored at or above the 60th percentile on some assessment in *third* grade would meet the grade-level standard, that doesn't necessarily mean that a student in the 60th percentile in *second* grade is truly "on track," since the rate of change of the 60th-percentile student over time may not be the desired rate of change in order to meet the grade-level standard.

Furthermore, in our experience, parents and school personnel in general seem to find scores described in reference to a set criterion to be easier to understand than scores described in reference to a norm group. Which leads us to a key aspect of the problem identification process: communicating information that clearly describes the nature and degree of the problem.

Communicating the Difference between What Is Expected and What Is Occurring

Let's look at some examples of how data can be easily communicated at the systems level, relevant to the problem identification step in our model. One simple visual is the bar graph in Figure 2.2 showing the percentage of students who are and are not above target. In the figure, this information is broken out in a bit more detail, with the lightest gray being used to denote students who are above target, slightly darker gray for students who are below target, and darkest gray for students who are well below expectations. Were this to be printed in color, the students would be represented by green, yellow, and red, respectively.

In this graph, performance on a local assessment of mathematics (the MAP) is summarized for a single school year. Students at each grade level were assessed in the fall and in the spring, so the bar farthest to the left represents the percentage of second-grade students above target (labeled "Meets Standards": 54%), below target ("Partially Meets Standards": 27%), and well below target ("Does Not Meet Standards": 19%) at the fall assessment. The next bar in sequence is the same cohort of second-grade students at the spring assessment, so we can see that the percentage in the lightest gray increased but so did the percentage in the darkest gray. Each pair of bars in the graph represents a different cohort of students' performances in the fall and the spring.

From this graph, we can see that there is a significant increase in the percentage of students well below target when moving from the fall to the spring assessment in the fourth grade. We also see that each of the fourth-, fifth-, and sixth-grade cohorts show a much higher percentage of students in the darkest gray than the second- and third-grade cohorts. So, we see that there is a significant discrepancy between what is expected and occurring for a large number of students in the later grades. We might further investigate the data to ask some additional questions. How do previous and ensuing years' graphs look? Do

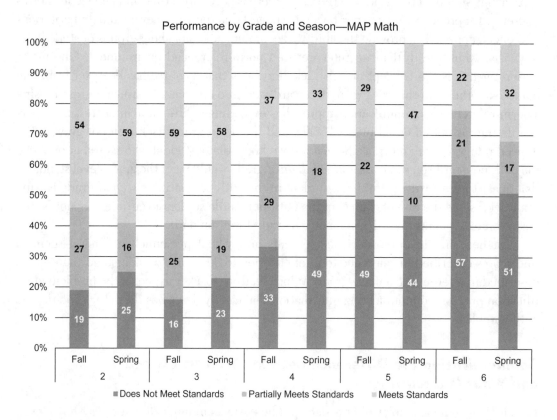

FIGURE 2.2. Bar graph showing percentage of students who are and are not above target.

we see the same pattern of decline in fourth grade, with lower performance in the later grades, regardless of the school year? If so, it would appear that we need to consider what is occurring instructionally in fourth grade that is causing students to fall further behind, or whether previous years' data show that current fourth graders have demonstrated a decline in performance over the past several years. If the latter is true, perhaps we have a cohort issue, where cohorts of students moving through the system have lower performance and a higher level of needs. If this is the case, then we can consider applying additional resources to these cohorts to support them and attempt to "catch them up." We often see cohort effects like this one where there are population shifts and demographic trends change across time.

In another example, we may look across multiple schools to see where there are successful practices that should be replicated. The next visual (see Figure 2.3) presents a line graph demonstrating the percentage of students above target by school across time on the MAP math assessment. Both the fall and the spring assessments are summarized for multiple school years for each selected school. The selected schools are also averaged together and each school is compared to this "District Total."

In this graph, we see that the trend for the district is generally upward, with a higher percentage of students above target in the more recent years. We also see that in each year, the percentage above target in the spring was higher than the percentage in the fall, so students are growing faster than the rate of growth of the target scores in each year. Comparing schools, three of the selected schools are consistently outperforming the district total:

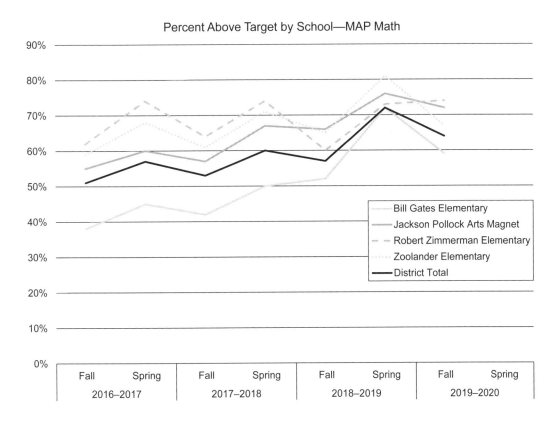

FIGURE 2.3. Line graph demonstrating the percentage of students above target by school across time on the MAP math assessment.

Jackson Pollack, Robert Zimmerman, and Zoolander. However, each of these schools is trending similarly to the district total—the gap between the schools' performance and the district is roughly the same at each time point. While Bill Gates Elementary remains just below the district total on the most recent assessment, the school has shown a strong trend upward relative to the district, and is effectively "catching up" to the other schools. Some additional questions need to be answered, such as "Was there a shift in population at Bill Gates?"; "What instructional practices were happening in math at the school?"; and "Did we see this trend across all grade levels?" A simple check of performance on the most recent assessment would have led to the conclusion only that this school is the lowest-performing school in the group, but an analysis of the trend over time reveals that in fact this school is one we may be able to learn from. Diving more deeply into the data can then help us to better understand how this school is closing the gap between what is expected and what is occurring more quickly than the other schools.

FOUR PURPOSES OF ASSESSMENT

Finally, we close the chapter on problem identification with an important consideration with regard to assessment. Problem identification can certainly be applied to a wide range of performance domains. However, many times (and, depending on your role in schools, perhaps most often) you will find yourself focusing on assessment results as a tool for guiding you through the steps of this model. For example, you may measure the difference between what is expected and what is occurring as the gap between current performance and target scores, as was described earlier in the chapter. But with the plethora of assessment data now available to most educators, it can be overwhelming. We hear calls to "triangulate" data (Altrichter, Feldman, Posch, & Somekh, 2008), but in our experience, the act of gathering multiple sources of assessment data no longer seems to be the problem (see Chapter 8 for a discussion on data warehouses). Despite the availability of robust assessment information, most educators are not sure which data should be examined, and when in the decision-making process they should be used.

Further complicating the situation is the now-deafening call for "formative assessment." The distinction between formative and summative assessment is an easy one: formative assessment, in our opinion, is any assessment that is used to inform instruction *while* it is occurring, just as summative assessment is used to assess the instruction *after* it occurred. (Summative data are affectionately referred to as "autopsy" data [DuFour, DuFour, Eaker, & Many, 2006].) As a side note, using this broad distinction is why the authors include GOM under the umbrella of formative assessment, earlier in the chapter. Unfortunately, this call for increased focus on formative assessment, while a step in the right direction, does not go far enough in helping data leaders make sense of their assessment plan, and in some cases is even misleading.

First, the very terms *formative assessment* and *summative assessment* are phrased in a way that makes it sound as if the assessments themselves are formative or summative. "I'm sorry, we can't use the results of the Chapter 2 test to reteach material that the class did poorly on, since that test was a summative assessment." This may sound ridiculous, but it is a common mistake to think that an assessment can only be used one way or the other, and often the result is that a teacher never even thinks to consider a strategy like reteaching, as is suggested in the above example. All assessments are used for a purpose (and frequently, for more than one purpose), and it is the purpose of the assessment that is either formative or summative in nature. So, in this example of the chapter test, it may have originally been planned to be used for a summative purpose, but when the teacher decided to modify instruction based on the results, it quickly shifted to an assessment being used formatively.

The second issue with this broad distinction between formative and summative assessment is that it is simply too broad to truly be useful. In order to develop a strategic assessment plan, it is helpful to think much more deeply about the purposes of assessment, and to understand how formative assessment can actually be divided into several purposes. The Reading First panel helped us to make better sense of all of the assessment data we see by breaking assessments down by four key purposes (National Institute of Child Health and Human Development, 2000; Torgesen, 2006). The four purposes of assessment, as first introduced in Chapter 1, are (1) screening, (2) diagnostic, (3) progress monitoring, and (4) outcomes. "Formative" assessment is now divided into three purposes (screening, diagnostic, and progress monitoring), providing more depth when building an assessment plan. Further supporting this more nuanced approach, these purposes overlay very nicely onto the problem-solving model, giving a framework for understanding which assessments should be used at which points in the process.

The order in which these key purposes are listed is no accident, as they make chronological sense when considering a path through the decision-making process. The first step in the problem-solving model is problem identification, and screening tools are effective assessments for establishing the difference between what is expected and what is occurring. As a rule, screening tools are quick and cheap (we don't want to spend a lot of time and money to find out simply that there is or isn't a problem). They do not need to give detailed information about performance within a domain—they simply give us an indication of overall performance and information about whether it is where we want it to be. For example, kindergarten/preschool screeners are in place in most school districts. They don't necessarily tell us what is wrong but they do give us a quick check as to whether a child is ready for kindergarten. If the screener reveals reason for concern, we dig more deeply (i.e., "diagnostic").

So, how do I know whether an assessment is a "screening" tool? The general rule of thumb is that it has to be quick enough to be easily administered to large numbers of students without significantly impacting instructional time, and it has to answer the question "Do I need to gather more information?" It does not need to provide enough information on its own to be used in making an instructional decision. Too often, we see educators taking the results from just one component of a screening tool (e.g., ORF) and using those results alone for placement in intervention groups. A screening tool (that includes multiple components) may be appropriate for instructional alterations in Tier 1 and for *initial* placement in Tier 2 intervention groups, but more data (i.e., progress monitoring, further diagnostic [drill-down] assessment) may be needed if students do not respond robustly to these efforts. The main question a screening tool answers is simply "Should I gather more data?" This streamlines the assessment process (and the decision-making process) because we can get a quick answer and rule out those areas where things are going well. We do not need to spend inordinate amounts of time identifying that a problem exists. However, after uncovering that a problem does exist, we do not jump to a solution without being properly informed. Note that this does not imply that you should wait for lengthy diagnostic assessments to be completed before providing additional instructional intensity for students. For instance, benchmark assessment may make it clear that a group of students needs something more than what they are getting in core instruction. As will be discussed later, in Chapter 6, the first step might be to provide a standard, evidence-based (Tier 2) treatment immediately for all students in this group. The treatment itself may end up providing the additional diagnostic information that is needed to support even more intensive (Tier 3) instruction for those students that need it.

Some other examples of popular screening tools include GOMs; many group-administered computer-delivered assessments, including those by NWEA and Scantron; vision and hearing screeners; and others. The list of examples is far too long for this book, so we encourage readers to apply some of the rules listed throughout the book to their own assessment plans, in determining how their assessment tools fit into each category, and how they might be streamlined.

Some nonexamples include specific skill-mastery assessments. These provide detailed information on which skills a student has performed to mastery, which is much too exhaustive for a simple screener. A tool we often see misused as a screener is the Developmental Reading Assessment (DRA; Beaver, 2006). This tool provides extensive diagnostic information but simply takes too much instructional time to be used as a screener.

We have worked with several schools where teachers complained bitterly about the amount of lost instructional time due to assessment, where we found that assessments like the DRA were being administered to 100% of the students in the school. The disruption to the classroom was enormous. The problem wasn't "too much testing"—it was "too much of the wrong testing." After streamlining their assessment plans, and moving tests like the DRA to later in the decision-making process, teachers remarked how they appreciated the data they were getting from their assessments. This is because the assessments were now being administered with a decision-making framework in mind. Quick screeners were giving staff regular information about which students were and were not on track. More detailed information was being gathered only on those students whose data indicated reason for concern. For those students, these additional data were necessary to help plan for their instruction, so they were not seen as a burden.

We return to the four purposes of assessment throughout Part I of this book, as we navigate the problem-solving model.

CONCLUSION

The problem-solving model represents a framework that we have found effective in helping educators to be systematic about using data at the organization level. It is intuitive, it is already in wide use when making decisions about individual students, and it ensures that educators will engage in some healthy metacognition about the processes they are currently using for data-driven decision making. It is likely that these processes are not systematic, and are typically based on external factors, such as what data are available. This is letting the assessment tail wag the data dog. Implementing the problem-solving model and engaging in the steps and activities outlined in this book ensures that educators will instead think first about what they need to make an informed decision, and then go about making certain the data to inform that decision are available.

The first step in the process is to identify the problem in observable and measurable terms: "What is the difference between what is expected and what is occurring?" We learned that we must start with the end in mind (what is expected), and work our way backward to what is occurring, in order to have a roadmap toward our destination. We considered backward planning as a tool to accomplish this, and learned how target scores are an essential component of this process. We considered strategies for communicating data in response to this first question in the problem-solving model, considering concepts such as "on track" to convey discrepancies from expectation at the systems level. Last, we considered the four purposes of assessment as a guide to developing an assessment plan that will facilitate the use of the problem-solving model.

Now that we have established the foundation for problem solving, we can move forward to the next step in the process. We have learned what our expectations are, and where our organization is performing relative to those expectations. Where there are gaps, we have defined those in measurable terms, which we can go back to later on to see whether we were effective at remedying these deficiencies. In response to seeing gaps, however, especially glaring ones, our first, most natural response is to ask "Why?" In the case of the problem-solving model, this is exactly the right question to ask. The next step, problem analysis, will let us explore how we can best ask and answer that question.

KEY ISSUES

- The systems-level problem-solving process begins with problem identification, which can be encapsulated by answering the question "What is the difference between what is expected and what is occurring?"
- Answering this question across a breadth of key outcomes is essential to a comprehensive systems-level decision-making process.
- To answer this question, we must first establish "what is expected."
  - This can be accomplished by setting target scores for each periodic screening assessment using a consistent process, such as logistic regression.
  - This can be accomplished for other non-assessment-related key outcomes, as well.
- The next step is to understand "what is occurring."
  - Effective visual presentation of data is an influential aspect of understanding current performance.
  - Analysis of assessment data within the four purposes of assessment helps to guide teams toward using the right information to answer the right question in the problem-solving process, at the right time.

CHAPTER 3

Systems-Level Problem Analysis

ROADMAP

1. Understanding the "why"
2. Data in problem analysis
3. Developing alterable hypotheses
4. Root cause analysis
5. Problem analysis in context
6. A step-by-step guide to problem analysis
7. Factors that often contribute to missing the problem analysis step
   a. School budgeting
   b. One-size-fits-all solutions
   c. Cursory problem analysis
8. Using problem analysis to address achievement gaps

PROBLEM ANALYSIS: UNDERSTANDING THE "WHY"

This chapter focuses on the use of data within the next step in the systems-level problem-solving model: problem analysis. This step is at the most basic level concerned with answering the question "Why?" In problem identification, we focused on the "what"—specifically, what is the discrepancy between what is expected and what is occurring. This required us to take some important steps in the process, including understanding and agreeing upon the "what is expected," as well as finding ways to measure the gap between current performance and these expectations.

In problem analysis, we attempt to understand the etiology behind this gap. The essential question "Why is this problem occurring?" is probably somewhat misleading, in that there may not be a single answer to the question. A more appropriate wording may be

"What are the whys behind this difference?" This establishes that there may be myriad factors involved, and encourages us to truly dig deeply into the problem, avoiding the natural tendency to stop searching and start solving as soon as we identify a single likely cause.

As in Chapter 2, the focus of this chapter is primarily on how to take what many readers already may know about using data-driven problem solving with individual students and show how the same approach can be implemented at the school or district level.

In situations where large numbers of students are not meeting expectations, due to the presence of a systems-level issue, data leaders who attempt to analyze problems student by student will likely quickly become overwhelmed. Since systems-level issues are nearly always present to some degree, systems-level problem analysis allows teams to more efficiently use data to address problems that may affect groups of students (or in some cases, the entire population) at the classroom, school, or district level, leaving more time and resources for the school to individually analyze the needs of those students who do demonstrate unique problems that cannot be addressed through systems-level problem solving. In a way, systems-level problem solving exemplifies the MTSS model. The first question in the MTSS model ("Is core instruction effective?") is, in fact, a systems question. The genius of this approach is that it looks to maximize the impact of data-informed instructional changes with the least possible overall effort. If we can examine data to identify systems issues, make changes to those issues, and resolve the identified problem for a large number of students, that is far more efficient than beginning by taking on the identified problem with each student, one by one. Similarly, systems-level data-driven problem analysis looks to address identified problems impacting large numbers of students, so that we can take the least resource-intensive approach possible to effectively support the needs of all students.

This chapter provides practical strategies for simplifying the systems-level data-driven problem analysis process, and for reminding the team that not having tools available is not a good reason to avoid investigating a question that the team feels we need to answer in order to truly understand the problem.

DATA IN PROBLEM ANALYSIS

In Chapter 2, we provided specific strategies for using data to answer the question "What is the discrepancy between what is expected and what is occurring?" We examined in depth a criterion-referenced approach to problem identification, establishing a criterion as the definition of "what is expected," as well as a method for measuring "what is occurring" that lends itself to comparisons to established expectations. We demonstrated ways to visualize and communicate these discrepancies, such as identifying the percentages of students below target, as an essential step in the process of rallying the team around a specific, measurable problem. Specifically, in the example shared in Chapter 2 (see Figure 2.3), we identified that (1) there was a much larger percentage of students in the fourth-, fifth-, and sixth-grade cohorts than in the second- and third-grade cohorts performing well below target, and (2) while three of the schools in the district (Jackson Pollack, Robert Zimmerman, and Zoolander) were outperforming the district total, trend data from another school (Bill Gates Elementary) suggested that it was closing the gap.

In problem analysis, we use data to broadly explore the underlying reasons why discrepancies such as these exist. We disaggregate the data, slicing and dicing to examine the performance of different population groups, not just by student demographics but by performance levels, profiles of strengths and weaknesses, attendance levels, behavior, and any number of other factors that may be relevant to the discrepancy. We also explore the data longitudinally, looking at trends in the discrepancy (as well as in related factors) over time, and looking at patterns in performance across years, grade levels, cohorts, and/or schools to understand changes in the discrepancy and related factors, which may lead to a hypothesis. We may also look broadly at related factors, including attendance and behavior, student engagement, family and student perceptions, environmental changes, and myriad other potential systems-level factors related to the discrepancy in performance.

In our discussion of the above example in Chapter 2, we posed several of these problem analysis questions, including:

1. Do we see the same pattern of decline in fourth grade in graphs of performance in previous and ensuing years, with lower performance in the later grades, regardless of the school year?
2. When looking at the previous year's data, do we see that it is in third grade where performance starts to look much worse?
3. Was the trend we identified in the data for Bill Gates Elementary present across all grade levels?
4. Was there a shift in population or a change in instructional practices at Bill Gates that might explain these trend data?

For several years, we created annual "data book PowerPoints" designed to guide school districts we consulted with, and the schools, grade levels, departments, and classrooms within those schools, in engaging in systems-level data-driven problem solving. This tool is discussed in greater detail at the end of Chapter 4, and a sample copy is available in the online supplement (see the box at the end of the table of contents). The graphs included within this tool, as well as the guiding questions around which they are organized, provide helpful examples of how systems-level problem analysis data can be communicated to allow data leaders and the data-driven schools with which they are working to ask and answer questions like those posed above.

For example, graphs within the data book PowerPoint depicting reading and math achievement include 4 years of trend data and allow the user to compare performance across schools within the district (see slide 13 in the online sample data book PowerPoint). The PowerPoint also includes graphs with performance broken down by grade level (see slide 15) and by performance quartile (see slide 34), to allow the user to drill down more deeply in examining the root cause of identified discrepancies. Finally, Guiding Question 2 (see slide 3) in the data book PowerPoint asks "Are all of your students in special population subgroups meeting standards or growing at a rate that will make them more likely to meet standards in the future?" Graphs in this section of the tool compare the performance of students receiving special education services with the performance of those not receiving special education, as well as the performance of those eligible for free or reduced-price lunch with the performance of those not eligible (see slide 41).

In a parallel example involving systems-level behavior data, teachers at an elementary school reported an increase in behavior issues. It was discovered that this increase began sharply, and its rise corresponded to a change in scheduling in which teachers were excused from the duty of monitoring the playground, replaced instead by paraprofessionals and other staff. By not interacting and observing students during free play, teachers no longer had access to information that they were using to make informed decisions about behavior management in the more structured classroom setting.

Some scholars refer to this type of analysis (at times disparagingly) as a "fishing expedition" because it deviates from the more academic approach of controlled, incremental progress within a line of research. In the research world, we are often able to control a number of variables, so that we can alter, and examine the effects of altering, a specific variable to establish evidence for cause-and-effect relationships. In practical settings, we are often left with messy, extant data, and faced with a problem for which we do not have the benefit of time or the structure to properly control the setting and wait to examine the change in relevant variables. In addition, we are often surprised by seemingly unrelated and easily overlooked factors, such as in the teacher playground example above. In problem analysis, if it feels like a fishing expedition, you are probably doing it right.

However, there are ways to structure your approach so that you don't get overwhelmed by the enormity of the available data and the volume of questions that could be asked of it. Effective systems-level problem analysis should be comprehensive, but at the same time efficient. Problem analysis that is too individualized too early on in the process can lead to "paralysis by analysis" and unnecessarily slow progress toward appropriate systems-level plan development. A sound approach provides some degree of theory to guide your data exploration, so that you aren't discovering that students who wear red socks are higher achievers. To continue the fishing analogy, you are going to cast your line where the fish are.

Next, we take a look at the goals of, as well as some tools for, approaching systems-level data-driven problem solving that help your team stay focused on a line of inquiry that is relevant to the problem, prioritize questions within that inquiry so we can get to implementing solutions quickly, and ensure that your team has a strategy for problem analysis that is driven by the questions you want to ask, not just the data you happen to have available. We then conclude the chapter by spending some time discussing one of the biggest hurdles to systems-level problem analysis—the fact that so many education systems are simply ignoring it—and applying what we have discussed to an example of addressing student achievements gaps in schools.

GOAL OF PROBLEM ANALYSIS: DEVELOPING ALTERABLE HYPOTHESES

The goal of problem analysis is to develop one or more hypotheses regarding why the problem exists. Burns and Gibbons (2011) define the hypothesis question as "What are the student's needs?" In this chapter, we adapt this approach to the systems level, asking "What are the students' needs," with "student" in its plural form. Within a systems-level context, we maintain the essential tenets of problem analysis within a problem-solving model (Batsche & Knoff, 1995; Knoff, 2002).

First, the hypotheses must be "alterable." We do not spend time on factors that are beyond our control. A popular and effective practice for teams engaged in the problem-solving process is, while brainstorming possible reasons for the problem, to divide up brainstormed ideas into "beyond our control" and "within our control." Some teams find Steven Covey's (1992) model (see Figure 3.1) helpful in highlighting this distinction between issues that fall primarily within what Covey terms the "circle of concern," which includes issues beyond our control, and issues that also fall within the "circle of influence," encompassing problems within our control as well.

This can be very helpful in refocusing the team on alterable factors, while limiting problem admiration and extinguishing the behavior of defeatism by not reinforcing it. Another effective tool for focusing on alterable problems is using an entirely data-driven approach to systems-level problem analysis, where the data themselves uncover the "whys" of the problem. The value in this approach is that alterable problems also tend to be measurable, and measurable problems are almost universally alterable. When the data themselves are the source for supporting our belief in a hypothesis, the solution is to find ways to change those relevant data. The data book PowerPoint described earlier provides a good example of this, since districts were coached to use the guiding questions and the data displays within the PowerPoint to help them analyze the potential reasons behind any identified discrepancies.

Another example, helpful in illustrating this point, is of a fourth-grade class with a high percentage of students in poverty and a significant number of students well below grade-level standard in reading. The relatively unalterable factor in this equation is poverty. However, the team uses a data-driven approach to examine the underlying data on student attendance, as well as the results of diagnostic assessments. The team discovers that interventions currently being prescribed to students are most effective with students who have a certain level of reading fluency—that is, beyond the level of the majority of students who have fallen behind in reading. Furthermore, the team identifies that student attendance within these interventions is low, due to scheduling conflicts at the school that cause intervention time to be usurped by other nonacademic activities. By taking a data-driven approach, with a focus on what is alterable, the team is able to generate two relevant hypotheses, both of which logically lead to plan development.

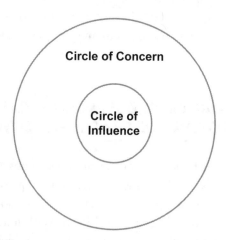

FIGURE 3.1. Steven Covey's circle of influence model.

Second, we consider the "whys" as a function of a mismatch between what the system is currently providing and what the needs of the students are. This is another tool to help the team focus on what it has the power to change, as well as leading the team to identify student needs, rather than student "problems." In fact, the entire model may be better worded as a "needs-fulfilling" model, instead of a "problem-solving" model, if only because human tendency is to think of a problem as something intractable, and a need as something that simply requires something to fulfill it. In the above fourth-grade class example, students needed support for their reading fluency, and they needed a fairly intensive dosage of intervention, neither of which was being provided by the system. With this mind-set, the hypothesis and plan development then focus on what changes to the system might be made to ensure fulfillment of these needs.

Third and finally, we take what appear at first to be unalterable factors that are at the root cause of the problem, and consider how we might, in fact, alter them. An important part of the systems-level problem-solving process is to consider the power the team has to rethink the entirety of the system. Systems are not limited to the walls of the school, the delivery of the curriculum, or the staff inside the building. Often, seemingly unalterable factors can be addressed through engaging the external resources of the community in creative ways, to partner in solving a problem. In one additional relevant example, we worked with an urban community where data-sharing agreements were established between county probation officers and the schools to provide the probation officers with real-time access to student attendance and course grades information. Attendance issues for these highest-need students may have previously been considered a relatively unalterable problem, but involving the broader resource network of the community created a systems-level plan to help address the issue.

ROOT CAUSE ANALYSIS

One model that can be used to identify these seemingly unalterable factors that are at the root cause of the problem and consider how we might, in fact, alter them is referred to as either "root cause" or "cause-and-effect" analysis (Love, Stiles, Mundry, & DiRanna, 2008). This method encourages data leaders to start by brainstorming multiple categories of potential causes of a systems-level problem. In order to drill down to the root cause—or the one cause that, if corrected, would prevent the recurrence of the problem—the model then calls for the team to use a "five-*whys*" strategy (Six Sigma, 2015) that involves repeatedly asking why each potential cause might contribute to the problem. Once data leaders believe they have identified the root cause, they must verify the cause by gathering and examining data to see whether the cause is supported by the data. Only after the root cause is verified would the model recommend that the team explore solutions to prevent recurrence of the problem.

Engaging in a five-*whys* strategy ensures that the process does not jump to a "solution" too quickly. It also ensures that the "why" that is eventually determined to be the root cause is, in fact, actionable. Here is an additional example of using the five-*whys* strategy to take a problem statement that does not on the surface appear to lead to a solution and transform it into an actionable problem and solution through problem analysis.

Problem: Our English language learner (ELL) students read fluently, but don't comprehend what they are reading. They are "word callers."

Why 1: Why don't they comprehend what they are reading?

Answer 1: Because they don't understand the words that they are reading.

Why 2: Why don't they understand the words that they are reading?

Answer 2: Because they don't have the background vocabulary that they need.

Why 3: Why don't they have the background vocabulary that they need?

Answer 3: Because it hasn't been taught to them.

Why 4: Why hasn't it been taught to them?

Answer 4: Because our instruction doesn't include a broad range of explicit instruction of vocabulary.

Why 5: Why doesn't instruction include a broad range of explicit vocabulary instruction?

Answer 5: Because our teachers aren't equipped with strategies for teaching morphemic and contextual analysis.

So, you can see from this conversation how the five-*whys* approach asks the team to drill deeply into the problem. Note that the conversation may not take place all in one sitting. If the team doesn't have the data needed to answer the "why" question, they should conduct the needed research to answer it. For instance, the answer about not including a broad range of explicit vocabulary instruction would require some data to support the claim, rather than simply trusting our gut instinct that it is true. If those data weren't readily available, the team may determine that this is a hypothesis that they need to test, gather data to do so, and then come back to the analysis process. An effective team will retain this focus on the process, and be able to pick up where they left off before the data were gathered.

At some point, the educator may take you down a path of answering the "why" with issues that are beyond our control. For example, "Why hasn't it been taught to them?" could easily have been responded to with "Because they missed years of exposure to English vocabulary." At that point, the team can simply redirect the conversation, reminding the group that our goal is to focus on issues that are within our ability to control. For instance, "poverty" is a potential "why" over which educators have no control. However, understanding poverty and adapting instructional practices to be more responsive to the needs of students in poverty is something that is within our realm of control. This "empowerment" of the team is a critical aspect of the root cause analysis process.

Finally, note that the process may need more than five *whys,* but likely not fewer. You will know that you are ready to act when the answer to the question leads to very specific action. For example, the group might think "because it hasn't been taught to them" is the actionable stopping point in the conversation. "We are going to teach vocabulary! But how? What methods? What are we already doing to teach vocabulary? What aren't we doing?"

In order to get to the "how do we act" step of the process, many additional questions still need to be answered. Continuing more deeply into the five-*whys* process unearths a deeper understanding of the root cause of the problem that leads to a clearer, more specific path of action. This tireless approach to problem analysis, refusing to be satisfied with an answer until we really understand it, and a willingness to peel back the layers of the onion on the problem are key characteristics to a team having the ability to truly be effective with the five-*whys* approach.

PROBLEM ANALYSIS IN CONTEXT

In their discussion of individual-level problem analysis, Burns and Gibbons (2011) stress the importance of establishing a hypothesis that considers all potential factors, especially those that are alterable within the school setting. We believe that it is just as important to consider this range of potential factors within systems-level problem analysis.

To ensure that data leaders engage in this type of comprehensive approach to problem analysis, we recommend that teams examine multiple measures and the intersections among them (Bernhardt, 1998). Victoria Bernhardt's multiple measures model (see Figure 3.2) contends that it is critical for effective problem analysis to include this examination of multiple measures and the intersections among them. As Bernhardt recommends, effective data-driven schools use data on both student learning and school processes to monitor and evaluate the success of systems-level school reform initiatives. Examples of student-level measures highlighted by Bernhardt include standardized tests, norm/criterion-referenced tests, teacher observations of abilities, and authentic assessments. These types of measures are likely quite familiar to most readers with at least some experience with systems-level data-driven decision making. Measures of school processes, however, are much more likely to be overlooked by data leaders and data-analysis teams. Even if viewed at the aggregate systems level, student learning measures focus on the "what" of learning: individual student outcomes. Measures of school processes instead focus on the "how" of learning: the evaluation of school procedures, programs, and initiatives.

A STEP-BY-STEP GUIDE TO PROBLEM ANALYSIS USING DATA INQUIRY

Appendix 3 includes a step-by-step process designed to provide a framework for taking the wisdom of the Bernhardt model and turning it into a systematic method for data inquiry. The process, which can be used at the district, school, grade, department, or even classroom level, takes the team through brainstorming the different data questions that need to be asked, organizing and prioritizing those questions, and making sure that an effective data management plan is in place to yield the answers to those data questions.

One of the significant benefits of the Bernhardt model is the depth of the questions that are asked when it is followed. Looking at how multiple aspects of the Venn diagram intersect, and asking questions at those points of intersection, naturally lead to questions that represent alterable hypotheses. They are also a strong complement to the root cause analysis discussed above. The goal of data inquiry and the problem analysis process is by nature to lead the team (in a way that they feel empowered) toward a focus on that which is alterable.

However, once the team gets the hang of the Bernhardt model and the five-*whys* process, they may begin to apply them to every problem they can identify. Since humans seem innately talented at problem identification, and perhaps less naturally inclined to problem

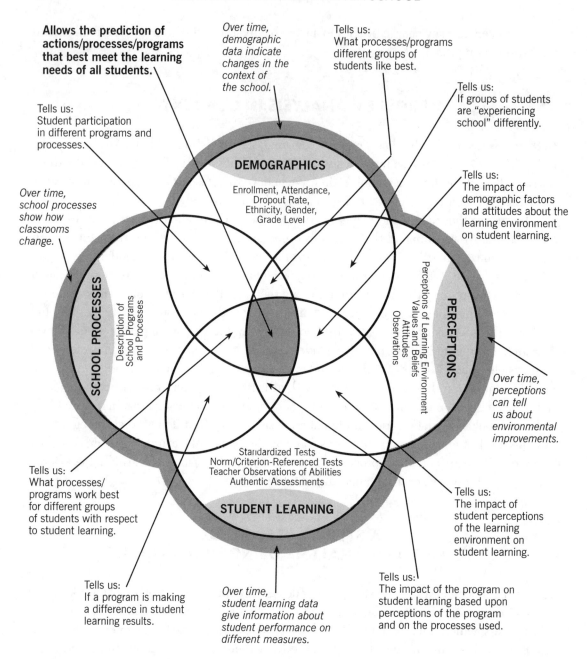

FIGURE 3.2. Victoria Bernhardt's multiple measures model. Reprinted with permission from Bernhardt (1998).

analysis, once they are equipped with a useful strategy for acting on the problems they have identified, there may be a tendency to attack every problem they see. This step-by-step data question activity encourages the team not to lose sight of those actionable questions, but organize them in a way that keeps the implementation of these deep inquiry processes more manageable. It keeps the team focused on the most pressing issues facing the system, whether that system is the district, school, grade level, department, or classroom. An example from a school district of a completed "Step 2" of this data analysis process is also included in Appendix 3, to provide a model for what this process may look like.

This step-by-step process also ties problem analysis into data management. A sound approach to data management, and the development of a data management plan, are discussed in greater detail in Chapter 8. This step-by-step activity directs the team's energy toward engaging in deep data inquiry, focused on actionable hypotheses. It takes the team further, by also providing a means for prioritizing those resulting data questions. Finally, it guides the team to create a systemic approach to managing the data that ensures that the answers to these data questions will be readily available, at the time they are needed, now and in future data inquiry cycles and school years.

PROBLEM ANALYSIS? PROBLEM ANALYSIS? WE DON'T NEED NO STINKING PROBLEM ANALYSIS!

In problem solving with individual students, it is a well-known fact that many teams fall prey to the tendency to jump immediately from problem identification into brainstorming ideas (Burns & Gibbons, 2011). Sadly, we have worked with far too many systems-level data-analysis teams that make the same mistake. Perhaps this is because problem analysis is considered by many to be one of the most difficult steps in the problem-solving model, and as a result they unconsciously avoid this challenge. It may be because the temptation to think they have the answer to the problem is simply too great. Whatever the psychological reason, the effects of moving directly from problem identification into plan development are disastrous, often resulting in a waste of time and educational resources spent addressing the gap between what is expected and what is occurring in ways that do not address the mismatch between what the system is providing and what the students' needs are.

There are a number of alterable behaviors that contribute to why the problem analysis step is so often missed, whether they be related to the process of how the school system itself operates, or the decision-making process of the team. While some of these may be difficult or beyond the power of the team itself to change, when identified and understood, at a minimum the team can be aware of and work to avoid the potential negative impact of these forces. We take a moment below to discuss how these factors may be playing into our tendency to overlook problem analysis.

School Budgeting

One key factor that ultimately leads schools to jump from problem identification to plan development is actually the school budgeting process. Typically, the school budgeting process is a constrained and relatively inflexible process. Often, schools by default take each budget line item from the previous year, and carry it forward to the coming year. Even when more significant changes in the budget are made, schools are reluctant to make changes to the staffing budget, either due to contractual obligations or simply a fear of losing people (Hess & Osberg, 2010).

This leads to the continuation of programs, and the staff that provide them, even after they are no longer a match with the needs of students. Since these programs are "around," kids get placed into the programs by default. We have seen countless schools where every student who is below target in reading gets "put" into a program that the school has had around for years, with entrenched staff, entrenched habits, and little to no evidence that this program yields any, let alone the best, return on investment. If school leaders are truly going to use data to drive decision making, we need instead to evaluate all of our programs at least annually, with the mind-set that programs that no longer match students' needs should be replaced with ones that do. This match is best identified not just by looking at the difference between what is expected and what is occurring but by reviewing the problem analysis process to understand students' changing needs, and ensuring that our programs are still addressing the "whys."

The timing of the school budgeting process also plays into the continuation of programs regardless of their effectiveness. School budgets for the coming school year are typically established months before the end of the previous year. In order to ensure that they get access to the funds they need, school leaders often must commit to the programs that they will be purchasing in the coming year at least 6–8 months prior to the beginning of that year. This makes it much more difficult to evaluate program effectiveness at the end of a school year, and then use that information to guide decision making about programs for the coming year. District leaders need to provide greater flexibility to schools, so that they can make decisions about which programs they will pay for, and how many and which staff they need in order to run them. The "use it or lose it" approach to claiming budget dollars and staff ultimately ends up with school leaders making decisions that are driven by a fear of losing funding, rather than by what would best serve students.

In the absence of a sea change in the school budgeting process, building leaders can take a much more data-based approach to school budgeting and purchasing. With a process in place that uses diagnostic assessment data to understand the systemic needs of the organization, and ongoing progress monitoring data (combined with fidelity data) to establish which interventions are effective, the informed school leader can make purchasing decisions that are responsive to the evidence. For example, if many students have difficulty with acquiring word analysis skills in the primary grade, intervention packages that feature enhanced phonics instruction should be budgeted for the following year. This demands that principals and other administrators who have a ground-level view of students' needs identify these needs and funnel this input up to central office administrators who plan for these purchases.

One Size Fits All

Another factor leading to schools skipping the problem analysis step is that intervention programs are often sold to schools as panaceas. We have worked with many schools where a well-established standard treatment protocol intervention is in place. However, all too frequently that intervention is either ill defined or is poorly matched to students. For example, in many schools, we see intervention lines on progress monitoring graphs that are simply labeled "Title I." We are fairly certain that the funding source used to pay for the intervention is not an adequate definition of that intervention. We would be concerned if on our medical chart we saw "private health insurance," instead of the specific treatment being delivered. Title I in this example becomes a "place" that we send students who are low performing, with either a loosely defined intervention plan, or an intervention that is prescribed to all students below target. This serves to encourage the behavior of moving directly from problem identification to plan development.

Again following the medical analogy, if problem analysis were skipped and we simply applied a single standard treatment protocol universally to all patients, then we might choose to administer acetaminophen to all patients exhibiting a fever. Based on a single data point, the discrepancy between what is expected (a temperature around 98.6°F) and what is occurring (a temperature higher than that), this single treatment is applied universally. This would certainly be a less expensive approach, since it is entirely likely that it will work for a significant percentage of patients, and we would have saved money by reducing the total cost of assessment.

Unfortunately, if modern medicine were to use this approach, a significant number of patients would die. By collecting multiple data points after the problem has been identified, medical professionals can establish the cause of the fever—for instance, it may be due to bacterial infection, viral, and so on. In the case of bacterial infection, antibiotics are an effective and well-established standard treatment protocol. But they have no impact and can even cause harm when the cause is viral. Similarly, when engaged in systems-level problem solving within schools, we should attempt to avoid implementing a single reading program with all students in a single group based on the students' performance on a state test. As in the medical example above, this one-size-fits-all approach is in danger of overlooking several different potential underlying reasons for the problem.

This is not to say that there aren't educational practices that we know to be broadly effective. And we aren't suggesting that every student requires a uniquely individualized intervention. One can certainly "prescribe" a common intervention (i.e., standard treatment protocol) to a group of students, provided that these supporting pieces are in place: the evidence gathered suggests that these students, in fact, have similar needs; that the intervention is well matched to those needs; and that ongoing data are collected on each student, to establish whether the intervention continues to be effective for everyone (Reyna, 2004).

Superficial Problem Analysis

We have worked with many systems-level data-analysis teams where problem analysis is not deep enough, leading to repeated cycles attempting to solve the same problem, or an abandonment of the process entirely. One frequent reason for this superficial problem analysis is that preexisting assumptions about the reasons for the problem are provided as a replacement for actual analysis. "Our ELL students are all 'word callers' and need comprehension instead of 'just' fluency," "Students who have been in our district from kindergarten have better outcomes than these kids coming in from other districts," and "We just have more mobility than district X" are all examples of assumptions we have heard given as the reasons behind pervasive systems-level issues, without conducting the data analysis to see whether they were actually true, alterable, and relevant to the problem. The practical example on the achievement gap, presented at the end of this chapter, is another example where trusting assumptions over analysis is prevalent. Trusting these assumptions, rather than using the problem-solving process to uncover the reasons for the problem, is not something we have seen to be an effective practice. As the saying goes, "Data are too often used like a drunk uses a lamppost. More for support than illumination."

Another reason for a lack of depth in the problem analysis process is simply that the team doesn't dig deeply enough. Sometimes the tools to quickly and easily analyze data are not available. Fortunately, technology can help with this issue (see Chapter 8). Even if your district can't afford a data warehouse and business intelligence tool set, there are low-cost tools available that can help you dig more deeply into your data. Sometimes the data themselves that are needed to answer key questions are not collected. Later in this chapter, we discuss a process for letting inquiry, rather than available data, guide the problem analysis process. When this happens, it exposes where these data may not be available, and motivates the team to resolve this issue in a way that would not be as likely if the team focused first on the available data, and then asked questions about it. Also, sometimes the team decides they've found the answer and moves to plan development before looking to see whether there might be more than one "why." More about this in the next section.

What Happens When You Skip It

Regardless of the reason, skipping the problem analysis process at the systems level has detrimental effects. Because the process is cyclical, the best outcome in this scenario is that the team will at least diligently walk through the problem-solving process again, for the same problem. In this case, while resources are spent in redundant work and critical time is lost while students continue to perform below expectations, there is still the possibility that the team will correct the errors made in the first go-round and address the problem more effectively. More frequently, however, schools abandon the systems-level problem-solving process and revert to individual problem solving with each student.

When viewed at the systems level, problem analysis is an incredibly easy step for the team to overlook. One way of describing it can help make more apparent why it is necessary. Without problem analysis, you basically have three steps: (1) Uh oh, we have a problem, (2) Oh no, let's throw this at it, and (3) Did it go away? When presented this way, it seems obvious that something is missing.

USING PROBLEM ANALYSIS TO ADDRESS ACHIEVEMENT GAPS

Problem analysis is particularly important in effectively addressing achievement gaps, an especially salient topic for schools today. It can help data leaders move beyond demographic markers of risk, such as race/ethnicity and poverty, and drill down to the core issues that truly account for gaps. The achievement gap issue is one where it is especially easy to focus on unalterable problems, blaming the problem on issues such as cultural differences in families' approaches to education, access to resources, and lack of enrichment outside of the school day. Approaching these problems as if these are static factors can lead to apathy, rather than empowerment. The moment we throw our hands up in the face of the magnitude of the problem, we have lost.

But focusing on the achievement gap in schools is simply an example of problem identification. Unfortunately, many of the practices to address the achievement gap that we witness in education today reflect the common issues that problem-solving teams encounter. Moving straight from problem identification to plan development, failing to ask deeper questions that explore how demographics and student learning intersect with perceptions and school processes, failing to prioritize data questions related to the achievement gap, and stopping the inquiry process before getting to the root cause are all mistakes that we see in education leaders' approaches to tackling the achievement gap issue. They are so frequent that, well, someone could write a book about it.

One school district that we worked with decided to tackle the issue of the achievement gap head-on. The underlying community had deep divisions along race and culture, with frequent, high-profile incidents motivated by racism and misunderstanding that fed the flames of these divisions. It would have been easy for this district to throw up their hands in the face of a communitywide issue.

Instead, the school district began to explore their data more deeply. One of the first things they learned was that their current approach to data analysis and reporting was not going deep enough to truly understand the problem. Federal and state reporting requirements led the district to compile their data across their broader African American population and their growing population of East African descent, many of whom were recent immigrants to the United States. While these were two distinct groups, with very different needs and backgrounds, all the disaggregation being done at the district and school levels was simply grouping these students into the single category of "Black, not Hispanic." Some of the East African students were also being grouped into the "ELL" category for data analysis, which pooled them with a large population of Hispanic students, many of whom were children of families employed through migrant labor, which represented a completely separate set of challenges. By beginning the process of disaggregating the data more thoroughly, the district began to ask questions in their inquiry process that were much more specific and actionable to the needs of each population. The types of school processes available to these population groups varied widely, as did the perceptions of the students and families, as well as the related demographic issues. The district focused first on their ability to disaggregate the student learning for each of these groups, ensuring that the technology tools they leveraged during their systems-level data analysis were equipped with the ability to distinguish these groups, and that their staff had the skills to use this technology to do so.

The district began to examine the data more deeply, exploring across Bernhardt's (1998) domains of data while maintaining a focus on identifying the separate issues and needs of each group. This helped tremendously in understanding the problems that each group was facing and the differences in resources available, as well as what approaches were likely to be accepted by the community. Maintaining a focus on alterable factors, the district will be equipped with the tools they need to make steady progress toward problem solving with each distinct population group. In our opinion, this is a clear example of responding to the alarm call that the achievement gap data have identified, but doing so with an eye toward a comprehensive problem analysis process, resulting in the very approach that the achievement gap issues necessitate: responding to the unique needs of each population group, and making sure that these needs are responded to equitably and in ways that are sensitive to the unique context of each population group.

KEY ISSUES

- The key question in problem analysis is: "What are the whys" behind the difference between expectations and occurrence that were uncovered in problem identification?

- Focusing on alterable factors is a critical mind-set needed for the problem analysis process to be successful.

- Root cause analysis is an effective method for ensuring adequate depth in problem analysis.

- Contextual variables, such as systems, perceptions, and the instructional environment, must be considered during problem analysis, in order to examine all potential factors contributing to the "whys."

- Commonly held practices, such as a school budgeting process that has deadlines that don't fit decision-making timelines, a love affair with panacea intervention "solutions," and a cursory process, are reasons why the problem analysis step is often skipped.

CHAPTER 4

Systems-Level Plan Development, Plan Implementation, and Plan Evaluation

One important caveat before we begin: While we have chosen to discuss plan development, plan implementation, and plan evaluation all in one chapter in this book, we agree that each represents a distinct, critical step within an effective individual- or systems-level problem-solving model. Specifically, we support the five-step problem-solving model introduced in Chapter 1.

This model is unique in comparison to some other popular problem-solving models in that it intentionally isolates and highlights the significance of plan implementation and implementation integrity. We believe that this is essential, since we must ensure that interventions are implemented as intended before we can expect to sensibly determine whether they have been effective with a student or group of students. Given this fact, whereas we have chosen to discuss plan development, plan implementation, and plan evaluation all in one chapter and acknowledge that they overlap to at least some extent, at the same time we highlight throughout the chapter the unique and integral importance of each as a separate key component of the systems-level problem-solving process.

As noted in Chapter 3, plan development must stem directly from the results of problem analysis, or we risk addressing the wrong problem and mistakenly determining that the plan has been ineffective. For example, in the playground story described in Chapter 1, by analyzing ODR data, interviewing the seven target students and their parents, and observing the students on the playground, the leadership team was able to more specifically operationalize the problem as a lack of cooperative play skills among the target students and plan an intervention that involved teaching these skills to all third-grade students and helping them practice the skills on the playground. If the team had not engaged in this intensive problem analysis and instead made the common assumption that the students had the skills but were just not adequately motivated to demonstrate them, they might have planned a very different intervention, focused primarily on incentives for the students to exhibit behaviors they may not yet have had, likely leading to the failure of the plan.

We agree that plan implementation is critical as well. The identified intervention must be implemented as intended in terms of the time allocated, individuals involved, and steps followed, or we risk mistakenly determining that it has been ineffective, when, in fact, it may not have been given an authentic opportunity to be effective. An addition to the opening anecdote provides evidence of this. A supplementary component of the plan not yet discussed involved collaborating with the county to sponsor a recreation program at the playground for the housing project where the seven target students lived. Unfortunately, it was unsuccessful at least in part due to the fact that the team members did not implement the plan as intended and attend the program with the students during the first 2 weeks. Because the adults were not able to attend, the students, who had shared a history of not feeling safe playing at the housing project playground, likely did not feel comfortable participating with only county personnel that they did not already know and trust.

Following development and implementation, a plan must be thoroughly evaluated to learn whether the problem has been adequately addressed with the target students or system. If it has not yet been adequately addressed, it is critical to cycle back to the first step of the problem-solving model, problem identification, to determine what to do next. Plan evaluation is also essential to ensure that we learn from this problem-solving experience and can more efficiently and effectively develop future plans for students and systems demonstrating similar problems. In the playground behavior example, the team examined changes in third-grade ODR data and found that the percentage of referrals coming from third-grade students declined significantly following the implementation of the plan to teach students cooperative games and help them practice the games at recess. This decline was particularly notable among the seven target students. As noted above, the county-sponsored recreation program at the housing project was much less successful. Evaluation of that component revealed that no students showed up for the first 2 weeks of the program, leading the county to cancel it.

SYSTEMS-LEVEL PLAN DEVELOPMENT

We now return to plan development for a more thorough discussion of what that step in the model can and should look like in data-driven schools engaged in systems-level problem solving. As highlighted in the five-step problem-solving model, effective plan development should be framed by three critical questions: (1) What is the goal?, (2) What is the intervention plan to meet this goal?, and (3) How will progress be monitored?

Identifying Research-Based Practices and Resources

As mentioned in Chapter 1, NCLB (2001), IDEIA (2004), and the data-driven personnel evaluation movement focused increased attention at the turn of the 21st century on the importance of systems-level data-driven decision making and the identification and implementation of research-based interventions. The most recent reauthorization of ESEA, renamed ESSA (2015), specifically directs states and local education agencies to consult with data leaders, including appropriate specialized instructional support personnel when designing and implementing research-based interventions (National Association of School Psychologists, 2016). It is therefore no doubt helpful, as a data leader, to develop your own library of research-based interventions with which you are familiar. To assist you in this process, there are many excellent online reviews and clearinghouses of interventions. Among the most popular at the time this book was written were the What Works Clearinghouse (*ies.ed.gov/ncee/wwc*), the National Center on Intensive Intervention at American Institutes for Research (*www.intensiveintervention.org/chart/instructional-intervention-tools*), and Intervention Central (*interventioncentral.org*). The former reviews evidence to support the effectiveness of purchasable intervention programs, whereas the latter two include scripts to implementing free research-based intervention methods and strategies.

Equally or even more important, however, than data leaders having their own library of research-based interventions is for them to be able to effectively facilitate problem solving among district, school, grade-level, or content-area team members and help them ask the right questions and access the right resources. This is especially critical given how frequently new interventions are developed and how quickly websites change. Keeping up with these changes can feel like a never-ending challenge. Students, interns, and early career data leaders often report struggling with this challenge, sharing their frustration as teachers repeatedly approach them with questions about the best interventions to address different academic and/or behavioral concerns. In addition to being effective problem-solving facilitators, it is also important for data leaders to be familiar with the characteristics of effective instruction and intervention at all tiers regardless of the problem they are attempting to solve. A strong understanding of these key elements of effective instruction can help leaders to better select any intervention. Burns, VanderHeyden, and Zaslofsky (2014) summarized this well in a recent *Best Practices in School Psychology* chapter, identifying the following five key characteristics of effective instruction: (1) correctly targets skills, (2) includes explicit instruction, (3) provides an appropriate level of challenge, (4) allows students frequent opportunities to respond, and (5) supplies students with immediate feedback.

Finally, it is critical to carefully investigate and take into account the function of a student's or group of students' problem before deciding upon an appropriate intervention. As discussed in Chapter 3, we often assume that the problem is either that the student or group of students has not yet acquired the skill with which they are having difficulty or that they are not motivated to demonstrate it. These, however, are only two of five potential reasons for academic or behavioral difficulty identified by Daley, Witt, Martens, and Dool (1997). According to Daley et al., the other three reasons include that the student or group of students (1) is not yet proficient in the skill, (2) is not yet fluent in demonstrating the skill, and (3) has not yet generalized demonstration of the skill to other settings.

T. Chris Riley-Tillman and his colleagues at the University of Missouri designed the Evidence-Based Intervention Network (*ebi.missouri.edu*) that helps users identify which of these reasons for academic failure best explains their student's or group of students' problem and which research-based interventions might best address the problem. The Network's website also includes scripts and brief videos demonstrating how users can implement these free intervention methods and strategies.

Planning How Progress Will Be Monitored

Data leaders must not only develop a plan for research-based intervention during this problem-solving phase but also specify a plan for monitoring the progress of the student or group of students in response to the intervention—the third purpose of assessment within a comprehensive assessment system. This progress monitoring plan allows the team to systematically assess the student's or group of students' growth trajectory and ultimately the effectiveness of the intervention. The plan should include (1) how often progress will be monitored, (2) for how long, (3) by whom, (4) with which tools, and (5) how the data will be used to make decisions.

How Often Will Progress Be Monitored?

Practitioners and systems have often looked for a single simple answer to the first question of how often progress should be monitored. Like most complicated questions, however, it does not have a simple answer. The answer is: It depends. It depends first on the sensitivity of the measure. Some progress monitoring measures, like the popular Reading-Curriculum Based Measure (R-CBM) 1-minute assessment of oral reading fluency, are sensitive to student growth if administered weekly or even twice a week. Other measures, such as math computation or math problem-solving CBMs, have not yet demonstrated consistent sensitivity to change in student skills over that short of a period of time. Because they do not appear to be able to pick up on student growth when administered weekly, we argue that it would likely be a waste of time and resources to administer them that frequently. The results would not be useful in determining whether an intervention was working. Instead, it may be more appropriate to administer these probes every other week, making it more likely they would pick up on any change that had occurred, or to use mastery monitoring tools, rather than GOMs, that track student mastery of specific math subskills. These mastery monitoring tools are discussed in greater detail later in this chapter. The bottom line is that it is critical for data leaders to be familiar with the evidence indicating how sensitive the measures they are using are to student growth before making a decision about how frequently to administer them.

Data leaders should also consider the intensity of the intervention being provided to the individual student or group of students in making their decision about how often to monitor progress. Shinn (2015) reminds us that sensitivity to growth may be partly about the psychometrics of the progress monitoring measure, but equally if not more important may be the level of support being provided to the student or group of students. If we want at-risk students to grow more quickly and close the gap toward their peers, we need to provide them with interventions that are more individualized, targeted to their needs, and delivered in larger time chunks over a longer period of time. If we do this, Shinn asserts that measures like math computation and math problem-solving CBMs—that might not appear sensitive to student growth when administered weekly under typical circumstances—will, in fact, show growth on a weekly basis.

For How Long?

The answer to the second question—How long should data leaders monitor students' progress before making a decision about adjusting the intervention?—is that it also depends. It depends on the stakes of the decision and on what research says about the intervention. If the progress monitoring data are being collected for a student or group of students already receiving general education and/or special education services to determine whether a research-based intervention is helping the student or group of students close the gap between their performance and expectations, the stakes are not as high as they would be if the data were being collected for the purpose of determining whether a student or group of students is not responding to intervention and meets eligibility criteria for special education services. In the former case, experts agree that a more liberal decision rule, such as the popular 4-point rule (National Center on Response to Intervention, 2012), may be appropriate. Under the 4-point rule, if the goal is to increase the target behavior (e.g., words read correctly per minute [wcpm]), then the 4-point rule would suggest that a change be considered following four consecutive data points below the aim line. If the goal is to decrease the target behavior (e.g., blurting out in class), the rule would suggest that a change be considered following four consecutive data points above the aim line. It is important to note that a "change" could include switching to a different intervention, but could in addition or instead include changing the frequency or intensity of the intervention. As discussed in greater detail below, depending on the fidelity with which the intervention was being implemented and how long research suggests the intervention should take to fully implement, it may also be that the team would consider, but reject, a change after the 4-data point decision rule is met. The rule only suggests that a change be considered.

In the case of a student or group of students being evaluated for special education eligibility, however, more stringent criteria are likely needed. Determining whether a student qualifies for and will receive special education services is a high-stakes decision that will likely change the student's access to peers without disabilities, so we need to hold ourselves to a higher standard in making our decision. Given these higher stakes, state education agencies should heed the work of scholars, such as Ted Christ and others, who have found that, given the reliability of the current tools we have for monitoring student progress, many more than four data points are needed before a reliable high-stakes decision can be made (Christ, Zopluoglu, Long, & Monaghen, 2012; Christ, Zopluoglu, Monaghen, & Van Norman, 2013). Some state education agencies have begun to require that practitioners gather 12 or more data points, in some cases over a specific number of weeks, to be able to more reliably document the inadequate response to intervention necessary for students to be eligible for special education under their SLD criteria (see Minnesota Department of Education, 2011, for an example).

All interventions are not, however, created equal. Data leaders are therefore cautioned to not only consider the stakes of the decision they are making regarding how often to progress monitor but to also consider what the research says about for how long the particular intervention being implemented needs to be administered before one can confidently evaluate its success with a student or group of students. With some interventions, it may take more intervention sessions and more than four—or even more than 12—data points before one can be sure whether an intervention appears to have been effective. As we discuss later, these estimates of how long an intervention must be implemented before its success can be evaluated are also dependent on the intervention having been implemented in a manner consistent with the way it was designed to be implemented in the research. A student's or group of students' response to an intervention that is implemented for what the research says is the necessary amount of time (e.g., currently 14 weeks) but that is not implemented with fidelity still cannot be sensibly evaluated.

By Whom?

As far as the third question is concerned—By whom should progress monitoring tools be administered?—we have observed three common models. The first involves general education and special education teachers or intervention specialists themselves screening and progress monitoring the students in their own classrooms, on their own special education caseloads or in their own intervention groups. In the second model, an identified assessment team of local data leaders—often including school psychologists, special education teachers, intervention specialists, or in some cases, trained paraprofessionals—conducts screening and/or progress monitoring with all students regardless of which classroom they are in, caseload they are on, or intervention group of which they are a part. In the third model, technology-delivered assessments are provided either in a group- or individually administered environment. All three models have potential advantages and disadvantages.

Under the first model, students may be more at ease during testing since they will likely have a more trusting relationship with the adults with whom they work on a regular basis. Screening and progress monitoring using this approach may also be more easily integrated into and arranged around instruction, since the teachers or interventionists themselves are determining when and with whom assessment will occur on any particular day. At the same time, concerns about the reliability of results may be greater under this model for a couple of reasons. First, because these teachers and interventionists are more intimately familiar with the students they are assessing, they may unconsciously and unintentionally drift from standardization in their administration or scoring of test items. For example, they may, without even realizing it, score what they believe they know the student *meant* to say, rather than what the student *actually said*. In addition, there is a significantly larger number of teachers or interventionists than there are members of an assessment team. As a result, it is more difficult to ensure that all those administering screening and progress monitoring measures have been adequately trained initially and have received adequate follow-up refresher trainings. Under the first model, this likely would contribute to greater variability in the way tests are administered and scored, making it harder to confidently use the results to measure student growth.

The second model has pros and cons as well. On the plus side, since there would likely be fewer assessment team members than general education and special education teachers, it would be easier to ensure that they continue to be adequately trained in administration and scoring. This more consistent training could contribute to increased confidence in the school's ability to use the results to make decisions about student progress. The fact that assessment team members would potentially not be as familiar with most students they were testing could be seen as both a pro and a con. One advantage of this lack of familiarity might be that assessment team members would be more likely to base their administration and scoring only on the current behavior and responses of the student and not on any prior knowledge of the student. A disadvantage, on the other hand, could be that students may feel less comfortable with assessment team members during the testing process and consequently may not perform as well, potentially calling into question the reliability of the data.

In the third model, the students are completing the assessment on a device. It is important to note that here we are referring to assessments that are computer administered, not just computer scored. Advantages of this third model include the fact that it standardizes administration, removing the possibility of observer drift referred to above, and reduces staffing issues. Among the cons of this method, however, are that it requires hardware availability, and that there is currently not as wide a range of assessments available in a technology-delivered format. Data leaders will need to carefully consider these advantages and disadvantages before making decisions about who will conduct screening and progress monitoring in their schools.

With Which Tools?

Data leaders must provide integral input into decisions regarding which tools to use in progress monitoring as well, addressing the fourth question about developing a progress monitoring plan. As mentioned previously, they need to either already have or be willing to develop strong data literacy skills and should possess expertise in knowing which sets of resources to seek out to help answer questions related to systems-level problem solving. One of those sets of resources may be websites that review the psychometric characteristics of screening and progress monitoring tools. At the time this book was written, the screening and progress monitoring tools charts on the previously mentioned National Center on Intensive Intervention at American Institutes for Research website (*www.intensiveintervention.org*) provide the most comprehensive resources of this kind. The data leader must be able to facilitate discussions and decisions within a data-driven school regarding the use of tools reviewed on sites like this. The characteristics of effective individual leaders in this respect, and ways in which developing leaders can enhance their skills in this area, are discussed in Chapter 9.

Websites like those described above primarily review GOMs. GOMs may not be available for all skills and at all grade levels, however. Data-driven schools must therefore also consider the use of alternative tools for frequently assessing student growth, including tools that Shinn (2012) refers to as "mastery monitoring" measures. These could include both CBMs focused on isolated skills (e.g., phonemic segmentation fluency, math computation) and common classroom formative assessments, which are designed by teachers through PLCs. With respect to both of these sets of tools, individual students or groups of students are monitored in terms of their mastery of specific skills, benchmarks, or standards, and instruction is adjusted to provide additional support as necessary to help them achieve mastery.

How Will the Data Be Used to Make Decisions?

These adjustments can be made effectively only if the progress monitoring plan includes specification of how the data collected will be used to make decisions. Too often in schools, we have seen educators chart progress monitoring data for individual students or groups of students seemingly for the sake of charting the data. In some cases, no changes in the intervention are ever made or even considered. The students are just provided with the stock intervention that the school happens to have available. In other cases, changes are made, but they are not clearly documented within the progress monitoring graph, making it nearly impossible to determine the impact those changes may have had on the students' growth. Many assessment-specific progress monitoring systems, such as AIMSweb, as well as assessment-agnostic systems, such as ChartDog 2.0 (*www.jimwrightonline.com/php/chartdog_2_0/chartdog.php*), allow users to indicate within progress monitoring graphs when an intervention is changed by inserting a vertical line. The slope of the student's progress is then recalculated from that point forward to indicate the impact of the change on the student's growth trajectory. Technology tools like these are discussed in more detail in Chapter 8.

SYSTEMS-LEVEL PLAN IMPLEMENTATION

A data-driven school engaged in effective systems-level problem solving must also plan how to monitor the way in which interventions are implemented. That is why the plan implementation step is so important. It helps the team answer the next key question in the problem-solving model: How will intervention integrity be ensured? As mentioned previously, it is meaningless to assess the degree to which a student or group of students within a system has responded to intervention if that intervention has not been implemented with fidelity to the way in which it was designed to be implemented.

In developing a plan, it is essential to first think critically about and document who will implement the plan that is developed. The person who delivers the intervention must have the time to deliver it, must be well trained initially, and must be provided with frequent refresher trainings in delivering the intervention. We have observed that in some schools, classroom teachers implement Tier 1 whole-class general education interventions, specialists (e.g., reading/math/behavior interventionists, Title I teachers) deliver Tier 2 small-group interventions, and paraprofessionals carry out Tier 3 individualized interventions with the most at-risk students. This is not the model advocated by most MTSS experts. While some paraprofessionals may be well trained in the Tier 3 interventions they are implementing, from our experience, many are not. Regardless of their specific training in the Tier 3 intervention, paraprofessionals likely do not have the same overall training and experience in working with at-risk students that a licensed general education or special education teacher would have.

We therefore advocate for readers to promote an alternative model more supported by the MTSS literature. We recommend that paraprofessionals instead cover Tier 1 general education classroom instruction during times when supplemental intervention is being provided to at-risk students, releasing the licensed general education teachers to be able to provide Tier 3 individualized support to the most needy students. We recognize that this may require some planning to ensure that the Tier 1 instruction taking place at that time can be implemented by a paraprofessional and that the paraprofessional is provided with any training necessary to deliver it. We believe that the potential benefits outweigh the challenges.

It is also critical for schools to reexamine their Tier 2 small-group intervention models to ensure that they are as efficient as possible, with minimal duplication of services. In our experience, many schools provide several parallel Tier 2 interventions to the same sets of students. More is not necessarily better, however. Adelman and Taylor (2012) illustrate this clearly in their "before" picture of the fragmented support systems in place in many traditional schools (see Figure 4.1).

Each of these Tier 2 interventions on its own may be beneficial to students, but if these interventions are not well coordinated, it can lead to valuable school resources being wasted. The time devoted to providing a large number of overlapping Tier 2 interventions to the same students can overwhelm the school's support systems, making it more difficult or even impossible to provide individualized Tier 3 general education support to the students most at risk. Instead, it may be more beneficial for schools to identify only the more limited number of Tier 2 interventions expected to be most effective with students in need of small-group support. This could free up some of the time of the teachers or specialists providing Tier 2 interventions to offer more Tier 3 general education interventions to those individual students who need that more intensive level of support.

As alluded to above in the review of the plan development step, effective plan implementation must also include devoting adequate time to implementing the intervention, providing staff involved in administering the intervention with adequate initial training, and ensuring that staff receive frequent, sufficient follow-up refresher training and coaching to guarantee that they do not drift from their initial training.

Research has shown that the one-time workshop approach to professional development (what is often referred to as a "spray and pray") is not associated with comprehensive understanding and ongoing effective implementation and application of interventions. Ongoing coaching and support is much more successful in achieving these outcomes, as shown in Figure 4.2, from Joyce and Showers (2002).

A key component of this ongoing coaching is regular fidelity checks using a combination of procedures, including self-assessments by the intervention implementers, direct observations of intervention implementation, and review of student work samples produced as part of the intervention. These fidelity checks help data-driven schools monitor the degree to which staff are following the key steps determined to be necessary for the intervention to have the opportunity to be effective with the student or group of students.

The first of these recommendations—devoting adequate time to implementing the intervention—may seem obvious, but in our experience, it is not as obvious as you might think. One example involves a consultation with a middle school regarding concerns about their students' progress in math. Data indicated that students in the school were not meeting expected proficiency or growth standards in math over the past several years. The team's initial hypothesis was that the new math curriculum the school had adopted a few years ago might not be appropriate to meet the needs of the students and that the school should consider replacing it. During the course of the conversation, however, it was revealed that the curriculum was designed to be administered in 75-minute sessions, but the school's sched-

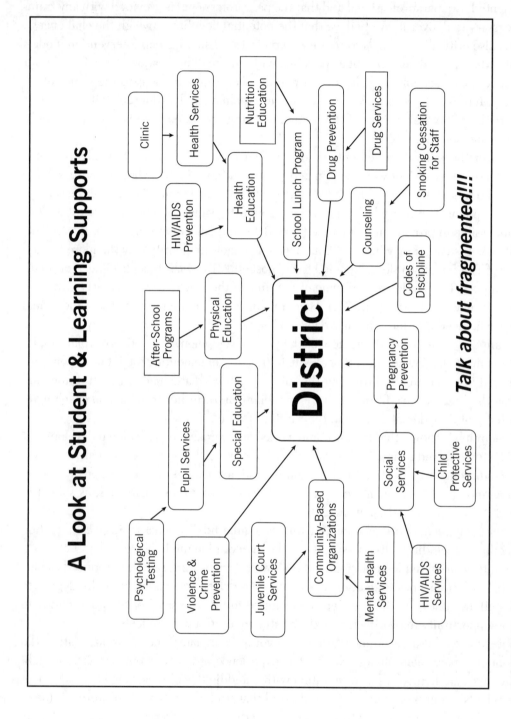

A Look at Student & Learning Supports

Talk about fragmented!!!

FIGURE 4.1. Fragmented support systems in place in traditional schools. Reprinted with permission from Adelman and Taylor (2012).

OUTCOMES Percentage of Participants Who Demonstrate Knowledge, Demonstrate New Skills in a Training Setting, and Use New Skills in the Classroom			
TRAINING COMPONENTS	Knowledge	Skill Demonstration	Use in the Classroom
Theory and Discussion	10%	5%	0%
...+ Demonstration in Training	30%	20%	0%
...+ Practice and Feedback in Training	60%	60%	5%
...+ Coaching in Classroom	95%	95%	95%

FIGURE 4.2. Results of Joyce and Showers's study of impact of ongoing coaching and support. Reprinted with permission from Joyce and Showers (2002).

ule called for 42-minute math classes. Further discussion uncovered the fact that currently, each math teacher was being left to decide on their own how to fit the 75-minute lesson into the 42-minute class period. Because each teacher was making these decisions individually, the team feared that there were likely significant differences in which components of the 75-minute lessons each teacher was choosing to include. Teachers were therefore not consistently implementing the intervention as intended and allowing students the opportunity to benefit from it.

The team agreed that it might still be possible for the students to be successful with this math curriculum without changing the school's schedule, but it would first be critical for the math teachers to collectively review the curriculum and determine which were the "non-negotiable" components that all of them would be sure to include in their lessons versus which were important, but not essential. If, based on this review, the teachers determined that the non-negotiable components could not be reliably implemented in 42 minutes, however, the schedule or curriculum would need to be reexamined.

It is important to remember that what gets documented is most often what gets completed. We believe that any forms and tools data-driven schools use to monitor implementation integrity must address any and all of the key components outlined above: (1) devoting adequate time to implementing the intervention, (2) providing staff involved in administering the intervention with adequate initial training, (3) ensuring that staff receive frequent, sufficient follow-up refresher training and coaching to guarantee that they do not drift from their initial training, and (4) conducting regular fidelity checks. Resources related to fidelity checks include both checklists of steps involved in specific intervention programs, methods, and strategies (available at *www.rtinetwork.org*), and checklists regarding implementation of any intervention regardless of content.

An extensive literature has developed in recent years about the need to assess and facilitate intervention fidelity (also known as treatment integrity; Hagermoser Sanetti & Kratochwill, 2009; Lane, Bocian, MacMillan, & Gresham, 2004). Simply stated, an evidence-based practice that is selected for implementation at the school level will be effective only if the local implementation of the practice is consistent with the way the practice was implemented in the research setting. The literature in this area has focused on two aspects. First, a number of procedures have been advanced to appraise the level of intervention fidelity, including checklists that detail specific steps of the intervention. (As noted previously, a representative sampling of such checklists is available at *www.rtinetwork.org/getstarted/evaluate/treatment-integrity-protocols*). These checklists can be used for teachers and interventionists to self-evaluate their adherence to intervention procedures, or may be used by specialists or administrators during teacher observations. The second aspect of this issue is how intervention fidelity, once it has been appraised, can be supported and facilitated. It has long been established that intervention fidelity is maximized when specialists or consultants meet with teachers to review fidelity data and discuss ways to improve adherence to the procedures (Noell, Witt, Gilbertson, Ranier, & Freeland, 1997; Noell et al., 2005). Kovaleski (2002) hypothesized that interventions are most likely to be implemented when problem-solving team members assist classroom teachers in "establishing" the intervention by actively participating as co-interventionists. These hands-on approaches are in contrast to ineffective problem-solving teams that make a recommendation for intervention and then assume that the intervention will be carried out without support, which in our experience, is highly unlikely.

A final aspect of effective team practice is planning and implementing the monitoring of student progress in response to the interventions. It has been known for over 30 years that teachers who monitor students' progress frequently and then make decisions based on graphed data realize better outcomes for their students than teachers who do not engage in these practices (Fuchs & Fuchs, 1986). Progress monitoring using graphed data has been advocated as a key component of MTSS (Batsche et al., 2005; Brown-Chidsey & Steege, 2010; Burns & Gibbons, 2012) and is embedded in most contemporary commercially available assessment platforms (e.g., AIMSweb, DIBELS Next, FastBridge, Star). Suffice it to say, "If you're not graphing data, you're not doing MTSS," and teams should ensure a total commitment to this practice.

SYSTEMS-LEVEL PLAN EVALUATION

The final step of the problem-solving model, plan evaluation, addresses the key question: Was the intervention/program plan effective? It does so by returning to the key question that was the focus of the model's first step, problem identification: What is the discrepancy between what is expected and what is occurring? To answer these questions, data targeting the fourth purpose of assessment within a comprehensive assessment system—outcomes— must be collected and analyzed.

The outcomes measured should address whether students have reached a level of proficiency consistent with expectations or whether they are growing at a rate that will make them more likely to reach proficiency in the future. In investigating outcomes data addressing whether students have reached a level of proficiency consistent with expectations, data leaders must clarify how their schools are defining expectations. As alluded to earlier in Chapter 2, two sets of criteria commonly used in schools in defining expectations are norms and proficiency targets. Norms evaluate the performance of a student or group of students compared to a sample of peers. The student's or group of students' performance can therefore be described in terms of where it ranks within the distribution of peer scores. In using this definition of proficiency, it is critical to identify and remain aware of the characteristics of the norm sample to which the individual student's or group of students' performance is being compared. In particular, data leaders must decide whether to use local (e.g., school, district, regional) or national norms. Some experts (e.g., Shinn, 2013) argue that local norms are preferable, since they are more likely to be representative of the characteristics of the individual student or group of students to which they are being compared.

We offer a few cautions if data-driven schools choose to use local norms, however. First, local norms are likely based on a smaller sample than national norms and consequently may be less stable from year to year or grade to grade. Second, local norms for measures given less frequently and to fewer students in a school district (e.g., math problem-solving probes) may be even more unstable and unreliable. Finally, local norms can lead to a lack of flexibility in identifying levels of risk and allocating necessary resources. For example, if a school wants to identify students in need of Tier 2 reading intervention, it may decide to target students who earn scores below the local 25th percentile on a reading CBM. This will always identify 25% of students as in need of Tier 2 intervention, regardless of grade level or year. Due to differences between cohorts of students, this may in some cases identify more students as in need of additional support than truly may need it, and in some cases, may not identify enough students. As a result, staff implementing Tier 2 interventions may not be allocated as efficiently, making it more difficult for them to effectively address the true needs of the students.

The second most common criteria used in defining expectations are proficiency targets. In Appendix 2, we describe how data leaders themselves can calculate these targets to predict proficiency on high-stakes outcomes (e.g., local, state, or federal accountability tests). They are typically calculated, however, by test publishers, states, or local agencies. For example, test publishers, school districts, consultants, and researchers have calculated targets predicting from performance on benchmark-screening tools, such as AIMSweb and the NWEA MAP, to performance on state accountability tests in reading and math. As explained in Chapter 2, these targets allow us to not only identify how students' performance ranks in comparison to that of their peers, as we can with local or national norms, but also to assess whether they are currently on track to be proficient on the high-stakes outcome. Data leaders must be educated consumers of these targets as well, leading data-driven schools in asking the right questions to determine whether the targets are appropriate to use for the purpose for which their school is considering using them. Below is a list of some recommended questions (Silberglitt & Hyson, 2014):

1. What method was used in setting the targets? Is this method consistent with what is understood to be best practice?
2. What are the characteristics of the sample that was used (e.g., size, demographic characteristics, national or local origin)? Do these characteristics suggest that the targets are generalizable to the population to be served?
3. How recently have the targets been calculated? Are the targets set to the most recent edition of the outcome test available? Have the sample characteristics changed significantly since the targets were set?
4. Is the outcome used in calculating the targets the same as or at least consistent with the

intended outcome (e.g., the same state accountability test or one of equal difficulty)? If the outcome is not similar to the outcome intended, then will the targets be artificially high or low, resulting in underidentification or overidentification of students at risk? (p. 498)

The reality is that some students or groups of students may not be currently proficient when their performance is compared to either norms or proficiency targets and may be unlikely to reach proficiency in the near future. In these cases, in completing the plan evaluation step, data-driven schools should also examine whether these students are at least growing at a rate that will make it more likely that they will reach proficiency in the future. To do this, data leaders must help schools analyze benchmark-screening or progress monitoring data and compare the growth trajectories of target students or groups of students to growth trajectories predicted to close the gap between what is expected and what is occurring. For example, CBM test publishers often provide rate of improvement (ROI) expectations for students that indicate by how much student scores need to increase from one benchmark-screening or frequent progress monitoring administration to the next for the student to stay on track or catch up with his or her peers. Similarly, computer-adaptive test publishers also frequently provide average growth norms that show at what rate a student needs to grow from one benchmark-screening administration to the next to be able to match the growth of other students in the norm sample who started at the same initial achievement level.

It is obviously preferable for students to meet these average growth targets rather than for them to not meet them, but it is critical for data-driven schools engaged in plan evaluation to realize that meeting average growth targets only ensures that an individual student or group of students is not falling further behind. It does not measure to what extent they are closing the gap—which is often significant—between their current performance and expectations. To address this question, data leaders are encouraged to set or examine already-identified *accelerated* growth targets. These targets should be set to allow data leaders to determine whether the student or group of students is on track to close the gap within a reasonable amount of time (e.g., 3 years). Data leaders are cautioned that, in many cases, these accelerated growth targets may be much higher than the average growth targets discussed earlier and therefore, are often difficult for schools to accept. It is, of course, much easier to set these accelerated targets than it is to help students meet them. However, this is the difficult job that we have signed up for as educators. If we truly believe, as our school district mission statements often state, that all children can learn to their full potential, we must make plans to ensure that that will happen and be willing to evaluate our plans to determine whether we have been successful in that goal. As noted earlier in our discussion of plan development, if we have planned for our progress monitoring to include clear indications of when we add, remove, or revise interventions, it will be much easier for us to determine the impact of these adjustments on the growth of student outcome data.

If the outcome data collected do not show that the student or group of students has met proficiency targets or grown at a rate that would make them more likely to be proficient in the future, as illustrated in the middle school math curriculum example shared earlier, it is critical for data leaders to consider all possible explanations. The most common hypothesis is that the intervention being implemented may not have an adequate research base supporting its use in addressing the needs of the target individual student or group of students and should therefore be discontinued. In the middle school example, this was the team's initial guess. They thought that the math curriculum must not be well validated to address the needs of their students, because students had not demonstrated the expected levels of proficiency and growth since they started implementing the curriculum a few years prior.

As demonstrated in the middle school example, it can be dangerous to too quickly jump to this conclusion. First, a data-driven school must closely examine the fidelity with which the intervention program or methods/strategies have been implemented to determine whether the target student or group of students had an authentic opportunity to benefit. If the problems with the effectiveness of the intervention are related to any of the four implementation integrity questions discussed earlier, the intervention may be perfectly appropriate, but the system may need to address issues with the implementation of the intervention before it can have the chance to be effective with the target student or group of students.

A PRACTICAL TOOL TO GUIDE SYSTEMS-LEVEL PROBLEM SOLVING: THE DATA BOOK POWERPOINT

For several years, the first author (Hyson) created annual "data book PowerPoints" designed to guide the school districts he consulted with, and the schools, grade levels, departments, and classrooms within those schools, in engaging in systems-level problem solving as discussed in the previous three chapters. Four guiding questions framed the data presented in the data books:

1. Are all of your students meeting standards or growing at a rate that will make them more likely to meet standards in the future?
2. Are all of your students in special population subgroups meeting standards or growing at a rate that will make them more likely to meet standards in the future?
3. What specific skill strengths or weaknesses do your students demonstrate based on standardized assessment results?
4. What are some sources of intervention resources to address these specific skill strengths or weaknesses?

A sample data book is available in the book's online supplement (see the box at the end of the table of contents). These PowerPoints were also used by Hyson in framing data retreats like the one described below.

> Each summer for several years in a row, Hyson facilitated half-day data retreats with a middle school with which he consulted. The purpose of the retreats was ultimately to help the school leadership team set a goal and develop an action plan for improving student outcomes.
> The first hour of the retreat took place in a computer lab and involved groups of two to three team members who rotated every 10–15 minutes through stations that included data displays designed to address the key guiding questions described above. Data addressed the summative, screening, and diagnostic pur-

poses of assessment within a comprehensive assessment system and were drawn from a variety of sources, including state accountability tests, computer-adaptive tests (e.g., NWEA MAP), and GOMs (e.g., AIMSweb's R-CBM). Parent perception survey data were also included when available. Teams were directed to review the data at each station and use the data to identify patterns and themes, generate questions, and begin to brainstorm goals. Hyson circulated throughout the room during this "data walk," answering questions and helping groups to interpret the data.

Following the data walk, the team transitioned to a conference room for the remainder of the morning to review and compare the patterns and themes, questions, and tentative goals they had come up with. Hyson then facilitated a systems-level problem-solving discussion through which the team identified the primary problem that had emerged from the data, analyzed why they thought the problem was occurring, developed a goal and action plan for addressing it, and outlined a process for implementation and evaluation of the plan.

• **Key Guiding Question 1: Are all of your students meeting standards or growing at a rate that will make them more likely to meet standards in the future?** If our discussions within data-driven schools are to follow this first guiding question, they must start with an examination of the performance of *all* students in response to Tier 1 general education instruction. If all—or at least 80–90% of—students are not meeting standards or growing at a rate that will make them more likely to meet standards in the future with the Tier 1 general education instruction provided, then it does not make sense to approach the needs of those not responding as a series of individual student problems. Determining whether students are meeting standards is not always easy, since it involves identifying the standard against which students will be compared, which measure(s) are most appropriate to use in assessing whether students are meeting standards, and determining the threshold on the measure above which students will be determined to have met the standard. Determining whether students are growing at a rate that will make it more likely that they will meet standards in the future is arguably even more complicated and is discussed in more detail in Chapter 5. The key is to set goals that are not just rigorous in attempting to close the gap but at the same time reasonable with the resources available. This was a particularly sensitive issue for the team described in the previously mentioned data retreat example, since the goal that they set would also be associated with performance incentives for district teachers. There was a desire, of course, to set a rigorous goal that would push teachers and students to their full potential, but there was also a simultaneous need to set a goal that would not appear overwhelming and would be potentially achievable within the current system.

Finally, this first question is critical because it provides teachers with data on their success with all students. It is important to recognize that these data can seem threatening to some teachers, since they may force teachers to acknowledge their potential lack of success in meeting student needs. The fact that the question includes a focus on growth, in addition to students' current proficiency in meeting standards, is key, however, since it allows data-driven schools to give teachers credit for helping students who have not yet reached proficiency to close the gap toward proficiency. This has often led teams we have worked with to set growth goals, as opposed to proficiency goals. All teachers, including those primarily working with low-achieving students, can help their students increase their growth trajectories, even if the students may still be unlikely to reach grade-level standards. Growth goals, as a result, are more likely to unite schools behind one goal.

- **Key Guiding Question 2: Are all of your students in special population subgroups meeting standards or growing at a rate that will make them more likely to meet standards in the future?** Patterns across these special population subgroups were often uncovered during the course of data walks like the one described earlier. The teams would then use the identified patterns (e.g., that students receiving special education services were less likely to be meeting grade-level standards than their general education peers) to set objectives related to their overall goals. For example, they might set an objective that at least 60% of students receiving special education services would meet accelerated NWEA MAP reading test growth goals designed to close the gap between students' current reading achievement and grade-level standards in 3 years, at most. If they met this objective, they would also be more likely to meet their overall goal of increasing the percentage of students who were already proficient or growing at a rate that will make them more likely to be proficient in the future. As can be seen, these first two guiding questions are key both to the first step in the systems-level problem-solving model (problem identification) and to determining the difference between what is expected and what is occurring, and to the last step in the model (plan evaluation) and to determining whether the plan is working.

- **Key Guiding Question 3: What specific skill strengths or weaknesses do your students demonstrate based on standardized assessment results?** The third question is particularly relevant to the diagnostic purpose of assessment discussed in Chapter 3 and to the problem analysis step in the systems-level problem-solving model. Within the data book PowerPoints being discussed here, grade-level subskill strand data from the NWEA MAP test and the state accountability test were provided to help teams address this question. As discussed in Chapter 3 and later in Chapter 5, however, data leaders must remain aware of the potential limitations of the data they are examining in identifying weaknesses. Before concluding that the data identify a weakness, they must ask themselves questions such as (1) Is the measure being used to identify the weaknesses appropriate for addressing the diagnostic purpose of assessment at the group level? At the individual level? and (2) What level of error is associated with the measure? How will this affect how a skill is identified as a significant and meaningful weakness? In this context, guidance was provided within the data book PowerPoints and in consultations regarding them, identifying the standard error of measurement of the strand scores shared and pointing out that this error was greater for individual student strand scores than it was for grade-level scores.

- **Key Guiding Question 4: What are some sources of intervention resources to address these specific skill strengths or weaknesses?** As highlighted in the Introduction, one of the keys to an effective data-driven school is the ability to connect data with instruction and intervention. The fourth key guiding question in the data book PowerPoints prompts teams to use the data gathered from the first three questions to inform instructional, intervention, and problem-solving processes within the school and engage in the third and fourth steps in the problem-solving model: plan development and plan implementation, respectively.

While the key guiding questions reviewed earlier appear to primarily involve examination of outcomes-related data, effective data teams must also examine how they can use formative assessment data to track their district's progress toward these outcomes. For example, screening data can be used to take snapshots along the way of progress with respect to the first two guiding questions. Screening measures that are highly correlated with the outcomes are most helpful in serving this role. See the discussion in Chapter 2 regarding target setting for more on this issue. We come back to the role that technology can play in helping us connect screening data with outcomes-related data in Chapter 8. Once the district-level team has determined whether the Tier 1 general education instruction is meeting the needs of most students and identified students who are not responding and in need of supplemental support, progress monitoring data can and should be viewed regularly by district-level teams to determine whether Tiers 2 and 3 supplemental support is helping students to close the gap toward proficiency. This was a critical part of the data retreat action planning discussions described above. The team needed to outline a specific process they would use to monitor implementation of their action plan so that they could see—before the end of the year—whether they were on track to meet their identified goal. Without this monitoring plan, they would just be waiting for the next summative assessment and hoping that their hard work had paid off and they had met their goal. They would have no structured way of assessing their progress and adjusting their plan if needed.

Diagnostic data must be used in an effective district-level team to determine why Tier 1 general education instruction may not be meeting the needs of most students. These data can then be examined to identify specific skills to which the district—or schools or grade levels within the district—can devote additional attention. We do *not*, however, recommend that district-level teams focus *solely* on weaknesses identified using diagnostic data at the expense of continuing to target the essential learnings/power standards identified within state standards and by district-level curriculum mapping efforts. This was also key during the data retreat action planning discussions addressed above. When the team identified a particular skill weakness through their examination of the data, their impulse was to revamp instruction to intensively target that weakness. Even if the data highlighting the weakness could be confirmed to be reliable, it was still critical for the team to be reminded that instruction as a whole should continue to more broadly target all relevant learning standards. Additional attention and support could be added to address the identified weakness, but it would be inappropriate to shift all attention to that one area. In addition, experts (e.g., Shinn, 2013) caution us that it is important to acknowledge that some students not responding to Tier 1 general education instruction may need to go straight to receiving Tier 3 support. If data suggest that students' needs are severe enough that individualized, targeted intervention is necessary, it would be irresponsible to require the students to receive Tier 2 standard treatment protocol interventions in a small group and for us to document that they were not responding before allowing them to access Tier 3 support.

What can and can't the data tell us about the effectiveness of our instruction and intervention programs? As discussed in detail earlier in this chapter in the context of the plan evaluation step of the systems-level problem-solving model, it is critical not to assume that lack of proficiency or growth toward proficiency is necessarily a result of the instruction or intervention being ineffective. District-level teams must examine other possible explanations for the patterns identified within the data. In examining these alternative explanations, district-level teams need to ask questions about the school processes, including the fidelity with which the instruction or intervention was implemented. Before recommending changing an instructional or intervention program, the team must determine whether the current program has been given an opportunity to be effective. If it has not been implemented for the duration and according to the protocol recommended in the research supporting its effectiveness, it will not be possible to make a judgment as to its success in meeting the needs of the students it was intended to target. As mentioned earlier, such a revelation emerged out of the data retreat discussion. The team determined that the lack of proficiency and growth their students were demonstrating in math was likely not due to the math curriculum, but more likely due to the fact that the curriculum—designed to be implemented in 75-minute sessions—was being delivered during 42-minute math classes, with teachers themselves individually choosing how to fit the 75-minute "square peg" into the 42-minute "round hole." They determined that, before they could consider replacing their math curriculum, they needed to have their teachers agree upon the essential components of the curriculum, implement the curriculum ensuring that those essential components were included in each 42-minute class, and then, once the curriculum had been implemented as intended and given an authentic opportunity to benefit students, reexamine their screening and summative outcomes to engage in plan evaluation and determine whether it had resulted in increased student proficiency and growth.

KEY ISSUES

- We talk about plan development, plan implementation, and plan evaluation all together in one chapter in this book, but it is still critical to recognize the unique importance of each of these three steps in the systems-level problem-solving model.
- Plan development is framed by three critical questions:
  - What is the goal?
  - What is the intervention plan to meet this goal?
  - How will progress be monitored?
- While it would be beneficial for data leaders to be familiar with specific research-based interventions, it is equally important for them to be well versed in the characteristics of effective instruction in general.
- Plan development must also include attention to:
  - How often progress will be monitored;
  - For how long;
  - By whom;
  - With which tools; and
  - How the data will be used to make decisions.
- Plan implementation must include devoting adequate time to implementing the intervention, providing staff involved in administering the intervention with adequate initial training, and ensuring that staff receive frequent, sufficient follow-up refresher training and coaching to guarantee that they do not drift from their initial training.
- Plan evaluation returns us to the first step in the systems-level problem-solving model, prompting us to assess whether we have narrowed any gap we identified in that step between what was expected and what was occurring.

■ To engage in effective plan evaluation, data-driven schools must clearly define what their expectations are for student learning, including considering the pros and cons of local and national norms, proficiency targets, and average and accelerated growth targets.

■ Before data-driven schools choose to use targets already developed by a test provider, cooperative, or state agency, data leaders are advised to use the guiding questions provided in this book to evaluate the appropriateness of those targets.

■ A tool like the data book PowerPoint highlighted at the end of this chapter can be used by data leaders to facilitate systems-level problem-solving discussions as a part of data retreats in their data-driven schools.

PART II

THE ROADMAP
FOR A DATA-DRIVEN SCHOOL
Data-Analysis Teaming
across Multiple Levels

CHAPTER 5

Data-Driven Problem Solving at the Grade, Classroom, and Student Levels

Initial Considerations

ROADMAP

1. Team format and membership
2. Sources of academic data
   a. Benchmark assessments: Universal screening
      i. Typically used benchmark-screening measures
      ii. Choosing benchmark-screening measures
      iii. Gating procedures
   b. Diagnostic (drill-down) assessments
   c. Progress monitoring
   d. Outcomes assessment
3. Sources of behavioral and social–emotional data
   a. ODRs
   b. Behavior screeners
   c. Classroom-level data
   d. Progress monitoring
   e. Functional behavioral assessment
   f. Psychoeducational evaluations

In Chapters 2–4, we illustrated how the problem-solving model can be used in a team format to identify needs and intervene when the problems are district and school based. This discussion is especially relevant to school functionaries who are asking the big questions about how well the overall program in the district is working. Moreover, trying to solve problems on an individual student level in systems where there are large numbers of students who are not performing to grade-level expectations either academically or behaviorally is counterproductive. Instead, a focus on "macro" issues is a more effective approach.

In this chapter, we set the stage for describing how the problem-solving model can be used in individual schools that operate within an MTSS to address the needs at the grade, classroom, and individual student levels (see Figure 1.3).

Just as teams are the vehicle for data-driven problem solving at the macro level for systemic issues, teams are the engine for problem solving at the micro level. The specific procedures along with extensive examples are presented in Chapters 6 (for academic issues) and 7 (for behavior and social–emotional issues). We address the format of teams and make recommendations as to their membership, with consideration given to differences between elementary and secondary schools. We also explain the various functions that are required for effective teaming and the consequent roles that various team members need to play during the meetings per se. Next, we provide details about the types of data that schools may use and access in implementing the problem-solving model at the grade, classroom, and individual student levels. We articulate the many assessment options and provide guidelines about how to select and use these assessments for the screening, diagnostic (drilldown), progress monitoring, and outcomes functions within a comprehensive assessment system. This information allows the reader to fully engage with our presentation of problem solving for academics (Chapter 6) and for behavior (Chapter 7).

TEAM FORMAT AND MEMBERSHIP

The basic format of the school-based team that we present in Chapters 6 and 7 is the grade-level team. In its most typical structure, the grade-level team is composed of all of the teachers in a particular grade in a given school (e.g., four third-grade teachers in hypothetical Washington Elementary School), along with the school principal and various educational specialists (e.g., remedial teachers and coaches, school psychologists, school counselors). Of course, the reader will immediately recognize that such a school may be common, but does not reflect the wide variety of school organizational structures in elementary, middle, and high schools. So, the first consideration in imagining the format and membership of various teams is school size. Starting with the elementary level, very small schools may not have enough teachers at a grade level to construct a viable team, and such schools likely share specialists or even principals. In these schools, our experience is that grouping teachers from two or three grades works well. For example, in a K–5 building with one or two teachers at a grade level, two teams could be formed: one for the primary grades (K–2) and a second for the intermediate grades (3–5). The downside of these arrangements is that teachers may not have other colleagues who teach the same grade and who can address particular curricular and instructional issues pertaining to that grade level. Nonetheless, this format does allow for pertinent data-based discussions within a similar developmental period. The opposite challenges pertain to very large elementary schools that may have six or more teachers at a grade level. In this situation, it is possible to construct two data teams at each grade level, which may help to maintain a manageable discussion of data, but does present logistical challenges. The decision as to whether to have one large team or to split teachers up should be guided by how and to what extent teachers share the same students. Generally, teams should be composed of those teachers who are responsible for a particular group of students (e.g., four classroom teachers who share 100 students).

Organizational structures in secondary schools vary widely and warrant special consideration with regard to the creation of data teams. In middle schools, it is typical to see a grade-level orientation, so empaneling data teams of teachers in a particular grade level, as described above, still pertains. Because many, if not most, middle schools are larger units than elementary schools, multiple teams at a given grade level would be common. For example, if seventh graders are assigned to "pods" of teachers, there would be a data team for each pod. Again, specialists assigned to the building would join the team or teams of teachers whom they support. Of course, multiple teams create challenges for the involvement of the principal, and it is acceptable for teams to be assigned to assistant principals. However, it is important for the school-based administrators to have active involvement in data teaming, as it is a critical vehicle for advancing the overall mission of the school.

High schools typically house large numbers of students and teachers who are generally grouped in departments by discipline rather than by shared students. This reality presents both challenges and opportunities. Challenges include complicated schedules, large numbers of teachers and specialists, and the sheer number of students to track. Nonetheless, these aspects do provide unique opportunities. Data teaming works best at this level when the activities described in Chapters 6 and 7 are split across different teams. As presented later in this chapter, in elementary and middle schools, data-analysis teams address both the performance of the group as a whole (Tier 1 analysis) and subsequently identify individual students for group interventions (Tier 2) or customized programming (Tier 3). In high schools, these functions might be undertaken by different groups. Tier 1 analysis and planning might be undertaken by departments. For example, the math department would analyze data from the state tests in mathematics that are given in grades 9 and 11 (the specific grades in which these high school state tests are given may, of course, vary by state), and consider how they should adjust instructional practices from grade 9 through 12. Then, groups of teachers and specialists at particular grade levels would take major responsibility for the analysis of individual student data to plan for skills remediation (Tiers 2 and 3 planning). Although these grade-level teams would have this function as their primary responsibility, it is also valuable for them to review whole-class Tier 1 data when considering instructional issues that cross departmental lines. For example, teachers could analyze results of state tests of written expression to reflect on their curricular and instructional practices in improving students' writing skills as they pertain to English, social studies, sciences, and other subjects.

Regardless of the organizational structure of the school and the particular membership of each data-analysis team, there are a number of roles that need to be filled in running the meeting. Before the first data meeting of the school year, the following roles should be decided upon by the team (rather than assigned by the principal). The team leader functions to open the meeting, initiate prompting questions, keep the meeting on track, maintain an appropriate pace, and summarize the meeting. In many cases, the principal or designated administrator serves this function, although in other cases, teams may tap a specialist (e.g., school psychologist) who has particularly good facilitative skills. In these cases, it is important to note that the principal needs to maintain an active role in the meeting, and not merely delegate his or her participation to the meeting facilitator. It is not recommended that one of the classroom teachers serve as the facilitator because the teachers will need to be "poring over the data" and actively engaging in discussions about instructional changes.

Perhaps the most critical role on a data-analysis team is the role of data manager. The data manager accesses the various databases (or data warehouse) to produce user-friendly summaries of data to be considered at each data-analysis team meeting. At the data-analysis meeting, the data manager accesses the databases (most contemporary teams use a projected display of the data), navigates websites, and is prepared to explain and interpret scores. Some schools also use the data manager to enter data into databases, although in other schools this function is decentralized by having teachers upload their own data. In our experience, a specialist who is data and technologically savvy is typically identified for this role, and in many cases these data management duties become part of the person's job description. (In some schools, this has become a full-time position.) So, unlike other roles to be filled on the data-analysis team, the data manager is most likely identified by administration rather than on an ad hoc basis by the team.

Two team members need to be identified to keep track of team proceedings. The meeting recorder is charged with maintaining thorough "minutes" of the meeting, typically by annotating the recording form that is described in this chapter. The display scribe is charged with creating a running display of the team deliberations by recording ideas on a whiteboard, blackboard, or computer. The team also needs to select a timekeeper who gives updates as to the progress on the task at hand and the amount of time left in the session.

SOURCES OF ACADEMIC DATA

A salient aspect of the progress of school teaming over the past 40 years has been the increasing use of data to inform the deliberations and to improve decision making. Contemporary data-analysis teams can and should access a number of important student data sources. These sources correspond to the key purposes of assessment identified by the National Reading Panel (National Institute of Child Health and Human Development, 2000). In regard to academic skills, these sources include screening (benchmark), diagnostic (drill-down) assessments, progress monitoring, and outcomes assessment (including statewide tests). In terms of behavioral functioning, the data sources are similar with respect to scope, but unique in regard to the form and method of collection. These sources, which include ODRs, behavior screeners, and direct behavior ratings (DBRs), are described in turn.

To provide some additional context we include a visual explanation (see Figure 5.1) of the process by which school teams in one midwestern district navigate sequentially through the key purposes of literacy assessment. In this diagram, across the top you see the key purposes identified, along with the critical question the team should be asking of the data. The appropriate assessments are listed in each column—note that the intensity of the assessment in each subsequent column is determined by the student's performance on the universal screening assessment.

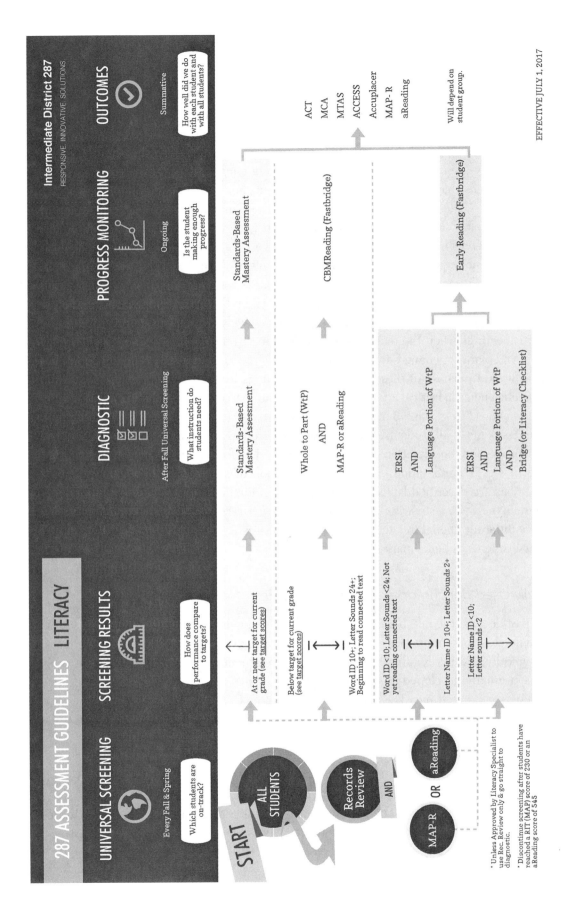

FIGURE 5.1. Navigating the key purposes of assessment. Reprinted with permission from Intermediate District 287, Plymouth, Minnesota.

Benchmark Assessments: Universal Screening

One type of assessment that is typically available for consideration by data-analysis teams are short tests of academic skills that are administered at preset intervals throughout a school year. Most districts administer these assessments three times per year in fall (e.g., September), winter (e.g., January), and spring (e.g., April). These assessments serve two purposes: first, they are used to determine to what extent students achieve desired academic targets on metrics that are presumed to be important. For our purposes here, we use the terms *benchmark* (designating scores at or above the benchmark level), *strategic* (designating scores below benchmark but above the intensive level), and *intensive* (designating very deficient scores in relation to the benchmark level). (Note that unlike state tests, these assessments do not typically identify an advanced range.) When the results of these assessments are used to categorize students within these performance levels, they are referred to as *benchmark assessments*. As described in Chapter 2 and presented in detail in Chapter 6, the percentages of students at various performance levels is a critical topic of discussion in Tier 1 meetings when the team addresses the effectiveness of the overall instructional program and plans for changes in core instruction.

The second purpose of these period assessments is to identify (screen) students who display deficiencies in critical academic skills and who therefore should receive supplemental interventions (Tiers 2 and 3 of an MTSS). Because it is typical for schools to administer these assessments to all students, this process is referred to as universal screening. Operating procedures for consideration of these assessment data for both benchmarking purposes (to inform Tier 1 deliberations) and for identification of students needing supplemental interventions are described later in this chapter. It is important to note that we are referring here to the same tests, with the terms *benchmark assessments* and *universal screening* denoting different (though related) purposes of the assessments. For simplicity, we refer to these assessments as benchmark-screening measures.

Typically Used Benchmark-Screening Measures

In the past decade, the number of commercially available benchmark-screening measures has proliferated, with most of the applications being pertinent to grades K–8. These measures typically address reading/language arts and mathematics. Some are based on procedures originally developed as CBMs, in which students are individually assessed, typically in one-to-one settings. These assessments serve as GOMs, short assessments that are intended to be a broad indicator of a given domain. In the area of reading, typical CBMs include:

- Reading fluency probes: the student is given a reading passage and asked to read orally; the number of wcpm is recorded.
- The "maze" technique: the student silently reads a paragraph in which words are removed and replaced by a choice of three words (the correct word and two distractors), with the score derived from the number of correctly identified words in a given time period.

- Vocabulary tests: the student is presented with a list of words and asked to identify a synonym in a multiple-choice format.
- Word analysis probes: the student reads orally from a list of decodable or nonsense words within a given time period; the number of items spoken correctly is recorded.
- Early reading measures: the student segments words into their constituent phonemes within a given time period, identifies initial/first sounds in words, names letters, identifies letter sounds, or identifies words that rhyme.

Other typically used benchmark-screening measures are computer-adaptive tests (CATs), which are based on item-response theory and are delivered in computer-adaptive formats, which allow for individual and group administration.

In mathematics, both CBM-based and computer-adaptive assessments are available. In various formats, these assessments include:

- Basic numeracy: typically measured by students' skills in identifying numerals, counting objects, identifying missing numbers in a sequence, and so forth.
- Computation: typically measured by number of problems correct or digits correct per minute in a timed format.
- Concepts and application: typically measured by number of correctly solved problems under timed conditions.
- Measurement: taps students' skills in geometry, money, and so forth.

As of this writing, prominent providers of benchmark-screening measures include AIMSweb (*https://aimsweb.pearson.com*); Acadience (previously known as DIBELS Next; *acadiencelearning.net*); easyCBM (*www.easycbm.com*); FastBridge Learning (*www.fastbridge.org*); the Northwest Evaluation Association (NWEA), which provides the Measures of Academic Progress (MAP) CAT (*www.nwea.org/assessments/map*); and Renaissance Learning, which provides the Star test (*www.renaissance.com*). Both CBM and computer-adaptive assessments frequently have versions in Spanish. A third-party review of these and other products has been conducted through the Center on Response to Intervention at American Institutes for Research and is available on its website (*www.rti4success.org*).

In recent years, commercially available assessments of written language have been developed, including AIMSweb's writing probes and the Language Usage assessment in NWEA's MAP test. In addition, extensive CBM procedures have been developed for assessing students' writing (Hosp, Hosp, & Howell, 2007). To conduct a CBM in written expression, the student is given a story starter (e.g., "Yesterday was an exciting day") and directed to write a paragraph on the topic for a specified amount of time (e.g., 3 minutes). The student's production may then be scored for total words written, words spelled correctly, percentage of legible words, correct writing sequences, incorrect writing sequences, and correct minus incorrect writing sequences. The benefit of these CBM measures is the ease of administration, which may be done individually or in a group. However, these measures are time-consuming to score and require extensive scorer training. In addition, benchmarks have been difficult to develop (Malecki, 2014). Of these measures, total words written may work as a universal screener, with the other measures serving as useful drill-down assessments.

In addition to CBM, another approach to benchmark screening of written expression is the use of holistic or analytic scoring rubrics for students' classroom writing productions (Miller, Linn, & Gronlund, 2013). When scoring a student's writing sample with a holistic rubric, an overall score on a quality dimension (e.g., 1–5) is given for the sample. In an analytic rubric, the student's writing sample is scored according to a set of identified criteria (e.g., focus, content, organization, style, conventions), with a score given for each criterion, which can then be summed. As with CBM, administration is efficient, but scoring is more challenging, particularly with analytic rubrics. Because the scoring criteria are more judgmental with rubrics (as contrasted with the clear criteria used with CBMs), consistency of rating across raters (teachers) can be especially problematic, and establishing benchmarks unfeasible. Consequently, holistic rubrics may work best for universal screening and analytic rubrics may be best reserved for diagnostic (drill-down) assessments. Thus, a combination of CBM (total words written) and a holistic rubric may work best for universal screening of writing.

Choosing Benchmark-Screening Measures

As described above, it is important that school districts choose wisely in designing a package of measures that work effectively and efficiently for benchmark-screening assessment. The following guidelines are suggested for making this important decision:

1. *Assessments should be good measures of the constructs that are considered important.* The first consideration is that the measures selected should include those subskills that the team considers to be important markers on the way to the terminal goal. For example, ORF might be a useful measure of overall reading skill at third grade, but less so in eighth grade, where a maze procedure or computer-adaptive assessment might work better (Silberglitt, Burns, Madyun, & Lail, 2006). In the early grades, assessments that break down basic skills into important marker variables (e.g., phonological awareness, phonics, numeracy) are particularly important.

2. *Assessment should be predictive of students' performance on a desired outcome measure.* As indicated above, performance on an outcome measure, such as the state proficiency test or a college-readiness test, is frequently seen as the standard by which schools and individual students are evaluated. Consequently, benchmark-screening measures should have a strong correlation with results of these outcome measures, so that the data-analysis teams can make good decisions about alterations to core instruction (Tier 1) and identifying students for intervention (Tiers 2 and 3). For example, a student who scores above target on the winter benchmark assessment should be expected to meet grade-level expectations on the state proficiency test in the spring. It should be noted, however, that the extent to which benchmark tests are predictive of state test results can vary by test and by state (Stage & Jacobsen, 2001). So, for example, widely used "national" target scores for performance on the benchmark test (e.g., Hasbrouck & Tindal, 2006) may not correspond to proficient performance on the state test in a specific state. It may be necessary for districts to conduct their own evaluations of benchmark testing to determine what cut points on their selected benchmark measures are most predictive of proficient performance on their

particular state test (see Chapter 2). Many CAT providers also provide state-by-state target scores, based on correlational studies conducted from their user group.

3. *Assessments should be efficient.* As we have indicated, we see the collection of benchmark-screening data as essential to the effective implementation of data-analysis teams. However, it is also important to maximize instructional time throughout the school year, and not overassess. To accomplish this balance, teams should select short-duration measures that can be efficiently administered to all students in a minimum amount of time. Schools have frequently met this goal by deploying assessment teams (teachers, specialists, aides, etc.) to conduct the assessments over a few school days in each assessment cycle. Computer-adaptive assessments and other group-administered measures hold particular promise in this regard and are often appreciated for the fact that, while they technically take longer than CBMs, the group-administration format often results in less disruption to overall instructional time and schedules. It is also worthwhile to refrain from using extensive tests that may be useful for drill-down assessments with individual students for benchmark screening. Although it would certainly be informative to have this information about all students, the cost of instructional time is too great, and shorter measures work well to both appraise the status of the entire group (Tier 1) and to identify individual students for more intensive assessments and interventions. For example, as discussed in Chapter 2, the DRA (Pearson Education, 2011), which may best be considered a diagnostic (drill-down) test, has been used in some districts as a benchmark-screening measure. However, it is our view that its overall length of administration (as much as 45–60 minutes per student) makes it impractical and unnecessary for this function. Kovaleski et al. (2013) provide a format for use in analyzing a school's battery of assessments in terms of effectiveness and efficiency.

4. *Assessments should have good psychometric properties.* Reliability and validity are essential aspects of any assessment procedure. Teams should select those measures that have published accounts of studies demonstrating that the measure is valid for the purpose for which it is used (benchmarking and screening) and is consistent across time (test–retest reliability), administrators (interrater reliability), and forms (alternate-forms reliability). These features are rated in the screening tools chart of the aforementioned Center on Response to Intervention at American Institutes for Research website (*www.rti4success.org*).

5. *Assessments should be reflective of student growth.* It is important that benchmark-screening measures be capable of reflecting students' gains as they acquire more skill on the construct being measured. Measures that have small increments (e.g., wcpm, standard scores on a computer-adaptive assessment) can readily indicate whether a student has made progress between fall and winter assessments. In contrast, measures that give a more amorphous "level" may not show growth during this time period even if the student is making real gains.

6. *Assessments should accommodate cultural and linguistic differences.* Although the number of languages spoken in the United States and other countries is daunting, assessment in the student's native language is ideal. As indicated above, a number of commercially available tests have Spanish-language versions. When such an assessment is not possible,

teams should be aware that students who are ELLs may display different growth patterns on tests administered in English (Vanderwood & Nam, 2008).

7. *Data should be readily accessed.* Most commercially available assessment platforms feature data-housing functions and sophisticated data-summarization and display options that are particularly useful in data-analysis team meetings. Part of the decision regarding the selection of assessment tools to use in the data-analysis process should therefore be how readily data can be uploaded and downloaded from the vendor's website, how intuitive it is to navigate the website, and the usefulness of the data displays. Although most schools use a data manager to be the primary handler of the data, as schools strive to develop a data culture, as described in previous chapters, the ease by which building administrators, specialists, and teachers can access the data becomes an important selection feature. It is also important to determine whether data from a particular assessment product can be readily uploaded into a data warehouse. Many schools use these warehouses to store various school data (e.g., attendance, state test scores, benchmark-screening data, ODRs) and data-analysis teams need to develop data sets that include certain aspects of these data (see Chapter 8; see also Runge, Lillenstein, & Kovaleski, 2016).

Gating Procedures

In the early elementary years, it is recommended that all students be screened in the requisite areas on an annual basis. Students' skills often develop irregularly and students may change their proficiency category during a given school year. At later grades, however, students' proficiency levels often stabilize and the need to track all students three times per year is attenuated. For example, students who have consistently displayed performance in the advanced range in a given academic area over a number of years probably do not need to be assessed at each benchmark period by the late elementary school grades. In these situations, a "gating" procedure should be considered in which some advanced students are not assessed and students warranting concern (intensive, strategic, and low benchmark categories) are assessed as usual. The annual state test results can serve as a check on students who are less frequently assessed. If this procedure is employed, it may compromise the ability to use the benchmark-screening data in making Tier 1 decisions, because the data set will not include all of the data. This concern can be addressed by using a data warehouse (see Chapter 8), so that students can be marked as "above target" even though they have not registered a score on the benchmark-screening test.

A related issue is that while benchmark-screening measures work well to inform Tier 1 decision making and identify which students need supplemental interventions, they do not provide sufficient information about which specific skill areas need to be addressed for individual students (typically in Tier 2). Here, school practitioners face a dilemma. As indicated above, screening needs to be efficient, and intensive, time-consuming diagnostic (drill-down) assessments cannot be used for all students. Yet, more information is needed to plan interventions for individual students and create viable intervention groups (see Chapter 6 for details). The gating procedure may again be used to address this conflict—that is, for students who perform above the benchmark target, no further assessment is needed. For those who perform somewhat below benchmark, short but targeted assessments may be used. These assessments are intended to be used for individual students and take about 5–10 minutes to administer. For example, if a district is using AIMSweb as their benchmark-screening assessment for all second graders, students who perform below the target level could be further assessed with the CORE Phonological Segmentation Test (Consortium on Reading Excellence, 2008) to identify which of these students should receive support in the reading subskill of phonological awareness. The results of these assessments are sufficient to conduct an initial problem analysis for each student and to assign students to intervention groups. For students who perform significantly below benchmark, more extensive assessments are needed, which we address next.

Diagnostic (Drill-Down) Assessments

As the name indicates, diagnostic (drill-down) assessments are extensive measures that are intended to perform a diagnosis of a student's component skills in a basic academic skill. They are used to create a tight instructional match for students who either display significant skill deficiencies as a result of benchmark screening in Tier 1, or perform poorly in response to initial attempts at supplemental interventions, as indicated by progress monitoring. Consequently, these assessments are typically associated with Tier 3 services, although they are often implemented during the course of Tier 2 supports.

In format, drill-down assessments follow the logic of curriculum-based evaluation (Hosp, Hosp, Howell, & Allison, 2014), in which a heuristic is used to plan a series of assessments that progressively work through a skill sequence to identify those skills on which the student is proficient and those on which the student is deficient. This sequential approach to assessment, in which testing proceeds only until the skill deficiency is identified (in contrast to the approach of conducting a comprehensive evaluation of all possible deficient areas), is why Kovaleski et al. (2013) used the term *drill down* to refer to this tactic. For example, an eighth grader who displays problems in reading might initially be administered a maze assessment to check his or her comprehension. If the student performs poorly on the maze, it is followed up with an assessment of the student's ORF. If the student has adequate fluency, an assessment of the student's vocabulary knowledge is administered to determine whether that is the cause of the comprehension deficiency. On the other hand, if the student displays poor ORF, the assessor drills down into the student's phonics skills or even phonemic awareness skills if needed. With this sequential procedure, two aims are accomplished. First, the student's precise point of deficiency is identified, which allows for the design of a more incisive intervention. Second, because these assessments are administered consecutively and are customized depending on the student's performance, efficiency of assessment is maximized. An example of a commercially available measure that follows this format is the CORE Multiple Measures (Consortium on Reading Excellence, 2008). Otherwise, the team can use CBMs or norm-referenced achievement measures that are designed to provide this level of analysis (e.g., the Comprehensive Test of Phonological Processing).

Progress Monitoring

A third source of important data that are useful in data-analysis teaming is the result of progress monitoring that is undertaken during the course of supplemental interventions. In most depictions of a three-tier system of support, students who are identified for supplemental interventions in Tiers 2 and 3 are administered additional assessments on a regular basis to monitor their progress and to appraise the effectiveness of the interventions. Numerous sources (e.g., Kovaleski & Pedersen, 2014; Kovaleski et al., 2013) have recommended that students' progress be monitored every other week in Tier 2 and weekly in Tier 3, as well as weekly in special education programs. These recommendations are based on both historical work on progress monitoring (Fuchs & Fuchs, 1986), as well as recent contributions that have addressed the number of data points needed to make defensible decisions (Christ et al., 2012, 2013). As discussed in Chapter 4, it is acknowledged that some measures may not be sufficiently sensitive to change to warrant frequent progress monitoring (e.g., maze, math concepts and application); in these cases, less frequent progress monitoring is advisable.

The measures used for progress monitoring are in many cases the same assessments that have been described above for benchmark screening. Most of the commercially available products described provide time-series graphic displays of students' progress on a weekly basis, including data paths, aim lines, trend lines, and intervention phase lines. Many also provide the calculated ROIs mentioned in Chapter 4, which describe the slope of the student's progress (e.g., wcpm per week or words gained per week). When the vendor does not provide ROIs, they can be readily calculated with software packages like Microsoft Excel (*rateofimprovement.com*) and ChartDog 2.0 (*www.jimwrightonline.com/php/chart-dog_2_0/chartdog.php*), as noted in Chapter 4. Both the graphed data and the calculated ROIs are critical metrics for Tiers 2 and 3 decision making. When choosing progress monitoring measures, the guidelines described above for benchmark-screening measures generally apply here, with the addition of the ability of the measure to provide graphed data and calculated ROIs. Particularly important is the ability of the measure to reflect very small increments of growth, as decisions are made on a much more frequent basis with these measures. A third-party review of progress monitoring measures has been developed by the National Center on Intensive Intervention at American Institutes for Research as well and can be accessed at *www.intensiveintervention.org/chart/progress-monitoring*.

Note also that, in later grades and in some content areas, GOMs may not be available for progress monitoring. In reading, for example, R-CBM's sensitivity to growth and the predictive relationship with outcome measures, such as statewide assessments, declines in the later grades. In content areas such as science and social studies, a GOM may not be available that accurately reflects the learning targets for the curriculum. In these cases, we see schools continuing to monitor progress, and shifting toward a specific skill-mastery approach to doing so (see Silberglitt, Parker, & Muyskens, 2016, for further discussion of these approaches). The team approaches that are presented in this book are still highly relevant to examining these kinds of formative assessment data, even if the measures themselves are different.

Outcomes Assessment

School districts typically collect summative data on their students, including statewide proficiency tests, spring CATs, tracking credit attainment and graduation rates, and so on. All of these measures reflect the outcomes of the process of schooling and are important indices in program evaluation efforts that have been discussed in previous chapters. These data may also be considered by school-based teams, as they evaluate the effectiveness of Tier 1 instruction. As of this writing, all 50 states require schools to administer statewide proficiency tests at various grade levels in reading, mathematics, writing, and other domains. The grade levels covered by these requirements vary widely, but it is typical for testing in reading and mathematics to begin in third grade and continue annually through the elementary years. In many cases, states have continued to assess reading and mathematics in various forms throughout the secondary grades, although often not on an annual basis. Written expression is assessed in many states, often on a sporadic basis, and content subjects (especially science) have been increasingly appraised, especially in high schools. Many states also require terminal examinations at the high school level, and sometimes tie performance on these tests to graduation requirements.

Our purpose here is not to debate the value of this widespread testing enterprise. Rather, the question at hand is what meaningful data are available that can be used by data-analysis teams to inform instructional decision making. An immediate issue is that these tests are frequently administered in the spring of the year and results are not available for teachers until late summer. Therefore, they can serve as a useful piece of the data package at the fall data meetings. In addition, in most districts and states, statewide tests are the "gold standard" by which the overall performance of the school is judged and the status of individual students evaluated. The percentages of students at various levels (in this book, we use the generic identifiers of advanced, proficient, basic, and below basic, although individual states often use different descriptors) are key markers regarding the overall performance of the school. In fact, the usefulness of other assessments (e.g., benchmark tests) is often appraised by the extent to which these tests correlate with and are predictive of performance on the state test. It is important to acknowledge here the uncomfortable reality that state tests have been shown to vary markedly in difficulty, so whether a school or an individual student has achieved desired targets (i.e., proficiency) can be spurious and misleading. Nonetheless, until a nationwide test is adopted, the state tests remain the de facto criterion measures.

The results of statewide testing are particularly usable in considering overall student performance in Tier 1. As described in detail below, in Tier 1 meetings, team members address whether their students as a group demonstrate proficiency in various areas (e.g., reading), analyze their current instructional practices, and plan for changes in instruction that can more effectively and efficiently facilitate the attainment of proficiency by the end of the academic year. So, the overall percentages of advanced, proficient, basic, and below basic that are identified at the beginning-of-year meeting can serve as a useful starting point for the team deliberations. It is especially useful if the state tests also allow for disaggregated data on particular component skills (e.g., the percentage of sixth graders who identified the main idea on the state reading test), as it allows for a more precise level of discussion.

The results of statewide testing are of limited usefulness in considering the needs of individual students in Tier 2 and 3 meetings. Although it is useful for team members to know the overall performance level of each student being reviewed, the level of fine-grained analysis needed to plan effective intervention programs is not available from these tests.

SOURCES OF BEHAVIORAL DATA

As reviewed above, there are a number of existing data streams for academics that are routinely collected in schools. In regard to behavioral data, the picture becomes a little less clear. As stated previously, there still is not an agreed-upon GOM for behavior. However, what is agreed upon is that the ideal universal screening data serves the purpose of problem identification at all levels of the system, as well as for both academic and behavioral data (Tilly, 2008). The data provide information about school climate, grade-level climate, and class trends; they allow for identification of groups and individual students who may require additional support; and they permit teams to make data-based tier placement decisions. A data-analysis team uses various sources of data that are summarized in an easily understood format in order to make informed and accurate decisions that guide how schools and classrooms are managed so that students can maximize their opportunities to progress as learners and individuals. In order to do this, the data team needs effective and efficient ways to gather data. There are a variety of data sources for behavioral concerns.

Several factors need to be considered prior to choosing a method. The method of data collection should be thought of as a GOM. It must serve as an indicator of student performance relative to the desired general outcome and then be able to be repeatedly administered throughout the academic year to track progress and show growth. Additionally, the method of data collection must be efficient *and* socially valid to be successful. As stated above, the data collection allows for the disaggregation in multiple levels and specifically by area of need. Finally, the method must demonstrate adequate psychometric properties.

The ultimate goal is to have the most complete picture of student behavioral functioning in order to efficiently and effectively provide support. No single source of data is sufficient in and of itself to accomplish this goal. Given that resources in the schools are finite and must be deployed to the greatest effect, it is vital to collect and analyze data that provide all of the necessary information. We propose a three-faceted approach to data collection: ODRs, behavior screeners, and classroom-level data. ODRs, the first facet and probably the most frequently used, are an important source of data—however, they give only a partial picture of behavioral functioning, that which is typically more severe in nature. The second facet, behavior screeners, allow for the collection of data that provide information regarding student social–emotional functioning and, depending on the choice of screener, can provide information regarding prosocial functioning, as well as problematic functioning. The final facet, classroom-level data, are collected on a daily routine basis within the context of a classroom management system. The importance of these data is that both positive and problematic behaviors are captured, as well as the chronic, low-level behaviors of concern—those behaviors that don't rise to the level of an office referral, as they are not as acute or severe, but manifest on a regular basis in the classroom and can contribute to a destabilized or dysfunctional environment.

Office Discipline Referrals

As mentioned above, efficiency of data collection is an important factor. ODRs often provide a source of behavioral data that is readily available in schools, either in paper form or electronically through student management systems. Some of the appeal of the ODRs is that they are familiar to staff, used on a regular basis, and occur naturally (Irvin et al., 2006; Sugai & Horner, 2002). Staff members do not have to change their day-to-day practices in order to collect this kind of data. It has been established that ODRs are a valid measure of school climate (Irvin et al., 2006) and they can be used to identify students in need of support (McIntosh, Campbell, Carter, & Zumbo, 2009). Additionally, there has been some initial research into establishing growth trajectories for ODRs that may help in predicting relative future ODRs and consequently overall level of risk (McIntosh, Frank, & Spaulding, 2010).

ODRs have their limitations. An important limitation is that ODR uses and outcomes are influenced by the differences in the cultural values systems of the individuals involved in the referral process (Irvin, Tobin, Sprague, Sugai, & Vincent, 2004). This is particularly important when considering ODRs for students across cultural subgroups. Another limitation of ODRs is that this method misses students who do not act out. As one study indicated, ODRs were not representative of teacher recordings of classroom behavior (Martella et al., 2010). If a student doesn't engage in a behavior that is significant enough (i.e., externalizing) to be referred to the office, then that behavior, while potentially still problematic, is not captured. There are a host of low-level chronic behaviors that are destabilizing to a classroom or school environment that are not reflected in this type of data. In order for a data team to function effectively to address the behavioral concerns of a building, these data are critical. Similarly, there are students who experience internalizing concerns that create issues for that student and potentially for a classroom or grade, yet these data are rarely included in ODRs.

If it is important to gather a picture of not only risk status but also the demonstration of prosocial behaviors, ODRs do not incorporate such positive behaviors. By definition, ODRs capture only negative behaviors. ODRs also suffer from inconsistent reporting of concerns by staff. Despite the fact that schoolwide PBIS (SWPBIS) attempts to create consistency of expectations and delineate what constitutes a referral to the office versus a classroom management issue, there remains inconsistency among teachers in terms of what constitutes an office referral. Even if teachers do agree on what constitutes a referral, they may still inconsistently report their concerns to the office (i.e., handle the problem in the classroom until it becomes unmanageable).

Behavior Screeners

Another option is behavior screeners: measures of behavior that are completed by teachers for all of their students (universal) or a targeted group. These should be administered once teachers have had the opportunity to get to know their students, generally after a minimum of 4 weeks. Behavior screeners can provide a picture of school climate, as well as identify school and classroom needs and students in need of intervention. Some of the major utilities of the brief screener are that it captures information regarding a global range of functioning and skills that may not be captured through direct behavior data collection/observation and that it can provide a context for behaviors that are manifested. There are numerous commercially available tools that are completed in either "paper-and-pencil" or online formats. A clear advantage of the online tools is that data are instantly scored and available for review. However, careful consideration must be given to the type of screening tool that is chosen, both in terms of the type of data yielded and the amount of staff time taken to complete the tool. For example, there are several screeners that are available online that require that an individual e-mail or link be sent to a teacher for each student with whom the teacher works. Then a 20- to 25-item scale is to be completed on each student. The data yielded are specific, but a significant concern with this approach is the large amount of time needed for a teacher to complete ratings for a classroom. The amount of time needed to complete this process is onerous and would likely be a barrier to teacher participation. Additionally, there is concern regarding the level of accuracy of the individual ratings with such a high-volume demand given that large numbers of the students for whom the ratings are completed will show no signs of risk.

Instead, it is recommended that a multigated approach be utilized that begins with more global ratings of risk (Dowdy, Ritchey, & Kamphaus, 2010). This approach can be used like a diagnostic (drill-down) academic assessment that starts broad and then gives further assessment to students who fall below a certain level and helps narrow down the need. Screeners of this type that are available include the Social Skills Improvement System—Performance Screening Guide (SSIS; Elliott & Gresham, 2008), the Behavioral and Emotional Screening System—Teacher Form (BESS; Kamphaus & Reynolds, 2015), the Behavior Intervention Monitoring Assessment System (BIMAS-2; McDougal, Bardos, & Meier, 2016), and the Social, Academic, and Emotional Behavior Risk Screener (SAEBRS; Kilgus & von der Embse, 2015).

Classroom-Level Data

Classroom-level data refer to information about individual student behavior performance, such as the frequency of calling-out behavior within the context of the classroom. Classroom-level data have the potential to be the most authentic and sensitive to change. They also prove to be potentially the most challenging to collect consistently. Teachers are constantly providing behavioral feedback to students in their classrooms—however, without clear parameters of what type of behaviors should be documented, it would be easy to get bogged down in the data collection process. The data that are of most value are those behaviors that do not rise to the level of an office referral but require teacher redirection due to being a disruption to the educational process. The next challenge is to use a method to capture the data that is relatively easy to use. As with most things, technology often provides a solution.

We first begin with a "low-tech" example. A direct behavior rating (DBR) (Miller et al., 2015; University of Connecticut, 2013) is an example of a tool that requires a teacher to circle a rating between 1 and 10 (1 being problematic and 10 being exemplary behavior) for an individual student's behavior in the classroom for a given time period. In general, it is relatively easy for the teacher to document, though the data are often less specific (i.e., there is a concern to a certain degree during a given time period) and will need to be entered electronically in order to be analyzed.

In terms of "high-tech" options, most student information systems have the capacity to capture these data. Typically, the teacher would need to log in to the system as they would for entering attendance data) and enter the concern. Many systems ask the teacher to categorize the behavior using a drop-down menu in addition to giving a narrative description. Often there is the option for notifying administrators and/or parents. The concern is date-

and time-stamped, administrators can access the data, and the data are available to be run as part of larger reports. What may be apparent in this brief description is that the teacher has to essentially stop instruction to enter the concern. The actual entry of the data usually takes several steps, thus reducing the likelihood of accurate data entry. In contrast to DBRs, the easy part is typically after the concern has been entered. There are some web-based products that allow for quick entry of both positive and negative behavior concerns on an iPad or other portable device. For some of these products, it is not as easy to get archived data for the running of different levels of reports.

As may be evident, classroom-level data hold promise in terms of rounding out the behavioral data picture at a universal level, but there are at this time logistical hurdles to overcome and trade-offs to be made.

Progress Monitoring

In the MTSS approach, a critical element of implementation is progress monitoring. The methods of universal screening approaches described above often can also be used as a tool for progress monitoring, but may have limitations to be considered. For instance, certain behavior screeners generally are not shown to be sensitive to change over short periods of time (National Center on Intensive Intervention, 2015) and are time-consuming to complete. In general, behavior screeners are best used at the universal level to serve as part of a baseline—however, many have developed a brief version for progress monitoring. Similarly, ODRs are valuable as an indicator of progress, but are not a consistent stream of data and the goal is an absence of referrals. Classroom-level data and DBRs provide the methods that can yield the most reliable and authentic information about response to interventions (National Center on Intensive Intervention, 2015). In the end, the most efficient and authentic method for progress monitoring is DBRs.

Functional Behavioral Assessment

Functional behavioral assessment (FBA) is a procedure to specifically identify a behavior of concern and the antecedents that exist prior to the behavior being exhibited with the goal of ascertaining the reason (or function) that a behavior occurs in response to a stimulus and the consequences that exist to maintain it so as to prevent it from occurring in the future. This is not intended to be an in-depth review of FBA procedures, but rather a brief overview of how the FBA process serves as a source of data for data-analysis teams. Depending on state education agency guidelines, it may be necessary to gain parental consent for FBA procedures, particularly if conditions are being manipulated. If so, clearly engaging in an FBA is intended for use at an individual level and therefore is not appropriate for Tier 1-level data-analysis teaming. However, at the Tier 1 level, giving consideration to the perceived function of the behavior would be appropriate for the team. At Tier 2, if the team deems it necessary, the type of FBA that is recommended is a basic FBA rather than a complex FBA. The basic FBA is intended for students who are demonstrating mild-to-moderate behavior concerns (Horner, Albin, Todd, Newton, & Sprague, 2011). It is relatively simple, efficient, and intended to support PBIS development using the existing data collected. The complex FBA is intended to be used at Tier 3 for a student who is engaging in moderate-to-severe behavior problems that may be dangerous and may occur in many settings. It is more time intensive and may involve coordinating with outside agencies as well (Horne et al., 2011).

Psychoeducational Evaluations

Finally, the most intensive form of data collection would be the formal psychoeducational evaluation. At this level, parental permission is secured and specific data about an individual student is gathered for the purposes of identification of the need for special education services and to inform special education programming. All of the previously collected data are considered as part of the evaluation, including how the student responded to any previously implemented behavior strategies. These data inform both whether the student is eligible for special education services, as well as the types of interventions that are to be implemented as part of the student's individualized education plan (IEP).

KEY ISSUES

- It is important to consider how teams are structured and who among school professionals serves on the teams; in general, grade-level teams are preferred, with appropriate adaptations made for secondary schools.

- To maximize effectiveness, identifying school staff to perform team roles is a critical step in creating data-based problem-solving teams; important roles include team leader, data manager, recorder, display scribe, and timekeeper.

- Within an MTSS, there are multiple sources of data on students' academic and behavioral functioning that provide ample fodder for informed decision making regarding overall student performance (Tier 1), and for developing and evaluating the performance of individual students (Tiers 2 and 3).

- Benchmark-screening data provide information to gauge the status of large groups of students (e.g., a grade level) and to plan and evaluate decisions about curriculum and instruction; grade-level teams meet at least three times per year to deliberate about these data.

- Diagnostic assessments allow teams to "drill down" into students' academic skills to provide incisive information that is used to plan supplemental interventions for groups and individual students.

- Data-analysis teams rely on graphed data from the progress monitoring of students receiving supplemental interventions to evaluate student progress and adjust intervention plans.

CHAPTER 6

Implementing Data Teaming at the School and Grade Levels for Academic Skills

ROADMAP

1. Purposes and aims of the teaming process at the school and grade levels
2. Sources of data
3. Forms and formats used in data-analysis teaming
4. The data-analysis teaming process for academics
   a. Beginning-of-year meetings
      i. Tier 1 teaming
         - Preparation and review of the data
         - Goal setting
         - Identifying instructional strategies
         - Planning for the logistics of implementation
      ii. Tier 2 teaming
         - Preparation and review of the data
         - Identifying students for group interventions
         - Setting group goals
         - Identifying interventions and planning progress monitoring
         - Planning for Tier 2 implementation logistics
      iii. Tier 3 teaming
         - Preparation and review of the data
         - Setting goals for individual students
         - Customizing interventions and planning progress monitoring
         - Deciding on referral for special education eligibility
         - Planning for Tier 3 implementation logistics
      iv. Final steps

    b. Formal follow-up meetings
      i. Tier 1 teaming
- Preparation and review of the data
- Evaluation of strategies used
- Resetting goals
- Identifying instructional strategies
- Planning for implementation logistics

      ii. Tier 2 teaming
- Preparation and review of the data
- Evaluation of strategies used
- Reconstituting the intervention groups
- Resetting goals
- Planning for implementation logistics

      iii. Tier 3 teaming
- Preparation and review of the data
- Planning for students who are newly identified for Tier 3 supports

    c. End-of-year meeting

In this chapter, we describe the step-by-step procedures for operating data-analysis teams at the school and grade levels. Similar to the process for guiding large-scale decisions that we described in the previous chapters, the operating procedures for decision making at the school and grade levels are based in the problem-solving model. We articulate how the functions of problem identification, problem analysis, plan development, plan implementation, and plan evaluation are implemented in this more localized context (see Figure 1.3 in Chapter 1). We describe how teams use data from various assessments to drill down into specific academic skills for both groups and individual students. The process of data-analysis teaming is contextualized within an MTSS, which has also been described as an RTI model (see Chapter 1). Decision making at each tier is highlighted, beginning with how teams use data to make classwide instructional decisions in Tier 1, and continuing with how decision making occurs with students who display academic deficiencies in Tiers 2 and 3. The focus of these decisions is on precise alignment of core instruction and specific interventions with students' assessed needs. How data analysis guides the selection of intervention packages and school scheduling is also addressed. This chapter uses a running example of student performance in reading because this is a commonly addressed issue at this level. It is hoped that this extensive example allows readers to extrapolate these procedures to other academic areas. Applications of the data-analysis teaming framework and procedures for student behavior and social–emotional functioning are addressed in Chapter 7.

PURPOSES AND AIMS OF THE TEAMING PROCESS AT THE SCHOOL AND GRADE LEVELS

As we have seen, school-based teaming is now understood as a process by which teams of educators utilize the problem-solving process to analyze student assessment data for a wide variety of purposes (see Figure 1.1). The primary purpose is to help teachers reflect on their own instructional practices by examining the impact those daily routines have on students' academic skills. As we describe later in this chapter, schools now have the tremendous (and rather new) ability to efficiently collect and manage meaningful and informative data that can be harvested to assist teachers in this reflective practice. It is our belief that data-informed teacher reflection and directed collaborative conversations about teachers' practices can have profound effects on the enhancement of teaching and the subsequent and consequent achievement of their students. It has been widely noted that the overall goal for Tier 1 instruction is that 80% of students will reach academic proficiency on the basis of core instruction alone (Batsche et al., 2005). Although this number should be considered as aspirational (and not derived from research to date), it does provide an ambitious, and we believe realistic, target for what we would expect in the way of student outcomes at this level. It is of course acknowledged that such overall school attainments are facilitated by standards-aligned curricula and research-based instructional practices and significantly hampered by hodgepodge curricula and instructional tactics that are not supported by research. No amount of useful data and collaborative analysis can overcome insufficient programs—nonetheless, we have found that data teaming even in these situations can help educators identify deficiencies in their instructional materials and weaknesses in their instructional practices, and use this information to change their overall program.

A related purpose is the use of these data to inform the planning, orchestrating, and support of school-based programs. The coordination of multiple personnel and programs in a single school toward the fulfillment of collective achievement goals is a daunting task that can be enhanced by the careful analysis of assessment data. We envision this analysis to be in the hands of teams of teachers and other school personnel under the leadership of the school principal, who is charged with the overall operation of the school, and who can create and support the changes necessary to meet the school's goals.

The next critical purpose of school teams is to identify students who demonstrate academic deficiencies in spite of team-supported core instruction, and more importantly, provide evidence-based supplemental interventions to groups of students (in Tier 2) and to individual students (in Tier 3). It is critical that school teams employ incisive assessments to identify students' academic needs and link the results of these assessments to intervention programs that have a strong probability of accelerating students' progress. Again, in popular conceptions of an MTSS, it is imagined that another 15% of students (beyond the 80% Tier 1 goal) would reach academic proficiency through Tier 2 supports with the final 5% succeeding with Tier 3 supports. (Note: These percentages are based on a typical general education population and do not include students with severe cognitive disabilities. It would, however, include students who are identified as needing special education in categories associated with nonintellectually impaired functioning [e.g., SLD, emotional disturbance].) These rather rosy projections are based on research that has demonstrated that the provision of substantial doses of research-based interventions has produced significant gains in reading skills of at-risk students (Torgesen et al., 2001). It is also presumed that the attainment of these targets will be further supported by the regular monitoring of student progress, which as we will see, is a critical aspect of the entire data-analysis system. It has been known for over 30 years (Fuchs & Fuchs, 1986) that weekly progress monitoring and graphic recording of those data maximally inform specialized instruction and improve student achievement.

SOURCES OF DATA

It is the central premise of this book that today's school teams should use data to inform their deliberations and to improve decision making. In Chapter 5, we described the many sources of data that schools routinely collect that should be used by school teams. In regard to academic skills, these sources include statewide tests, universal screenings (benchmark tests), drill-down assessments, and progress monitoring. Unfortunately, in some schools, these assessments are conducted but are not used in a systematic manner to make important decisions. Rather, they seem to be a perfunctory attempt to satisfy calls for accountability. In contrast, in the data-analysis teaming process, these assessments are placed front and center as key data for teachers and other team members to consider to guide day-to-day instruction, identify students for interventions, monitor students' progress, and evaluate instructional and intervention effectiveness.

FORMS AND FORMATS USED IN DATA-ANALYSIS TEAMING

As we begin now to address the specific operational procedures of data-analysis teaming for academics, it is important to first consider the forms and formats that are used in the process. In our experience, the quality of the team process is strongly related to the forms and formats it uses. Forms that are designed well not only provide an efficient way to memorialize the data analyzed and decisions made, but more importantly, actually guide the meetings themselves. Teams generally use the assigned form as an outline for their deliberations. As a result, good forms facilitate effective and efficient team processing and poor forms often mire the team in extraneous details at the expense of the critical intent of the deliberations. For example, we have seen many evaluation reports and IEP forms in various states that appear to have been created to minimize litigation rather than to design an effective special education program, which may play a role in the failure of many special education programs to display robust student outcomes.

For these reasons, we developed the data-analysis team recording (DATR) forms for meetings in which data on students' academic performance is analyzed and discussed (see Forms 6.1 and 6.2 at the end of this chapter). Note that there are separate forms for meetings that occur at the beginning of a school year (Form 6.1) and those that occur after the first meeting as follow-up meetings (Form 6.2). Parallel forms for data analysis of students' behavior and emotionality are presented in Chapter 7. Our field experience with Forms 6.1 and 6.2 indicates that they provide for the recording of critical data analyzed and decisions made in data-analysis team meetings and work well to guide the agenda and pace of the meetings, keeping team members on track and preventing unnecessary, irrelevant, and tangential discussions. We next describe how these forms are used as we discuss the data-analysis teaming process.

THE DATA-ANALYSIS TEAMING PROCESS FOR ACADEMICS

In the following pages, we present step-by-step procedures for operating data-analysis team meetings that address students' academic skills; we present parallel procedures for team meetings addressing student behavior in Chapter 7. In doing so, it is not implied that schools need separate teams or allocated meeting days and times to address these domains that are, in fact, closely related. It is a local decision as to how best to orchestrate discussions about these two areas of concern. So, for example, some schools may find it most effective to have separate meetings for consideration of academic and behavioral data. Others may find that a division by tier rather than domain works best. In this format, a meeting could be held to address Tier 1 issues. The team would first analyze the overall academic performance data and make plans for changes in core instruction and then analyze the overall behavioral data and discuss schoolwide discipline procedures. The same options probably pertain to Tier 2 discussions in which students are identified for group interventions. For Tier 3 discussions, in which customized plans are developed for individual students, it likely makes the most sense to consider both academic and behavioral data for each student, as both areas need to be taken into consideration in the development of a comprehensive plan. One commonality for all of these options is that the grade-level team will remain the default structure, as described in Chapter 5. It should be noted that data-analysis teams may also access other relevant student data addressing domains beyond student learning (see the Bernhardt model in Chapter 3), as needed throughout their deliberations, including data on student engagement, student perceptions, and so forth. We do not include these types of data in our examples in this chapter, however, in the interest of presenting the data-teaming procedures in as clear and concise a manner as possible.

In describing the data-analysis teaming process, we first discuss the meeting format and procedures that occur at the beginning of the school year, and then address procedures for follow-up meetings that occur later, because these meetings address different issues (i.e., developing a plan vs. evaluating the effectiveness of the plan). In doing so, in the description of procedures we embed an illustration that pertains to students' reading skills, using grade 3 as our running example. It is hoped that readers will generalize from this example to other domains and grade levels.

A complete flow chart illustrating the steps involved in the data-analysis teaming process described here is included at the end of this chapter (see Figure 6.9). For the reader's benefit, sections of Figure 6.9 illustrating each of four stages in the process are also included within the text of the chapter immediately preceding the discussion of that particular stage (i.e., Tier 1, Tier 2 and Tier 3 beginning-of-year meetings and follow-up meetings). The first example of this is Figure 6.1 on page 100 illustrating the steps within Tier 1 beginning-of-year meetings.

Beginning-of-Year Meetings

Initial meetings to discuss student academic data should occur at the beginning of the school year (typically in late September or early October). The data to be discussed should include the results of the previous year's state tests (if available) and the benchmark-screening data that were collected at the beginning of the school year. In these meetings, data are first analyzed in terms of the performance of the entire grade cohort (Tier 1), students are identified for group interventions (Tier 2), and finally, customized plans are made for individual students (Tier 3).

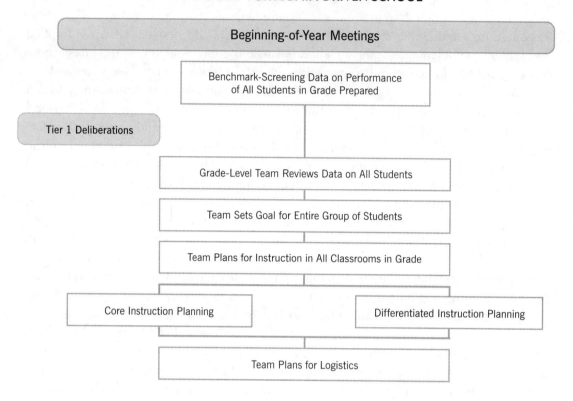

FIGURE 6.1. Flowchart of steps in Tier 1 beginning-of-year meetings.

Tier 1 Teaming

The first purpose of data-analysis teaming, and the function that should come first sequentially, is the analysis of whole-grade data. In this meeting (or meeting segment), data are displayed and disseminated that pertain to the grade level as a whole (e.g., percentage of students in advanced, proficient, basic, and below basic categories of the state test and at the benchmark, strategic, and intensive levels on the most recent benchmark-screening assessments). The aim of this meeting is to identify the overall academic performance of the group, to set goals to be accomplished by the winter meeting, to identify what aspects of the curriculum (e.g., reading series) should be emphasized during the coming months, and to discuss strategies that should be used in core instruction to maximize the probability that the set goals will be attained.

PREPARATION AND REVIEW OF THE DATA

As the meeting begins, the top section of the DATR Form is filled out (date of meeting, grade level, and meeting attendees and their positions). (See Figure 6.2 for the DATR Form used in this example.[1]) The data summaries are distributed and/or displayed via projector. A simple, but crucial tip to consider is to provide only group data to the team at this point and specifically refrain from providing any data on individual students. We have found that

---

[1] Note that Figures 6.2, 6.7, 7.3, 7.4, and 7.5 include excerpts from a completed form. A fully completed form (see Forms 6.1, 6.2, and 7.1) may include more students in the boxes for each group.

Date:	October 1, 20XX		Grade:	3	

Meeting Attendees	Position
Camilla Pascual	Principal
James Kaat	Teacher
Victoria Powers	Teacher
Rachel Rollins	Teacher
Erline Battey	Teacher

Meeting Attendees	Position
Cesar Tovar	School Psychologist
Allison Mincher	School Counselor
Toni Oliva	Reading Specialist

TIER 1

Critical Target Skill(s): Note number and percentage of students at designated level based on benchmark/standard assessment. Name of test(s):	Oral reading fluency (ORF), computer-adaptive test (CAT)
Advanced	Not addressed.
Benchmark	ORF: 52% scoring at 70 wcpm or better. CAT: 40% scoring at 310 or better.
Strategic	ORF: 36% scoring between 56 and 69 wcpm. CAT: 35% scoring between 200 and 309.
Intensive	ORF: 12% scoring below 56 wcpm. CAT: 25% scoring below 200.

Goals: Note number and percentage of students who should display improvements on benchmark/standard assessment. Date of goal review: February 1, 20XX

ORF: 80 students (80%) will attain the winter benchmark of 86 wcpm by the next data-review meeting.

CAT: 50 students (50%) will attain the winter benchmark of 350 by the next data-review meeting.

(continued)

FIGURE 6.2. Sample completed Data-Analysis Team Recording (DATR) Form: Beginning-of-Year Meeting.

Strategies: Describe strategies identified for core instruction.

Reading fluency (all students): Repeated reading with student pairs.

Reading fluency (differentiated small groups): BEST strategy (phonics okay, need support with multisyllabic words), FCRR strategies and supplemental lessons from grade 2 book (need support with phonology).

Comprehension: Building vocabulary by identifying age-appropriate root words.

Logistics: Describe actions to be taken to support strategy implementation.

Teachers will meet during the week of 10/8/20XX to choose FCRR strategies. Ms. Oliva will consult.

Ms. Pascual will cover Mr. Kaat's class so that he can observe Ms. Powers using the FCRR strategy during small-group instruction.

Teachers will self-rate on implementation of the repeated reading and phonics strategies with checklists supplied by Mr. Tovar.

Ms. Oliva will visit each classroom to conduct fidelity checks on implementation of the repeated reading and phonics strategies, and will provide feedback to teachers individually.

TIER 2

Students Identified for Tier 2 Interventions: Insert instructional focus of intervention groups and list students assigned to each group. Identify any student needing further assessment and indicate the type of assessment needed.

Group 1: Monitor		Group 2: Comprehension		Group 3: Fluency	
Susie V	Liam H	Mary N	Jasmine C	Khloe F	
Kevin C	Serenity G	Jean M	Emma F	Aaliyah H	
Frank J		Tyrone S		Addison O	
Anelys P		Igor H		Jaxson B	
Jake B		Rita P		Aubree T	
Jayne B		Eddie K		London B	
Noah D		Latitia W		Sam O	

Group 4: Fluency–Comprehension		Group 5: Phonics		Further Assessment	Name of Assessment
Xavier J	John B and others	Bob S			
Caleb Z		Shaquille O			
Kaylee G		Ginger B			
Juan R		Jack B			
Asher L		Eric C			
Camilla H and others					

(continued)

FIGURE 6.2. *(continued)*

Goals: Indicate goal for each group.　　　　　　**Date of goal review:** 1/30/20XX

Group 1: Monitor	Students will gain 27 wcpm on the ORF R-CBM assessment by the midyear assessment.
Group 2: Comprehension	Students will gain 60 scaled score points on the CAT by the midyear assessment.
Group 3: Fluency	Students will gain 27 wcpm on the ORF R-CBM assessment by the midyear assessment.
Group 4: Fluency–Comprehension	Students will gain 27 wcpm on the ORF R-CBM assessment by the midyear assessment.
Group 5: Phonics	These students are receiving Tier 3 supports; refer to each student's individual plan.

Strategies for Intervention Groups: Note strategy (or program) to be implemented with each group. Indicate the progress monitoring measure to be used and the frequency of monitoring.

Group	Strategy/Program	Progress Monitoring (PM)	PM Frequency
Group 1: Monitor	General education program	ORF R-CBM	Monthly
Group 2: Comprehension	Reading Apprenticeship with emphasis on preteaching vocabulary and summarizing	CAT	Biweekly
Group 3: Fluency	Read Naturally	ORF R-CBM	Biweekly
Group 4: Fluency–Comprehension	Reading Apprenticeship and Read Naturally (alternating days)	ORF CAT	Biweekly
Group 5: Phonics	These students are receiving Tier 3 supports; refer to each student's individual plan.		

Logistics: Describe actions to be taken to support strategy implementation.

Group	Frequency of Intervention (Days, Times)	Intervener	Other Logistics
Group 1: Monitor	N/A	N/A	Classroom teachers will monitor progress.
Group 2: Comprehension	Daily; 30 minutes	Ms. Battey	Fidelity checks: Ms. Pascual
Group 3: Fluency	Daily; 30 minutes	Ms. Rollins	Fidelity checks: Ms. Oliva
Group 4: Fluency–Comprehension	Daily; 30 minutes	Mr. Kaat	Fidelity checks: Ms. Oliva
Group 5: Phonics	Daily; 40 minutes	Ms. Oliva	See individual Tier 3 plans.
All:	Monthly	Teachers; reading specialist	Follow-up meetings

(continued)

FIGURE 6.2. *(continued)*

Student Identified for Tier 3 (Customized Intervention): | John B

Assessment Measures and Scores

ORF (median grade 3 probes) — 53 wcpm (intensive level)

CAT — 234 (strategic level)

Maze — 9 (strategic level)

Phonics Survey (Letter Names and Sounds) — 83 (benchmark level)

Phonics Survey (other subtests) — All 14–15 (benchmark level)

Goal: John will gain 27 wcpm and reach an ORF level of 80 wcpm by the midyear assessment.	**Date of Goal Review:** 1/15/20XX
Intervention: Reading Apprenticeship and Read Naturally (alternating days)	**Location and Frequency:** Tier 2 fluency–comprehension group. Daily, 30 minutes.
Progress Monitoring Measure: ORF	**Frequency of Monitoring:** Weekly
Intervener: Mr. Kaat	**Progress Monitor:** Mr. Kaat

Student Identified for Tier 3 (Customized Intervention): | Bob S

Assessment Measure and Scores

ORF (median grade 3 probes) — 27 wcpm (intensive level)

CAT — 148 (intensive level)

Maze — 3 (intensive level)

Phonics Survey (Letter Names and Sounds) — 60 (intensive level)

Phonics Survey (Short Vowels CVC) — 14 (benchmark level)

Phonics Survey (Long Vowels) — 13 (strategic level)

Phonics Survey (Consonant Blends, Digraphs) — 8–9 (intensive levels)

Phonics Survey (R-Controlled Vowels) — 5 (intensive level)

Phonics Survey (Variant Vowels) — 4 (intensive level)

Goal Bob will gain 27 wcpm and reach an ORF level of 54 wcpm by the midyear assessment.	**Date of Goal Review:** 1/15/20XX
Intervention: Multisensory reading intervention with explicit teaching of phonics	**Location and Frequency:** Phonics group. Daily, 40 minutes.
Progress Monitoring Measure: ORF R-CBM	**Frequency of Monitoring:** Weekly
Intervener: Ms. Oliva	**Progress Monitor:** Ms. Oliva

(continued)

FIGURE 6.2. *(continued)*

TO-DO LIST

Person Responsible	Task
Ms. Oliva	Check progress of Bob S, Shaquille O, and Ginger B on 11/1/XX and consider referral for special education determination if insufficient progress is noted (as per their ROIs).
Ms. Oliva Mr. Tovar	Coordinate academic interventions and behavior plans created for Jack B and Eric C.

FIGURE 6.2. *(continued)*

when team members receive a "pack" of data forms that include individual student data, they invariably page through the sheets to find their students' data, and the meeting degenerates into a discussion of individual students. This level of discussion is handled in the Tier 2 and 3 segments of the meeting, but derails the focus on changes to core instruction that is the intention of Tier 1 teaming. The data presented should also not be disaggregated by classroom—rather, it should reflect the performance of the entire grade cohort.

To begin, the facilitator directs the group to examine the data. In the current example, the third-grade team is analyzing data from two assessments: an ORF R-CBM and a CAT. Both of these measures function primarily as GOMs of the broad domain of reading, and as such may seem redundant. However, the team has chosen these assessments because third grade is a point at which students should be consolidating basic decoding skills and focusing primarily on comprehension. The R-CBM allows the team to ensure that students have grade-appropriate decoding skills, while the CAT gives some initial information about students' emerging comprehension skills. These measures will also be useful during subsequent Tier 2 discussions regarding which students might have deficiencies in fluency (the R-CBM) and which have deficiencies in comprehension (the CAT). To facilitate ease of understanding, the data manager has created a bar graph that depicts both sets of results in one display (see Figure 6.3). (See Chapter 8 for ideas on how data managers can use a data warehouse to create such displays.)

Because this is a beginning-of-year meeting, the team analyzes the data according to the fall benchmarks on each assessment. Referring to the "Critical Target Skill(s)" section of the DATR Form (see Figure 6.2. page 101), the facilitator prompts the group to articulate the percentages of students at various performance levels according to Figure 6.3. This step conforms to the problem identification phase of the problem-solving process depicted in Figure 1.1 in Chapter 1. As indicated in this sample DATR Form, the team notes that 52% of the students are at the benchmark level on the ORF measure, having attained 70 wcpm;

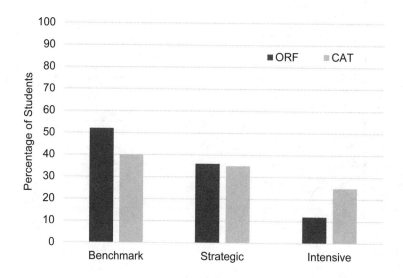

FIGURE 6.3. Percentages of students at benchmark, strategic, and intensive levels of performance on ORF and CAT in fall screening.

36% are in the strategic range, having scored between 56 and 69 wcpm; and 12% are in the intensive range, scoring below 56 wcpm. On the CAT measure, the team records that 40% of the group is at the benchmark level, scoring above 310 on the computer-adaptive metric; 35% are in the strategic range, scoring between 200 and 309; and 25% are in the intensive range, scoring below 200. Note that we have included a space on the DATR Form for annotating the performance of students who have scored in the advanced range, for use in cases in which the team is considering data that include that category (e.g., state tests), or if the team wishes to identify a selected level of performance on a benchmark-screening measure as indicative of advanced performance. Data for these levels are not used in this example.

Generally, the next step of the problem-solving model is problem analysis. However, we temporarily set this step aside during deliberations about overall student performance in Tier 1 during the beginning-of-year meeting, because it is premature to address underlying reasons for the performance of the entire group of third graders at this time. This step has more salience for other tiers and at other times of the year.

GOAL SETTING

The next step for the team to engage in is the first step of plan development (see Figure 1.1). A goal is set for each metric for the next meeting, in this case the winter meeting, which will be held shortly after the winter universal screenings have been conducted. Goal setting is not an exact process, although some useful parameters have been offered (Shapiro & Guard, 2014). In general, teams should set ambitious but realistic goals that reference the amount of gain that typical students display during a given time period (e.g., half year) and the benchmark scores that pertain to the next assessment—that is, the team uses backward planning, working from the level of proficiency that is expected of students at the end of that grade. These established expected levels of proficiency should be based on the same levels used in systems-level decision making, described in Chapter 2. This ensures continuity of decision making across individual, classroom, grade, school, and district levels.

For this example, the fall, winter, and spring R-CBM benchmarks are indicated in Table 6.1. Now, analyzing the raw ORF data in Table 6.2 (which sorts the data from high to low on ORF), the team notes that four of the students in the strategic range scored at 68 and 69 wcpm, and if they can gain the number of wcpm per week that is gained by typical peers (for this example, we use 1 wcpm/week), they should attain the winter benchmark score of

TABLE 6.1. Example of Benchmark, Strategic, and Intensive Levels for Two Measures in Fall, Winter, and Spring

	Fall		Winter		Spring	
	ORF	CAT	ORF	CAT	ORF	CAT
Benchmark	70	310	86	350	100	400
Strategic	56–69	200–309	68–85	225–349	80–99	260–399
Intensive	<56	<200	<66	<225	<79	<260

TABLE 6.2. Fall ORF Scores of Third Graders Used in Example

109	85	71	60
108	85	70	60
106	84	69	59
105	84	69	59
104	83	68	59
101	83	68	58
100	81	66	58
99	80	65	58
98	80	65	57
97	80	65	57
95	78	64	57
94	78	64	56
93	78	64	56
93	78	63	54
93	77	63	53
90	77	63	53
89	77	62	52
89	76	62	49
89	76	62	38
88	75	62	37
87	75	61	36
87	74	61	27
87	73	61	23
85	72	61	20
85	72	60	15

86 in the 18 weeks until the next universal screening (4% of the group[2]). Assuming that the students at benchmark do not regress (currently 52% of the group), that puts the percentage of students at benchmark at 56%. Thinking ambitiously, the team aspires to facilitating gains at 100–150% of the typical rate of improvement for the rest of the group. Projecting an improvement of 150% (or 1.5 wcpm/week) for the other students would mean that students would gain 27 wcpm in 18 weeks. Considering a winter benchmark of 86 wcpm, any student currently at 59 wcpm or greater would hit the winter benchmark, which would add an additional 24% of students attaining benchmark on ORF. So, the group sets the overall goal at 80% (56% + 24%) of students reaching benchmark by the winter meeting and records it in the "Goals" section of the DATR Form (see Figure 6.2). It should be noted that individual goals for these students, as well as those at the lower end of the ORF distribution, will be addressed during the Tier 2 and 3 discussions. However, at this point, the focus is on projections to overall benchmark performance, which leads to a discussion of those strategies in core instruction that not only allow for continued progress of students at the benchmark level but also facilitate accelerated progress for those who are behind on that skill.

---

[2] For demonstration purposes, we have set the number of students at this grade level at 100.

A similar procedure is used for the computer-adaptive measure (CAT). By midyear, students in third grade should reach a scaled score of 350 on this instrument (see Table 6.1). Information from the publisher indicates that typical students grow at 10 scaled score points per month, with individualized growth goals ranging from 8 to 12 scaled score points per month.[3] At this point, as shown in Figure 6.3, 40% have reached the fall benchmark (310), and are on track to attain the winter benchmark of 350. However, a larger number of students are lagging behind at the strategic level (35%) and an additional 25% are at the intensive level. As indicated in Table 6.3, the data have been sorted high to low on CAT scores, and the prevalence of subbenchmark scores for the group is apparent. Even with gains of 150% of individualized growth goals, only 10 additional students (10%) will reach the winter benchmark. Using backward planning, the team decides that it is critical that all students meet the overall ORF benchmark by the end of the year because the curriculum

**TABLE 6.3. Fall CAT Scores
of Third Graders Used in Example**

572	351	283	194
483	350	278	193
453	347	273	192
453	343	271	191
451	341	271	189
449	341	268	188
448	339	264	188
447	338	257	187
443	333	257	186
438	332	255	168
438	329	253	160
434	325	253	151
428	315	249	150
414	310	249	150
412	306	245	149
403	298	244	148
399	296	243	144
398	295	241	136
394	294	239	127
394	293	238	114
382	292	237	114
368	291	210	112
366	290	210	84
360	290	202	82
358	284	201	78

[3]CATs typically provide growth goals that are tailored to a student's starting point, so the typical growth would be different across students, depending on their initial score. It is important to use these individualized growth goals when setting group-level goals, to account for regression to the mean.

after third grade de-emphasizes word study and fluency and focuses increasingly on comprehension skills. Consequently, it sets a goal of 50% of students achieving the comprehension benchmark by the next (winter) meeting and records this goal in the "Goals" section of the DATR Form (see Figure 6.2).

The team also indicates in the "Goals" section of the DATR Form the date on which progress toward the goal will be evaluated. This date typically coincides with the date of the next data-analysis team meeting during which benchmark-screening data are considered (e.g., winter). It should also be noted that the minimal target to be set at this time is in regard to the proficiency of the overall group. Subgoals can also be set for disaggregated groups (e.g., low-income students, students in special education) if so desired.

IDENTIFYING INSTRUCTIONAL STRATEGIES

Following the DATR Form sequentially, the next step is for the grade-level data-analysis team to engage in the second step of plan development (see Figure 1.1) by identifying instructional strategies to address the goals that have just been set. Because these strategies are intended to be used by all classroom teachers at this grade level (or for secondary schools, all teachers in the "pod" or department—note that for reading strategies these may be across several content areas/departments), the team engages in an in-depth discussion of the instructional goal, the performance of the current group of students, and how the current curricular-instructional plan addresses this instructional target. In cases in which the school district has provided instructional materials that neatly match with students' instructional needs at particular grade levels as well as corresponding explicit instructional activities to meet these needs (e.g., has implemented a reading series that carefully and intensively addresses the "big ideas" in reading that are appropriate for that grade), this step serves as a review of those materials and the instruction provided. In the current example, it is apparent that many students in the third grade are below benchmark in ORF. An initial question for the team to address is the extent to which the third-grade level of the district reading series provides explicit instruction to advance ORF. A related issue that the team needs to address is how teachers can differentiate instruction across the always prevailing reality that students have widely varying performance levels. For example, the team in this case would need to discuss how during the 90 minutes of allocated time for language arts instruction the teachers can create flexible groups and use different materials and strategies that span this range for students who are at intensive, strategic, benchmark, and advanced levels. Unfortunately, in many cases, teachers have not been provided with a core curriculum that is reasonably calculated to produce gains for all students, but is based on misguided educational theories or false advertising. In these situations, the team has to identify supplemental materials or practices that can "plug the holes" in the basic curricular instructional program.

The concept here is that although teachers invariably have preferred teaching routines in their individual classrooms, there should be common curricular and instructional procedures that are delivered with a realistic degree of consistency, as the entire notion of curriculum design is to guarantee a common, basic level of instruction for all students. In this regard, a major function (and benefit) of data-analysis teams is to give teachers an opportunity to reflect on and discuss together the curriculum they are implementing and the instructional strategies that they are using, a practice that is often not incorporated in school operations. By emphasizing particular aspects of the curriculum and particular instructional strategies, the teachers in attendance at the meeting are committing to use these strategies during the coming months. In this way, at the end of that period of time, the teachers will be ready for plan evaluation (see Figure 1.1) in which they determine whether the strategies have been successful in meeting the goals the team has set. This evaluation allows teachers to hone their instructional program from year to year toward those practices that are most effective in facilitating student gains.

How the strategies are selected in data-analysis team meetings merits particular attention. In the early days of teacher assistance teams (e.g., TATs), teachers were encouraged to brainstorm ideas on instructional strategies. In contemporary data-analysis teams, during this segment of the meeting, the team facilitator might initiate the discussion with a prompt, such as "Let's list some effective strategies that will assist our students to meet our goals." Like traditional meetings, the team would respond by generating ideas for strategies and the scribe would record them on a visual display (e.g., whiteboard). The difference here is that the team needs to generate specific ideas with regard to meeting the particular goals, which should be distinguished from open brainstorming in which widely varying ideas that are not targeted to precisely defined objectives are listed. The second important nuance is the emphasis on the word *effective*. Data-analysis teams need to focus on strategies that have a solid research base. In the current era of education, a substantial research base is available for almost all instructional domains, and teams should have the identification of these strategies as a foundational principle and practice. If teams maintain this awareness, the generated list of strategies should be specific to the skills assessed and supported by research.

Once an adequate list of options is created, the facilitator leads the team through a series of questions that are designed to facilitate the selection of one or two strategies that are research based and that are also deemed by the teachers to be practical and readily assumed into their daily instructional routines. The suggested prompts are:

"Let's rate these ideas."
"Which ones have a good research base?"
"Of those, which ones are most practical?"
"What materials do we have available?"
"What materials do we need?"
"Based on what we see on the display, what's our choice for the best strategy(ies)?"

In our third-grade example, the team has created a dual-pronged approach to help the students improve their ORF (see Figure 6.2). The first strategy, repeated reading (Samuels, 1979), is selected as a whole-group strategy for use with all students using carefully selected student pairs. For the second strategy, the team's problem analysis results in the hypothesis that the third graders with particularly low rates most likely need additional work with phonics instruction. For students whose basic phonological skills are adequate, but who struggle with multisyllabic words, the team selects the BEST strategy (O'Connor, 2014).

For students who lack phonological skills, the team identifies a set of strategies from the Florida Center for Reading Research (FCRR; *www.fcrr.org*), along with reteaching lessons from earlier books in the reading series. (It should be noted that many of these students will be identified for supplemental interventions in the second phase of the data-analysis teaming process, but at this point, the focus is what is planned for them during core instruction.) The team also decided that, although the core curriculum provides ample coverage of instruction in comprehension, some additional comprehension strategies needed to be implemented during core instruction, particularly for those students who were closing in on the winter CAT benchmark. The team identified a number of age-appropriate comprehension strategies and selected building vocabulary by identifying age-appropriate root words for implementation during the next 4 months and recorded their choice on the DATR Form (see Figure 6.2).

PLANNING FOR THE LOGISTICS OF IMPLEMENTATION

It is unrealistic to imagine that teachers will implement the selected strategies without support during the following months leading up to the next benchmark assessment. In the plan implementation step (see Figure 1.1) for Tier 1 instruction, the team needs to identify those supports. The first issue to address is the extent to which all the classroom teachers have the requisite materials, understand the components of the selected strategies, and have skill in implementing the strategy. The building administrator (the principal) attending the meeting is a particularly important ally at this stage, as she can arrange logistics to maximize the likelihood that the strategy will be implemented with fidelity. For example, if most teachers know a particular strategy, but one does not, the principal can arrange for coverage of classes so that teachers can model the strategy for one another. The principal may also arrange for certain teachers to meet to create or adapt materials.

This segment of the meeting also allows for the team to address another key feature of plan implementation by articulating how it will monitor adherence to the selected strategy in terms of the critical questions "Is the strategy being used as planned?" and "Is the strategy being implemented as designed?" As described in Chapter 4, these matters pertain directly to the concept of intervention fidelity. The specialists on the team (e.g., reading coaches and specialists, school psychologists) can be particularly useful here as nonadministrative adjuncts to visit classrooms, assess fidelity, and give teachers feedback. Of course, it is best practice for principals to also monitor strategy use and fidelity during their routine observations of teachers. The principal can also arrange for interim "mini-sessions" for teachers and other team members to discuss how strategy implementation is progressing.

In the current example (see Figure 6.2), the team agrees that all third-grade teachers have adequate materials to implement the interventions, but need to work together to identify the specific strategies from FCRR to use in small-group phonics instruction during core reading time. The team also notes that one of the teachers is somewhat unsure about the phonics plan. The principal indicates that she will cover that teacher's class so that the teacher can observe another teacher during differentiated group time in core instruction. The team also plans for each teacher to self-appraise his or her use of the repeated reading and phonics strategies using fidelity checklists and for the reading coach to visit each classroom to conduct a second fidelity check. Because all teachers were familiar and comfortable with the selected comprehension strategy, no logistical supports were needed for this aspect of the Tier 1 plan.

Tier 2 Teaming

In the next phase of the data-analysis teaming process, the grade-level team analyzes the results of benchmark-screening assessments and other available data for individual students and sorts them into supplemental intervention groups (Tier 2). As indicated above, this activity can follow immediately after the Tier 1 discussion or be reserved for another time or date. As with Tier 1 discussions, the Tier 2 deliberations should be held shortly after the results of the benchmark-screening assessments have been completed in the early fall (i.e., late September or early October). In this section, we describe the steps for conducting this analysis in the beginning-of-year meeting (see Figure 6.4) and then describe in a separate section the procedures to follow in subsequent meetings during the school year.

PREPARATION AND REVIEW OF THE DATA

For Tier 2 decision making, data from all available assessments are needed on all students who are not at the benchmark (and above) level. This data set would include the results of

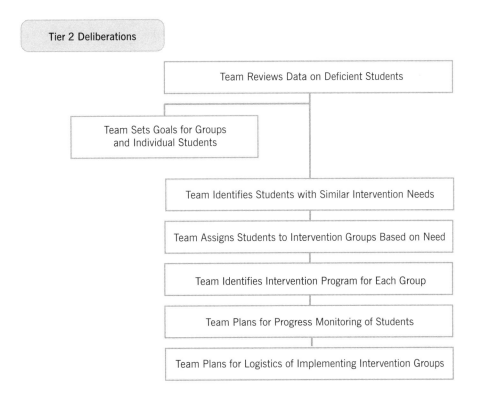

FIGURE 6.4. Flowchart of steps in Tier 2 beginning-of-year meetings.

the fall benchmark-screening, state tests from the previous spring (if available), and other data. There has been some suggestion (Fuchs, Fuchs, & Compton, 2012) that individual assessments (that we have referred to previously as diagnostic or drill-down assessments) be administered and included in decision making at this stage. However, such data collection is time intensive, and teams need to weigh the benefits of enhanced data with time and staff limitations along with the concomitant encroachment on students' instructional time. Our position is that benchmark-screening data are often sufficient for initial placement of students into instructional groups, particularly those who would be identified for Tier 2 interventions. More extensive drill-down assessments may be needed at this time for very deficient students depending on the particular grade level and what skills are covered on the benchmark-screening assessments. (See the discussion below regarding Tier 3 decision making.) Additional students who fail to show adequate progress in response to Tier 2 interventions can be scheduled for drill-down assessments later, as their progress monitoring data are analyzed.

The first step is for the data manager to create a data display of all the students below benchmark who are in the strategic range—in this case, displaying scores of individual students by name. The display should efficiently indicate in one view all of the available scores. In the current example, the display would include data on the students' ORF (R-CBM) and comprehension (CAT). As indicated in Table 6.4, these data are organized according to

TABLE 6.4. Students Designated for Tier 2 Consideration Based on ORF and CAT Scores

Group	Student	ORF	CAT	Group	Student	ORF	CAT
M	Susie V	69	283	F	Khloe F	61	257
C	Mary N	69	249	FC	Xavier J	61	238
M	Kevin C	68	271	F	Aaliyah A	61	298
C	Jean M	68	243	FC	Caleb Z	61	241
M	Frank J	66	253	FC	Kaylee G	60	84
M	Anelys P	65	350	FC	Juan R	60	239
C	Tyrone S	65	210	F	Addison O	60	284
C	Igor H	65	187	FC	Asher L	59	223
M	Jake B	64	329	FC	Camilla H	59	219
C	Rita P	64	168	F	Jaxson B	59	268
C	Eddie K	64	198	F	Aubree T	58	273
M	Jayne B	63	288	FC	Cooper P	58	233
C	Latitia W	63	220	FC	Leslie N	58	244
C	Jasmine C	63	230	FC	Grayson L	57	249
M	Noah D	62	253	FC	Sofia U	57	210
C	Emma F	62	245	FC	Mackenzie S	57	222
M	Liam H	62	264	F	London B	56	255
M	Serenity G	62	278	F	Sam O	56	257

Note. Groups are designated as monitor (M), comprehension (C), fluency (F), and fluency–comprehension (FC).

scores on one measure from highest to lowest. In this example, the team has sorted the data based on the students' ORF scores (from high to low).

IDENTIFYING STUDENTS FOR GROUP INTERVENTIONS

With the aforementioned data display in place, the team initiates problem identification through an analysis of the data. The DATR Form (Form 6.1, pages 146–150) has been prepared for five intervention groups with space for listing individual student names in each group. There is also space for indicating additional assessments if so desired at this time, with space to annotate the recommended assessment procedure. Before committing names to the DATR Form, however, it is best to work out student groups on a whiteboard, blackboard, or computer display, with the scribe creating written lists of students in groups. This tactic allows for team members to survey group instructional targets and assign students and make changes and adaptations as needed.

The first task to address is which students are close enough to benchmark to project that they will reach the benchmark without supplemental intervention. At first, it may seem surprising to not provide supplemental interventions to any student who has not yet reached the benchmark. However, the plans made in the Tier 1 deliberations to move the entire group forward in their skill acquisition should be robust enough so that many of these students will increase their performance to reach or approximate the benchmark level as a result of these adaptations to core and differentiated instruction—that is, students who are slightly below the benchmark are not being ignored—rather, Tier 1 planning should include discussions about how core instruction will be differentiated to address their skill deficits within the classroom setting (e.g., by using small, flexible groupings of students with similar skill deficits).

In this example, the team has decided to identify students who are close to the ORF and CAT benchmarks for no supplemental interventions outside of core instruction. These nine students, designated by "M" in the "Group" column in Table 6.4, have ORF scores between 62 and 69 and CAT scores above 250.[4] The team further indicates that they will monitor progress of these students on a monthly basis using an ORF R-CBM and a comprehension CAT. The names of these students have been entered in the "Group 1" column of the DATR Form (Figure 6.2, page 102)—the group has been designated as "monitor group."[5]

It should be noted that in an environment in which target scores have been set using logistic regression as outlined in Appendix 2, one would assume that any student below benchmark needs some change to instruction (either via changes to core instruction or the addition of a supplemental intervention) to catch up. When this process is used to set targets, the rate of increase of each of those targets is set with the same process of linking to a common outcome, and thus reflects expected growth for a student right at target.

---

[4]Decisions involving various cutoff scores in this example are for purposes of illustration and are not meant to be understood as cutoffs to be used in actual practice. Those decisions depend on the psychometric characteristics of the actual measures used and their relation to the curricula used in an individual school.

[5]Only a limited number of spaces have been allocated for student names in these figures; teams should adapt the DATR Form to accommodate multiple students.

However, when the means and needed sample sizes to perform logistic regression are not available and the school district does not use a commercially available assessment tool for benchmark screening, using less well-coordinated norms, such as those popularized by Hasbrouck and Tindal (2006, 2017), may be appropriate. Again, it is a team decision as to whether the changes needed for these students require supplemental intervention or differentiated activities during core instruction are sufficient to accelerate their growth.

The next step is for the team to sort the remaining students into intervention groups according to their assessed needs (problem analysis). Generally, students are sorted according to their predominant instructional need at the time. In the current example, the team reviews the data as a whole and decides that three intervention groups are needed (in addition to the monitor group described above), which they annotate on the DATR Form: a group focusing on comprehension skills, another group to address ORF, and a third group to address both fluency and comprehension (Figure 6.2, page 102). (The phonics group designated on this form consists of students receiving Tier 3 supports and is described in the next section.) The team reviews the data on each student who has scores in the strategic range on the corresponding metric and designates each student for the appropriate group. The team here identifies nine students (designated as "C" in the "Group" column in Table 6.4 for the comprehension group and enters their names in the designated section of the DATR Form (Figure 6.2, page 102). The team made this decision because these students' ORF was in range to be accommodated in the general education classroom (scores between 62 and 69 wcpm), but they had concerning comprehension scores (below 250 on the CAT). Next, the team designates students who need support in a group that focuses on ORF. They designate seven students for this group who have low ORF scores (<62 wcpm), but whose comprehension is within a range that can be accommodated in the general educational program (CAT scores above 250). These students are designated with an "F" in the "Group" column in Table 6.4, and their names are entered into the DATR Form in the designated space (Figure 6.2, page 102). Finally, the team creates a group that has both fluency and comprehension needs, as indicated by scores below 62 in ORF and below 250 on the CAT. These 11 students are indicated by "FC" in the "Group" column in Table 6.4 and their names are added to the designated area of the DATR Form (Figure 6.2, page 102).

Not all students fit perfectly into the designated groups, and careful consideration of which group is most appropriate for each student should be undertaken. Nonetheless, because all students in Tier 2 receive more frequent progress monitoring (e.g., every 2 weeks), a less than ideal assignment to a particular intervention group can be caught in a relatively short period of time and the student can be reassigned. The reader will also note at this point that we have deferred our analysis and planning for students in the intensive range to a later segment of the process.

The size of the intervention groups is also an important consideration. In an analysis of 41 schools implementing RTI (MTSS), Mellard, McKnight, and Jordan (2010) noted that in Tier 2, around half of the schools in their study used intervention groups of two to five students with the second most frequent group size being six to 10 students. They also noted that decreasing group size is one method (though not the only one) of increasing intervention intensity, and in Tier 3, they found that although half of the schools used intervention groups of two to five, few used larger groups in this tier, and the number of schools using one-to-one formats increased. Although the research evidence is unclear as to the optimal group size for each tier, a reasonable approach would be to allow for larger groups (e.g., six to 10 students) for interventions aimed at students whose deficiencies are not substantial and to plan smaller groups (e.g., two to five students) for students with more significant skill deficiencies. Although other researchers argue the benefits of one-to-one instruction (e.g., Slavin, Lake, Davis, & Madden, 2011), such arrangements are not feasible in most schools.

In the current example, the team would consider how many groups are needed for the students identified as needing Tier 2 support. In some cases, such as the fluency group of seven students, one intervention group might suffice, while the fluency–comprehension group of 11 students might be broken up into two intervention groups. There will also be additional need for supplemental instruction when the most deficient students are considered for Tier 3 interventions, which will necessitate the creation of additional groups (as described below). How many total groups and the size of each group should be guided by best-practice recommendations from the research literature. However, it is acknowledged that teacher and staff availability may put realistic limits on these arrangements. In Chapter 4, we briefly discussed the exigencies that impact these decisions, such as how intervention periods are scheduled in the school day and week, how teachers, specialists, and paraprofessionals are assigned to groups, and so forth. The reader is also referred to other resources regarding the implementation of MTSS for guidance on these matters (Brown-Chidsey & Bickford, 2015; Burns & Gibbons, 2012; *www.rtinetwork.org*; *www.rti4success.org*).

SETTING GROUP GOALS

Like the goal-setting step in the Tier 1 section, the team next sets a measurable goal, this time for each intervention group (Step 1 of plan development). The goal should be based on an ambitious, yet realistic target score on the most relevant assessment instrument. In this example, for the comprehension group, the team decides to use the students' performance on the computer-adaptive assessment (CAT) for goal setting, because this measure is a better metric for assessing comprehension. For the fluency and fluency–comprehension groups, the team decides to set the goal using ORF. For all groups, because supplemental interventions are being planned, the team sets ambitious goals of 150% of the individualized growth goal for each student. As indicated in our discussion of goal setting in Tier 1, for the CAT in this example, individualized growth goals ranged from 8 to 12 scaled score points per month—so an overall goal for the comprehension group would be calculated by multiplying the goal for each student by 150% and then by the number of months until the next benchmark-screening administration (i.e., for a student with a growth goal of 10, the formula would be $10 \times 1.5 \times 4 = 60$). (If proficiency targets were available predicting from the CAT to the state accountability test, Chapter 4 would also suggest that these accelerated growth targets could be set to allow the team to determine whether students were on track to close the gap toward proficiency within a reasonable amount of time [e.g., 3 years]). For the fluency and fluency–comprehension groups, a typical student makes a 1 wcpm increase in ORF per week, so, using the 150% figure, the team would set a goal of a 27 wcpm gain over the 18 weeks between assessments ($1 \times 1.5 \times 18 = 27$).[6] The team also sets a goal for the students who are not being provided with supplemental supports but who are being monitored. Again, using the CBM metric, a goal of 27 wcpm is set. (A goal using CAT would certainly also be appropriate in this situation.) These goals are entered into the appropriate space on the DATR Form (Figure 6.2, page 103).

It is noted here that the practice of setting a groupwide goal results in projecting students at varying performance levels at different targets after the intervention period. Students with higher scores might be close to the benchmark if they meet the goal, while lower-performing students would remain substantially behind. Nonetheless, it is our opinion that goals need to be reasonable and those students who do not hit benchmark levels by the next assessment are still making meaningful improvement in skills and are achieving "traction" in their skill improvement that can be capitalized on in the future, provided you have accounted for regression to the mean in the ways discussed above. As we describe later in the chapter, in follow-up meetings, the progress of each student is reviewed in relation to the set goal. In addition, the overall performance of the group in relation to the group goal is appraised to determine whether the intervention was effective for the group as a whole.

IDENTIFYING INTERVENTIONS AND PLANNING PROGRESS MONITORING

Following the DATR Form, the team next identifies an intervention for each group that is matched to the identified need (Step 2 of plan development). In our experience, most practitioners of the MTSS approach use commercially available intervention packages for supplemental interventions in Tier 2. Most of these packages have an established evidence base and use a standard-protocol format (Vaughn & Fuchs, 2003)—that is, the interventions are manualized and designed to be used in a strictly formatted and scripted manner to maximize intervention fidelity. As discussed in depth in Chapter 4, third-party reviews of available intervention packages have been published by the Institute of Education Sciences via the What Works Clearinghouse (*ies.ed.gov/ncee/wwc*) and the National Center on Intensive Intervention at American Institutes for Research (*www.intensiveintervention.org/chart/instructional-intervention-tools*). Chapter 4 also includes other sources of research-based strategies (e.g., Intervention Central, Evidence Based Intervention Network).

In the current example, the team identifies intervention packages for each of the three intervention groups. It designates *Reading Apprenticeship* (Schoenbach & Greenleaf, 2017) for the comprehension group, with emphasis on preteaching vocabulary and summarizing; *Read Naturally* (Ihnot & Ihnot, 2015) for the fluency group; and both of these programs used on alternate days for the fluency–comprehension group. The team annotates these plans on the DATR Form (Figure 6.2, page 103), and indicates that the monitor group receives only the general education program.

---

[6]Like with CATs, expected rates of growth differ for R-CBM, depending on a student's starting point (Silberglitt & Hintze, 2007). Unfortunately, national norms on expected growth rates by starting point were not available at the time of this writing. The practitioner is advised to set especially ambitious goals for students below target when setting group-level growth goals on R-CBM, in order to account for regression to the mean.

The final task to be accomplished at this stage of the data-analysis process is to plan for progress monitoring for each group of students undergoing supplemental Tier 2 interventions (Step 3 of plan development). Using the space next to the identified intervention program on the DATR Form, the team selects and annotates an assessment procedure that matches the goal set and the focus of the intervention. In the current example, the team indicates that it is using ORF R-CBM for the fluency group, CAT for the comprehension group, and both measures for the fluency–comprehension group. With regard to the frequency of progress monitoring, many sources (e.g., Kovaleski et al., 2013) indicate that progress monitoring in Tier 2 should occur every other week (biweekly). The team in this example selects this frequency for the intervention groups and decides to monitor progress monthly for the monitor group. These decisions are annotated accordingly in the "PM Frequency" column of the DATR Form (Figure 6.2, page 103). As discussed in Chapter 4, in deciding on how frequently they will use GOMs or CATs to monitor student progress, teams should also be sure to confirm the reliability of these measures since some may not be sensitive to change when given weekly or even biweekly.

PLANNING FOR TIER 2 IMPLEMENTATION LOGISTICS

The creation of supplemental intervention groups often involves substantial logistical issues and therefore requires careful consideration in the implementation planning stage for Tier 2. First and most obviously, time for intervention needs to have been built into the daily school schedule before the school year has begun. As indicated in Chapter 1, the data-analysis teaming process is designed to be conducted in the context of an MTSS that involves periods of time each day wherein interventions can take place (known variably by terms such as *power hour, tier time*, etc.). Next, the staff member in charge of the intervention group needs to be identified. In many MTSS, there are four classes of personnel who are typically available to deliver interventions: intervention specialists (including remedial teachers), classroom teachers, specials teachers (e.g., special education, music, physical education), and paraeducators (aides and volunteers). As discussed previously, personnel should be assigned to intervention groups so that the most capable, experienced, and well-trained staff work with the students who have the most significant academic deficits. In the current example, the team has identified one of the classroom teachers who has received special training in early literacy skills for the fluency–comprehension group (Mr. Kaat) and two other classroom teachers for the fluency and comprehension groups (Figure 6.2, page 103). Because of the size of these groups, paraprofessionals (instructional aides) are also deployed to reduce group size. (The team reserves the highly trained reading specialist for work with students in Tier 3, as described below.)

The next issue to be addressed in implementation planning is the frequency of the intervention, with regard to number of days per week and number of minutes per day. In many schools that have an MTSS, students receive supplemental interventions for at least 30 minutes each day, although the length of time and number of days vary in different schools. It should also be noted that some students may need interventions in more than one domain (e.g., reading and math) and may therefore need to be scheduled for interventions on alternating days. In the current example, the team has designated that the intervention groups meet daily for 30 minutes.

Another important plan implementation issue to discuss is developing a plan for the assessment of intervention fidelity. As discussed in Chapter 4, the effectiveness of the teaming process and the MTSS approach in general is the delivery of interventions with sufficient fidelity to realize meaningful student progress. The team needs to designate the approach to be used to assess fidelity, choosing among teacher self-appraisal, observation by colleagues and specialists, and/or observations by the principal. The team also needs to ensure that there is a viable checklist of intervention features for each intervention to be used in the fidelity checks. As indicated in Chapter 4, fidelity checklists for many contemporary intervention packages and instructional strategies are available at *www.rtinetwork. org/getstarted/evaluate/treatment-integrity-protocols*. In the current example, the team has designated the principal and reading specialist as the personnel who will conduct the fidelity checks during the next few months in the designated space on the DATR Form (Figure 6.2, page 103).

Finally, any other logistics that pertain to the implementation of Tier 2 intervention groups are discussed at this time. An important consideration that should be addressed is how the team can ensure that Tier 2 supplemental interventions are congruent with differentiated instruction for these students during core instruction (Tier 1). In the current example, the team plans for monthly follow-up meetings among the classroom teachers and the reading specialist to discuss how the core instruction matches with the interventions being implemented. It also annotates that the classroom teachers monitor progress of the students in the monitor group.

Tier 3 Teaming

In the final stage of the beginning-of-year data-analysis teaming process, data on individual students who display significant deficits in academic performance are reviewed and customized plans are made for these students (see Figure 6.5). Like the previous phases of the process, formats have been included in the DATR Form (Form 6.1, page 146) for this purpose. It should be noted that each Tier 3 page of the DATR Form has space for two students; the page can be copied as needed for additional students.

PREPARATION AND REVIEW OF THE DATA

The data to be considered for students being reviewed for Tier 3 interventions include the same data as were considered for the Tier 2 group, including state tests (if available), fall benchmark-screening, and any other available data. In addition, because these students display the most significant deficiencies (e.g., below basic on state tests, intensive range on benchmark-screening assessments), in-depth problem analysis is needed for these students. In many cases, the team would have conducted drill-down assessments on these students during the previous year. If not, new drill-down assessments should be conducted as soon as it is feasible in the current school term. This will provide a comprehensive set of data that allow for precise identification of students' academic skills and set the stage for an in-depth

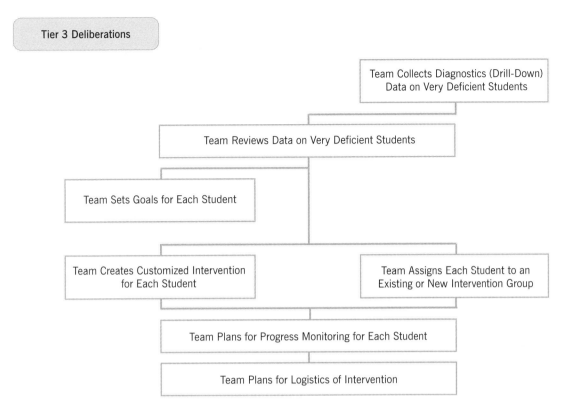

FIGURE 6.5. Flowchart of steps in Tier 3 beginning-of-year meetings.

discussion of intervention options. The data manager should prepare a display that includes all of these data in an easy-to-view format, again organized from highest to lowest scores on a salient measure.

Table 6.5 shows a typical display of students at this level. Following our running example, the team notes that three students have IEPs for reading. Because their needs are being met in the special education program, no further deliberations are needed for these students. Although drill-down assessments would be arranged for all of the remaining students, we focus on just two of these students for demonstration purposes: John B and Bob S.

The team in this case uses a commercially available test of early reading for its drill-down assessment. The instrument includes a maze test and a set of tests of early reading skills. The maze test is useful because, although it is a direct measure of silent reading fluency, it can also be used as an indicator of comprehension. The early reading tests give the team information about the students' skills in phonics, phonological and phonemic awareness, and alphabetic principle. John's scores on the ORF test and the CAT are transcribed onto the DATR Form (Figure 6.2, page 104). The team then adds his scores on the maze and a phonics survey; John has scored at the strategic level on the maze test and at the benchmark level on all of the early reading tests. The team concludes that John has the phonics prerequisite skills to read connected text and is actually comprehending a fair amount of material in spite of his deficient ORF.

TABLE 6.5. Students Designated for Tier 3 Consideration Based on ORF and CAT Scores

IEP	Student	ORF	CAT
	Jimmy H	54	149
	John B	53	234
	Bernadette P	53	160
	Hillary R	52	150
	Eric C	49	114
	Jack B	38	206
	Ginger B	37	150
	Shaquille O	36	271
	Bob S	27	148
Yes	Isaiah M	23	82
Yes	Lloyd T	20	114
Yes	Tomi M	15	112

Bob presents a very different profile. The team has transferred his scores on the ORF measure and the CAT, both of which are in the strategic range, as well as his new scores on the drill-down assessment (see Figure 6.2, page 104). In line with his CAT score, his performance on the maze test is in the intensive range, indicating poor comprehension. To test the hypothesis that his poor ORF and comprehension difficulties are caused by deficient phonics skills, the drill-down assessment of his phonics skills indicates that Bob has acquired most of his letter names and sounds and is getting traction with words in a consonant–vowel–consonant (CVC) pattern with short-vowel sounds and with words with long-vowel sounds (both scores in the strategic range). However, he demonstrates very deficient phonics skills when attempting to read words that have consonant blends, digraphs, r-controlled vowels, and variant vowels.

SETTING GOALS FOR INDIVIDUAL STUDENTS

For Tier 3, plan development begins with goals being set for each student, using the DATR Form (see Form 6.1, page 149). As indicated for students being considered in other tiers, the goal is set using a measure that has the most relevance and utility for the student's most critically deficient skill. In spite of the fact that students needing intensive Tier 3 interventions have a history of slow progress on these measures, the goal should again be ambitious and be indexed on the progress made by typical students during half of a school year (backward planning). The rationale is that it is intended that the intensity of the intervention should markedly increase the student's ROI. In addition, students who have very deficient skills often display relatively large gains from month to month because they have more "room" to grow in comparison to typical students, particularly on measures such as CBM and CAT. In our example, in spite of their very different skill deficiencies, the team decides that an ORF R-CBM should be sensitive to growth for both of these students and designates a gain of 1.5 wcpm/week as a goal, which is rendered as an overall gain of 27 wcpm between the current meeting and the midyear meeting in January. In both cases, the target overall level is indicated: 80 wcpm for John and 54 wcpm for Bob.

CUSTOMIZING INTERVENTIONS AND PLANNING PROGRESS MONITORING

The next steps in plan development for students in Tier 3 is to customize interventions and plan for progress monitoring for each student. Although the analysis at this phase of the process is on individual students, the data should first be analyzed to determine how students at this level of deficiency can be grouped for intervention. The need to design customized, individualized interventions does not mean that these interventions must be delivered in a one-to-one intervention format. Although some well-known interventions (e.g., Reading Recovery) feature a one-to-one teacher–student ratio, most intensive interventions utilize small groups, which have been shown in some studies to be as effective as one-to-one arrangements (Elbaum, Vaughn, Hughes, & Moody, 2000; Mellard et al., 2010) and are more feasible given the staffing patterns in most schools. Accordingly, the data for students are first analyzed to determine whether any of the students can be reasonably accommodated in existing intervention groups, as indicated by the proximity of their performance levels to the other Tier 2 students. If so, they can be assigned to those groups. If not, additional intervention groups should be created, with each group focused on a particular area of need.

In our example, the team decides that John needs supplemental instruction in fluency building and comprehension and reasons that the Tier 2 fluency–comprehension group would meet his needs and adds him to the DATR Form (Figure 6.2) in that group (see Figure 6.2, page 102). However, because John is in the intensive range in ORF, an individual plan is articulated for him on the Tier 3 section of the DATR Form (see page 104). To address Bob's phonics needs, the team prescribes a multisensory reading intervention with explicit teaching of phonics (e.g., an Orton–Gillingham approach) for 40 minutes each day. In most cases, other students would be identified with similar needs and a phonics group would be created for these students. It should be noted that interventions in Tier 3 should be delivered in very small groups (e.g., three to five students) so that the probability for rapid academic gains can be maximized. The team also notes on the form that the reading specialist will work with the phonics group. We have designed the DATR Form so that all group assignments are organized on the second page of the form, so in this case, the phonics group is created on page 102 (Figure 6.2) and the team populates the group with Bob and the other students so designated for this Tier 3 intervention.

The final step for each student is to plan for the monitoring of each student's progress. As with other tiers, the progress monitoring measure should match the deficient area as indicated in the goal-setting step. The frequency of progress monitoring in Tier 3 is once per week, because interventions may need to be adjusted or changed if the student does not display sufficient progress in a timely fashion. In addition, as described below, sufficient data points will be needed if the student needs to be referred for an evaluation for eligibility for special education (Kovaleski et al., 2013). In the current example, having set an ORF goal for both John and Bob, an ORF R-CBM is designated on the DATR Form as the weekly progress monitoring measure. It should also be noted that, as a member of the fluency–comprehension group, John will also be monitored every other week with a CAT.

DECIDING ON REFERRAL FOR SPECIAL EDUCATION ELIGIBILITY

A special note is needed here regarding when students should be referred for a comprehensive evaluation to determine eligibility for special education. Some students may be identified in the review of students with the most deficient skills as potentially in need of referral for this service. Teams should be aware that federal regulations governing special education have consistently been interpreted by the U.S. Department of Education to indicate that the provision of interventions during an MTSS process should not serve as a bar to expedient referral of students for special education eligibility determination if the student displays a clear need for those services. Nonetheless, unless the student presents with obvious indications of a severe disability (e.g., blindness, intellectual disability, autism, traumatic brain injury), these referrals will generally not be made at the beginning-of-year meetings for a number of reasons. First, students with significant academic deficiencies who attended the same school the year before were likely tracked by that data-analysis team, and if a referral was indicated, it would have been made in the previous school year. Second, students who may have moved into the school over the summer months and who display significant deficiencies during the fall benchmark-screening assessment may not have had access to standards-aligned core instruction and targeted interventions in their previous schools. If so, a course of Tier 3 intervention for a sufficient amount of time in the fall term is needed to determine how the student responds to a research-based intervention. This assessment of the student's RTI is necessary as part of the required determination as to whether the student's assessed academic deficiency is a function of a lack of instruction, as would be indicated if the student displayed good progress during the intervention period. Needless to say, any student who may be considered as potentially eligible for special education referral should be carefully and frequently monitored during the intervention period, and a decision about referral may need to be made in a shorter time period than the typical three-times-per-year review. In most cases, decisions about referral for special education are made during the school year, as the team appraises the student's ROI to the response to intervention plan. Detailed procedures for making these determinations have been articulated elsewhere (Kovaleski et al., 2013).

PLANNING FOR TIER 3 IMPLEMENTATION LOGISTICS

The coordination of actions needed to implement individual interventions in Tier 3 (intervention planning) can be challenging and the team needs to keep track of which personnel are assigned to which follow-up activity. To record these actions, the DATR Form includes a final page (Form 6.1, page 150), which has space for the designation of the person responsible and the task assigned. For example, students who display deficiencies in multiple academic areas (e.g., reading, writing, math) often display behavior problems as well. In these cases, both the academic and the behavioral data should be organized, displayed, and analyzed during this phase of the data-analysis process, which entails a combination of procedures addressed in this chapter. Some illustrative examples of "to-dos" associated with Tier 3 services are included in Figure 6.2, page 105. It is likely that a given team meeting will generate many more annotations.

Final Steps

As the team completes its analysis of three tiers of data and plans accordingly, the final step would be to schedule any follow-up meetings. The next formal data-analysis team meeting would be scheduled for the winter, just after the collection of winter benchmark-screening data. However, teams may need interim meetings to stay on track; these should be scheduled before the close of the data-analysis meeting. A useful step is to designate one person (typically the facilitator) to send a follow-up reminder e-mail to all participants. It is also important as the meeting ends to make plans for the DATR Form to be disseminated to all participants.

Formal Follow-Up Meetings

The data-analysis team meetings at the beginning of the year should work well to set a course for instructional improvements to the core program (Tier 1) and identify students for supplemental interventions (Tiers 2 and 3). Data are gathered, organized, and analyzed, and plans are made for both the entire group and individual students. Throughout the fall, teams may meet as needed to continue to review students' progress and to refine strategies selected in the fall. At midyear, after the winter benchmark-screening assessments are conducted, we recommend a second formal data-analysis meeting. At this time, the focus changes from initial planning to a review of student progress and an evaluation of the success of the planned changes to core instruction (Tier 1) and the interventions designed for groups (Tier 2) and individual students (Tier 3). So, although the initial steps of the problem-solving process (problem identification, problem analysis, plan development, plan implementation) are again covered in these meetings, special attention is given to the final step of the process (plan evaluation) as interventions implemented during the preceding months are appraised as to their effectiveness (see Chapter 1, Figure 1.1; Figure 6.6).

The DATR Follow-Up Form (Form 6.2) has been designed to guide the data-analysis team through this meeting to summarize the winter data and to memorialize the decisions made in that meeting. The team members are the same as those who met in the fall meeting, including grade-level classroom (or department at high school) teachers, specialists, and the principal or designated building administrator. Continuing the current example of a team of third-grade teachers and personnel, the names of attendees, the meeting date, and grade level are annotated accordingly on the DATR Follow-Up Form (see Figure 6.7).

Tier 1 Teaming

The follow-up process begins with a review of the data on all students to determine the progress of the group as a whole (e.g., all third graders) and to evaluate the efficacy of the strategies selected for emphasis during core instruction and differentiation.

PREPARATION AND REVIEW OF THE DATA

Similar to the fall meeting, the data manager would provide a data display that features only group data without individually listing data on isolated students. Continuing our example,

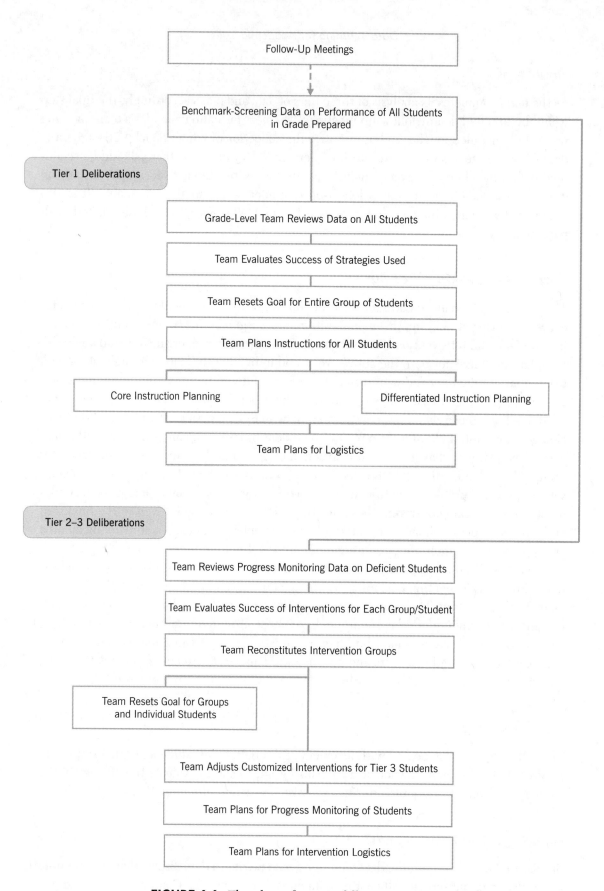

FIGURE 6.6. Flowchart of steps in follow-up meetings.

Date:	January 20, 20XX		Grade:	3	

Meeting Attendees	Position
Camilla Pascual	Principal
James Kaat	Teacher
Victoria Powers	Teacher
Rachel Rollins	Teacher
Erline Battey	Teacher

Meeting Attendees	Position
Cesar Tovar	School Psychologist
Allison Mincher	School Counselor
Toni Oliva	Reading Specialist

TIER 1

Critical Target Skill(s): Note number and percentage of students at designated level based on benchmark/ standard assessment. Name of test(s):	Oral reading fluency (ORF), computer-adaptive test (CAT)

Data since Last Assessment	
Advanced	Not addressed.
Benchmark	ORF: 82% scoring at 86 wcpm or better. CAT: 45% scoring at 350 or better.
Strategic	ORF: 12% scoring between 68 and 85 wcpm. CAT: 40% scoring between 225 and 249.
Intensive	ORF: 6% scoring below 66 wcpm. CAT: 15% scoring below 225.
Was overall goal met?	Yes for ORF. No for comprehension.

Review of Strategies Used: Note the strategies for core instruction and differentiation planned in the last meeting. Rate their fidelity of use and their effectiveness in producing goal achievement.

Strategies	Fidelity	Success
Repeated reading	Very good (>90% on checklists)	Effective
BEST strategy, FCRR strategies, supplemental lessons from grade 2 book	Very good (>90% on checklists)	Effective
Vocabulary root words strategy	Very good (>90% on checklists)	Not effective at this point.

(continued)

FIGURE 6.7. Sample completed Data-Analysis Team Recording Form (DATR): Follow-Up Meeting.

Reset Goals: Note number and percentage of students who should display improvements on benchmark/standard assessment. Date of next goal review: 5/1/20XX

ORF: 95 students (95%) will attain the spring benchmark of 100 wcpm by the next data-review meeting.

CAT: 75 students (75%) will attain the winter benchmark of 400 by the next data-review meeting.

Strategies: Describe strategies selected for core instruction and differentiation for the next time period. (Strategies may be maintained, revised, or replaced.)

Reading fluency: Repeated reading, BEST strategy, and FCRR strategies should continue as implemented so far.

Comprehension: Preteach vocabulary, graphic organizers.

Logistics: Describe actions to be taken to support strategy implementation.

Coaching between Mr. Kaat and Ms. Powers is discontinued.

Teachers will do self-ratings of their use of preteaching vocabulary and graphic organizers with checklists supplied by Mr. Oliva. Ms. Pascual will observe teachers' use of these strategies.

TIER 2

Student Progress since Last Assessment: Note the progress made by each student in each group as indicated by midyear benchmark and rate of improvement (ROI) assessments.

Group 1: Monitor

Student	Goal Attained?	Progress
Susie V	Yes	Satisfactory: ORF = 99, ROI = 1.2, CAT = 340
Kevin C	Yes	Satisfactory: ORF = 97, ROI = 1.0, CAT = 333
Frank J	Yes	Satisfactory: ORF = 97, ROI = 1.0, CAT = 323
Anelys P	Yes	Satisfactory: ORF = 94, ROI = 0.9, CAT = 330
Jake B	Yes	Satisfactory: ORF = 98, ROI = 1.3, CAT = 341

(continued)

FIGURE 6.7. *(continued)*

Group 2: Comprehension		
Student	**Goal Attained?**	**Progress**
Mary N	Yes	Satisfactory: CAT = 310
Jean M	Yes	Satisfactory: CAT = 305
Tyrone S	Yes	Satisfactory: CAT = 272
Igor H	Yes	Satisfactory: CAT = 253
Rita P	No	Not satisfactory: CAT = 200

Group 3: Fluency		
Student	**Goal Attained?**	**Progress**
Khloe F	Yes	Satisfactory: ORF = 88, ROI = 1.5, CAT = 288
Aaliyah A	No	Satisfactory: ORF = 86, ROI = 1.3, CAT = 345
Addison O	Yes	Satisfactory: ORF = 87, ROI = 1.2, CAT = 337
Jaxson B	Yes	Satisfactory: ORF = 90, ROI = 1.1, CAT = 310
London B	No	Satisfactory: ORF = 71, ROI = 0.7, CAT = 275

Group 4: Fluency–Comprehension		
Student	**Goal Attained?**	**Progress**
Xavier J	Yes	Satisfactory: ORF = 90, ROI = 1.3, CAT = 270
Caleb Z	Yes	Satisfactory: ORF = 87, ROI = 1.2, CAT = 300
Kaylee G	Yes	Satisfactory: ORF = 89, ROI = 1.1, CAT = 150
Sofia U	No	Not satisfactory: ORF = 77, ROI = 0.9, CAT = 222
Mackenzie S	No	Not satisfactory: ORF = 80, ROI = 0.8, CAT = 221

(continued)

FIGURE 6.7. *(continued)*

Group 5: Phonics		
Student	Goal Attained?	Progress
Eric C	Yes	Satisfactory: ORF = 79, ROI = 0.9, CAT = 200
Jack B	Yes	Satisfactory: ORF = 80, ROI = 1.0, CAT = 222
Ginger B	Yes	Satisfactory: ORF = 69, ROI = 0.8, CAT = 198
Shaquille O	No	Satisfactory: ORF = 62, ROI = 0.6, CAT = 207
Bob S	No	Satisfactory: ORF = 45, ROI = 0.5, CAT = 150

Review of Strategies Used: Note the strategies planned in the last meeting. Rate their fidelity of use and their effectiveness in producing goal achievement (e.g., percentage of students reaching their goal).

	Strategies	Fidelity	Success
Group 1: Monitor	General education program	Acceptable	100%
Group 2: Comprehension	Reading Apprenticeship with emphasis on preteaching vocabulary and summarizing	Strong	80%
Group 3: Fluency	Read Naturally	Acceptable	60%
Group 4: Fluency Comprehension	Reading Apprenticeship and Read Naturally (alternating days)	Questionable for Reading Apprenticeship; acceptable for Read Naturally	60%
Group 5: Phonics	Multisensory phonics	Acceptable	60%

Students Identified for Tier 2 Interventions: Insert instructional focus of intervention groups and list students assigned to each group based on the most recent data. Identify any student needing further assessment and indicate the type of assessment needed.

Group 1: Monitor		Group 2: Comprehension		Group 3: Fluency	
Frank J Addison O Jaxson B Mary N Jean M Aalliyah A		Tyrone S Igor H Rita P Khloe F Xavier J Kaylee G		Eric C Jack B Ginger B London B Grayson L	
Group 4: Fluency–Comprehension		Group 5: Phonics		Further Assessment	Name of Assessment
Sofia U Mackenzie S Jimmy H John B Bernadette P Hillary R		Shaquille O Bob S Florence P		Shaquille O	CBE

(continued)

FIGURE 6.7. *(continued)*

Strategies for Intervention Groups: Note strategy (or program) to be implemented with each group. (Strategies may be maintained, revised, or replaced.) Indicate the progress monitoring measure to be used and the frequency of monitoring.

Group	Strategy/Program	Progress Monitoring	PM Frequency
Group 1: Monitor	General education program	CAT	Monthly
Group 2: Comprehension	Reading Apprenticeship with emphasis on preteaching vocabulary and summarizing	CAT	Biweekly
Group 3: Fluency	Read Naturally	ORF R-CBM	Biweekly
Group 4: Fluency–Comprehension	Reading Apprenticeship and Read Naturally (alternating days)	CAT	Biweekly
Group 5: Phonics	Multisensory phonics	ORF R-CBM	Weekly

Goals: Indicate goal for each group.   Date of goal review: 5/1/20XX

Group 1: Monitor	Students will gain 50 scaled score points on the CAT by the end-of-year assessment.
Group 2: Comprehension	Students will gain 50 scaled score points on the CAT by the end-of-year assessment.
Group 3: Fluency	Students will gain 20–30 wcpm on the ORF R-CBM assessment by the end-of-year assessment.
Group 4: Fluency–Comprehension	Students will gain 50 scaled score points on the CAT by the end-of-year assessment.
Group 5: Phonics	These students are receiving Tier 3 supports; refer to each student's individual plan.

Logistics: Describe actions to be taken to support strategy implementation.

Group	Frequency of Intervention (Days, Times)	Intervener	Other Logistics
Group 1: Monitor	N/A	N/A	Classroom teachers will monitor progress.
Group 2: Comprehension	Daily; 30 minutes	Ms. Battey	Fidelity checks: Ms. Pascual
Group 3: Fluency	Daily; 30 minutes	Ms. Rollins	Fidelity checks: Ms. Oliva
Group 4: Fluency–Comprehension	Daily; 30 minutes	Mr. Kaat	Fidelity checks: Ms. Oliva
Group 5: Phonics	Daily; 40 minutes	Ms. Oliva	See individual Tier 3 plans.
All:	Monthly	Teachers; reading specialist	Follow-up meetings

(continued)

FIGURE 6.7. *(continued)*

Student Newly Identified for Tier 3 (Customized Intervention): | Florence P

Assessment Measures and Scores

ORF (median grade 3 probes) — 40 wcpm (intensive level)

CAT — 199 (intensive level)

Maze — 4 (intensive level)

Phonics Survey (Letter Names and Sounds) — 59 (intensive level)

Phonics Survey (Short Vowels CVC) — 14 (benchmark level)

Phonics Survey (Long Vowels) — 12 (strategic level)

Phonics Survey (Consonant Blends, Digraphs) — 6–7 (intensive levels)

Phonics Survey (R-Controlled Vowels) — 6 (intensive level)

Phonics Survey (Variant Vowels) — 5 (intensive level)

Goal: Florence will gain 27 wcpm and reach an ORF of 67 wcpm by the midyear assessment.	**Date of Goal Review:** 5/1/20XX
Intervention: Multisensory reading intervention with explicit teaching of phonics	**Location and Frequency:** Phonics group, daily, 40 minutes
Progress Monitoring Measure: ORF R-CBM	**Frequency of Monitoring:** Weekly
Intervener: Ms. Oliva	**Progress Monitor:** Ms. Oliva

Student Previously Identified for Tier 3 (Customized Intervention): | Bob S

Student Progress since Last Assessment: Note the progress made by the student as indicated by graphed data and rate of improvement (ROI).

Assessment Measure	Data	Goal Attained?
ORF R-CBM	Fall: 27 wcpm; winter: 45 wcpm	No
ORF ROI	0.5 wcpm/week	
CAT	Fall: 148; spring: 150	

Was the intervention effective? No	**Was the intervention delivered with fidelity?** Yes
Reset Goal: Bob will gain 27 wcpm to attain 72 wcpm. He will display an ROI of 1.5 wcpm/week.	**Date of Goal Review:** 5/1/20XX
Intervention: Continue multisensory reading intervention with explicit teaching of phonics. Refer for evaluation to consider special education services.	**Location and Frequency:** Phonics group, daily, 40 minutes
Progress Monitoring Measure: ORF R-CBM	**Frequency of Monitoring:** Weekly
Intervener: Ms. Oliva	**Progress Monitor:** Ms. Oliva

FIGURE 6.7. *(continued)*

the data manager has again prepared a graphic summary of the third-graders' performance on the ORF R-CBM and the CAT comprehension assessments, this time using the winter screening data (see Figure 6.8). Focusing on the "Critical Target Skill(s)" section of the DATR Follow-Up Form (Figure 6.7), the team describes and summarizes the percentage of students who are at various levels of performance as per the winter assessment, including benchmark, strategic, and intensive levels, as well as those at the advanced level, if so desired and designated by the team. The team then reviews the completed fall DATR Form (Figure 6.2) for the goal that the team set in terms of percentage and number of students whom they projected to reach proficiency by the winter benchmark-screening assessment, and makes a judgment about whether the goal was met as indicated by the winter data.

Reviewing the data in Figure 6.8, the team annotates on the DATR Follow-Up Form (Figure 6.7, page 127) the following percentages of students at the various levels on the ORF R-CBM: benchmark—82%, strategic—12%, intensive—6%. The goal set in the fall meeting was that 80% would reach the benchmark level by the winter assessment; the team concludes that the overall goal was met. The team also notes the percentages of students at various levels on the comprehension CAT: benchmark—45%, strategic—40%, intensive—15%. The goal set in the fall meeting was 50% of students meeting proficiency, so the team decides that the comprehension goal has not been met. An overall statement about the goal attainment is then included on the DATR Follow-Up Form in this section.[7]

EVALUATION OF STRATEGIES USED

The next step is a new one for the team and unique to follow-up meetings: plan evaluation. Focusing on the "Review of Strategies Used" section of the DATR Follow-Up Form

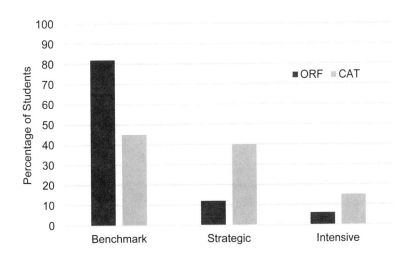

FIGURE 6.8. Percentages of students at benchmark, strategic, and intensive levels of performance on ORF and CAT in winter screening.

---

[7]It should be noted that the team needs to consider the levels appropriate for the winter assessment, as indicated in Table 6.1.

(Figure 6.7, page 127), the facilitator draws the team's attention to the two strategies that were identified for core instruction and differentiation in Tier 1 at the fall meeting, as the recorder transcribes the strategies from the fall DATR Form (Figure 6.2). The facilitator then prompts the team to discuss the extent to which the strategies were implemented with good fidelity during the months preceding the current meeting, first calling on the classroom teachers to self-evaluate, and then asking those charged with conducting classroom observations to check fidelity to weigh in. If the facilitator is the principal, they should also render an opinion at this point. As stated earlier, this guided reflection of the use of the agreed-upon strategies is a key aspect of the process, as teachers consider their use of the strategies, what was easy and difficult to implement, and whether the strategies were delivered with sufficient fidelity for them to connect their use with the students' progress (or lack thereof). (It is noted that this is a self-reflective process for the team and not an evaluation of teacher performance.) Because the team next considers whether the strategies were successful and should be continued, whether the strategies were used and implemented with good fidelity is critical to those decisions. For example, if the strategy was used with good fidelity and goals were attained, the team may have good reason to relate those gains to the strategies used. If the strategies were used with good fidelity and goals were not reached, the team would likely not continue those strategies in the coming months and not select those strategies in the future. Conversely, if the strategies were not implemented with fidelity but the students met their goals, the team may want to consider what other factors were working well during the preceding months. If the strategies were not used with fidelity and the students did not meet the overall goal, whether the strategy was effective or not cannot be ascertained. It is only by verifying that a strategy was implemented with high fidelity that the effect of the strategy can be evaluated.

At this point, the literature on assessing and making decisions about intervention fidelity is in its infancy and clear links between the level of fidelity recorded and student outcomes has not been established. For example, if a checklist of actions undertaken during the implementation of a strategy is used for teachers' self-appraisal or by an observer, it is not known whether certain percentages of items are needed for the strategy to have a demonstrable effect. This situation is further complicated by the probability that not all items on a fidelity checklist are of equal importance, so simple quantitative summaries may be misleading. Given this reality, we recommend that teams consider the data available from the fidelity checklists and provide a qualitative descriptor of their judgment of the overall fidelity of implementation by the classroom teachers. In the current example (Figure 6.7, page 127), the team annotates the strategies selected in the fall (repeated readings, etc.), records that the average number of items completed by all raters was above 90%, and applies the descriptor "very good" on the DATR Follow-Up Form.

After the fidelity is rated, the team then makes a judgment as to the success of each strategy. Again, strict causation may be elusive, but the team should have some sense as to whether the progress displayed by the students could be reasonably related to the strategies used. In the current example, the team judges the strategies to be effective in terms of improving students' ORF. They also note that the strategies have helped some students improve their comprehension, which followed from becoming better at fluently decoding. However, the strategies were not effective alone in terms of improving comprehension.

RESETTING GOALS

Having completed the plan evaluation step, the team now returns to the beginning of the problem-solving cycle (see Chapter 1, Figure 1.1). Before deciding upon what strategies will be emphasized in the next part of the school year, the team analyzes the winter data (problem identification and analysis) and resets the goal for the end of the year (the first action of plan development). Again using backward planning, it is noted that most students should reach the benchmark on the target measures by the end of the year, so the team should again set ambitious goals to achieve proficiency. Nonetheless, some students may still be very deficient and unlikely to make extraordinary leaps during this time, so reasonable, but ambitious, projections about their performance should be taken into consideration. In the current example, the team decides to set a goal that 95% of the students will be at benchmark in ORF by the spring benchmark-screening assessment and 75% will hit benchmark on the comprehension CAT (see Figure 6.7, page 128).[8]

IDENTIFYING INSTRUCTIONAL STRATEGIES

Having set the goal for spring, the team then discusses the strategies that will be emphasized in core instruction during the coming months (Step 2 of plan development). This decision should be based on the success of the strategies used in the fall and their continued relevance in terms of the goals that were set. In the current example (Figure 6.7, page 128), the team concludes that three strategies should be highlighted for use in the spring. First, repeated readings should continue with those students who are approaching the ORF benchmark, but who need to increase their fluency to that level. Second, because some students still struggle with phonics skills, small-group work on phonics during core instruction should continue. The team also notes that most of these students are receiving supplemental interventions in Tier 2 or 3 arrangements, so the strategy should be congruent with those interventions. Finally, the team notes that comprehension skills should be emphasized for the entire group to address the comprehension goal and identifies two strategies for emphasis by all teachers: preteaching vocabulary and graphic organizers. Progress of the entire group of students is appraised using their performance on the spring benchmark assessment.

PLANNING FOR IMPLEMENTATION LOGISTICS

The last task for the Tier 1 section of the meeting is for the team to review the logistic issues identified in the fall meeting and discuss whether they need to be continued and/or whether new logistical concerns have emerged that need to be addressed. In the current example (Figure 6.7, page 128), the team notes that the support that the teacher who was unfamiliar with the phonics strategy received was appreciated and helpful, but does not need to be continued. The teachers agreed to do self-appraisals of their use of the selected comprehension strategy, and the principal indicated that she will include a fidelity check in her upcoming teacher observations.

---

[8]It should be noted that the team needs to consider the levels appropriate for the spring assessment, as indicated in Table 6.1.

Tier 2 Teaming

The team next turns to a review of progress for students who were assigned to Tier 2 intervention groups in the beginning-of-year meeting. Here again, the focus is on the plan evaluation phase of the problem-solving cycle.

PREPARATION AND REVIEW OF THE DATA

For the review of students who received Tier 2 interventions, data from two sources need to be gathered, summarized, and displayed for the data-analysis team. Data should be gathered for individual students and organized by intervention group. The first data source is the results of the midyear (winter) benchmark-screening assessments. In the current example (Figure 6.7), the team prepares data on the midyear ORF R-CBM and the comprehension CAT. The second source of data that is now available to the team is the ROI data that are generated from progress monitoring. Generally, particularly with CBM, data from progress monitoring on individual students can be graphed and can also be transformed into a metric that indicates the average rate at which the student improved per week during the intervention period (i.e., ROI). Although there are a number of approaches to calculating ROI, the consensus of researchers at this time (e.g., Christ et al., 2012, 2013) is that using ordinary least squares is the most psychometrically appropriate approach. The datum provided by this approach is typically indicated as a per week indicator. For example, for ORF R-CBM, the ROI metric of wcpm *per week* would indicate how many words read correctly a student *gained* on average during the weeks of intervention. ROI data are often provided by commercial vendors of assessment systems that include progress monitoring. Alternatively, ROI calculators are available via Excel formats (see *rateofimprovement.com*) and ChartDog 2.0 (*www.jimwrightonline.com/php/chartdog_2_0/chartdog.php*). An example of a Tier 2 data set that includes both the benchmark-screening and ROI data is presented in Table 6.6. This time the data are presented by intervention group.

As the team reviews this data set, the recorder transcribes the students' names into the designated group (Figure 6.7, pages 128–130).[9] The group then examines the level (benchmark-screening scores) and ROI (if available) attained by each student and indicates in qualitative terms whether the goal was attained and the progress made. For example, in Figure 6.7, the team notes that all of the students in the monitor group met their goal of gaining 27 wcpm since the fall assessment. Their ROIs also look appropriate (around 1 wcpm/week). They note that this progress is "satisfactory." For the comprehension group, the team notes that some students met their goal of gaining 60 scaled score points since the fall assessment, while others did not. Their progress is rated as "satisfactory" or "not satisfactory," respectively. The goal set for the fluency group was a gain of 27 wcpm. Examining the performance of students in this group, the team notes that although not all students met this goal, all hit or approximated the winter ORF benchmark (86 wcpm) and all displayed ROIs that were typical of other third graders. So, the team notes satisfactory progress for all listed students. The team then notes mixed progress for the fluency–comprehension group, with some students attaining the goal of an increase of 27 wcpm and some not. They rate the students' progress accordingly. Finally,

---

[9] Only some of the students identified for Tier 2 interventions earlier in this chapter are indicated in this figure. In actual practice, all students receiving interventions would be listed.

TABLE 6.6. Data Considered during Example of Follow-Up Meeting

Monitor group	ORF	ROI	CAT	Fluency group	ORF	ROI	CAT
Susie V	99	1.2	340	Khloe F	88	1.5	288
Kevin C	97	1.0	333	Aaliyah A	86	1.3	345
Frank J	97	1.0	323	Addison O	87	1.2	337
Anelys P	94	0.9	330	Jaxson B	90	1.1	310
Jake B	98	1.3	341	Aubree T	85	1.0	318
Jayne B	90	1.0	334	London B	71	0.7	275
Noah D	90	1.1	349	Sam O	81	1.1	305
Liam H	87	1.1	336				
Serenity G	86	1.0	338				

Comprehension group	ORF	ROI	CAT	Fluency–Comprehension group	ORF	ROI	CAT
Mary N	100	1.3	310	Xavier J	90	1.3	270
Jean M	97	1.2	305	Caleb Z	87	1.2	300
Tyrone S	95	1.0	272	Kaylee G	89	1.1	150
Igor H	96	1.1	253	Juan R	87	1.0	266
Rita P	92	1.0	200	Asher L	86	1.0	281
Eddie K	90	0.9	225	Camilla H	81	0.9	224
Latitia W	87	1.1	273	Cooper P	84	0.8	294
Jasmine C	86	1.0	288	Leslie N	82	0.8	292
Emma F	89	0.9	305	Grayson L	75	0.7	299
				Sofia U	77	0.9	222
				Mackenzie S	80	0.8	221
				Jimmy H	76	0.7	224
				John B	75	0.8	277
				Bernadette P	73	0.9	220
				Hillary R	70	0.6	215

Phonics group	ORF	ROI	CAT	Special Education	ORF	ROI	CAT
Eric C	79	0.9	200	Isaiah M	45	0.5	121
Jack B	80	1.0	222	Lloyd T	44	0.4	145
Ginger B	69	0.8	198	Tomi M	33	0.6	133
Shaquille O	62	0.6	207				
Bob S	45	0.5	150				

in Figure 6.7 on page 130, the performance of students in the phonics group is listed. This group was constituted during Tier 3 deliberations in the fall. These students are reviewed individually in the forthcoming Tier 3 follow-up discussions.

EVALUATION OF STRATEGIES USED

On the DATR Follow-Up Form (see Form 6.2, page 151), the recorder transcribes the strategies used for each group and the team facilitator leads the group in a discussion of the level of fidelity achieved in the implementation of the strategy. As described previously, the assessment of intervention fidelity is a serious and purposeful undertaking, and has direct bearing on the team's appraisal of the effects of the intervention. For example, the team in the current example (Figure 6.7, page 130) has judged that the fidelity for the monitor, fluency, and phonics groups was acceptable, and the fidelity for the comprehension group was strong. However, the fidelity for the fluency–comprehension group was mixed because it was judged as acceptable for *Read Naturally*, but questionable for *Reading Apprenticeship*. Less than satisfactory fidelity should be discussed by the team with regard to issues such as teachers' belief in and commitment to the strategy, the level of difficulty presented by its implementation, and whether logistic issues intended to support strategy implementation have been effective and sufficient.

The team then reviews the progress of students in each group (Figure 6.7, page 130) and annotates the percentage of the students who have reached their goal in the "Success" column. This combination of fidelity appraisal and performance of the instructional group should lead to an objective evaluation of the relative success of the intervention used (plan evaluation), which will drive the decision about whether the intervention should continue for the group. A number of possibilities emerge here. If the strategy produced success for the majority of students in the group, the strategy should be continued for those students who made acceptable progress. If the strategy was not successful for the majority of the students, two aspects should be checked. First, the team should revisit whether the strategy was really implemented with fidelity. If not, efforts should be made to enhance the fidelity. Second, the team should check whether the intervention group was really a correct match for the constituent students. This issue should have emerged as the students' progress was monitored and as the teacher worked with the students. If the intervention was correctly matched and implemented with fidelity, the viability of this intervention may be questioned for use in this school. This prospect is perplexing if the school has chosen research-based intervention programs, but it is possible that interventions that have a good research base still may not scale to all implementation sites. For example, there may be inherent conflicts between the procedures of the intervention and how the core curriculum is delivered. Coherence between the core and the selected interventions is critical, but sometimes overlooked when intervention packages are purchased.

RECONSTITUTING THE INTERVENTION GROUPS

Depending on the decisions that were made regarding the evaluation of the interventions, the team next uses the new data to reconstitute the intervention group, using the DATR Follow-Up Form (see Form 6.2, page 154) to populate students into groups. Using problem analysis, the team reviews the data set that was created for this follow-up meeting (as described above), and identifies students in the following categories:

- *Students who have made substantial progress and now are not substantially discrepant from the benchmark. Tier 2 interventions can be discontinued at this point.* Some teams decide to continue to monitor these students on a periodic basis (e.g., monthly) to ensure that their progress is sustained. In our example (Figure 6.7, page 130), the team identifies students for monitoring who hit benchmark on ORF and made good progress on the comprehension CAT.

- *Students who were at or above benchmark in previous assessments (and therefore received no supplemental supports), but who have now slipped below benchmark in the current screening-benchmarking assessment.* A Tier 2 intervention would be considered for these students at this time. In our example (Figure 6.7), there are no students who fit this category, but the team will continue to monitor this possibility in each follow-up meeting.

- *Students who made good progress during the first course of intervention, but who continue to need that intervention.* These students should be slotted for that intervention group. In our example, Tyrone S, Igor H, and Rita P fall into this category; they continue to need support in comprehension.

- *Students who attained proficiency on a lower-level skill, but continue to need intervention on a higher-level skill.* These students should be placed in the intervention group that addresses the higher-level skill. In our example, Khloe F, Xavier J, and Kaylee G have hit the benchmark in ORF, but still need intervention in comprehension, so they will join the comprehension group at this point.

- *Students who have not made adequate progress.* Assuming that the intervention was appropriate and delivered with fidelity, further drill-down assessment is indicated for this group to discern more precisely their instructional need. The names of these students and the assessment identified for them should be annotated in the appropriate column (Form 6.2, page 154). It should be noted that the timing of when to perform these additional assessments is critical, and the decision to assess further may have been made at an earlier point. After the assessment is completed and the new data reviewed, the team decides whether the student should continue in the current group, or be placed in a different group. For many of these students, the increased intensity of Tier 3 interventions would likely be indicated. In our example (Figure 6.7), Shaquille O would receive a drill-down assessment (curriculum-based evaluation) because of his lack of progress during Tier 2 intervention.

The next step is for the team to engage in plan development to specify the intervention for each newly constituted group, and identify the progress monitoring assessment and frequency. The DATR Follow-Up Form (see Form 6.2, page 155) is designed for this annotation. In our example (Figure 6.7), because most interventions had acceptable fidelity during the first half of the year, they are continued during the second half. Progress monitoring would again match the construct being assessed. Because many of the students in this example are attaining ORF goals, but not comprehension goals, more frequent use of the CAT as a monitoring measure is indicated. The frequency of progress monitoring in Tier 2 is again biweekly. (The progress of the phonics group, consisting of students in Tier 3, is monitored weekly.)

RESETTING GOALS

Next, the team resets goals for each Tier 2 group. The procedure follows the guidance offered earlier for beginning-of-year meetings—that is, using a backward planning approach, the percentage of improvement for all members of the group is the suggested format. The targets for each group are annotated on the DATR Follow-Up Form (see Form 6.2, page 155). In our example (Figure 6.7, page 131), increases in CAT scaled scores of 50 points (commensurate with typical growth) are projected for the monitor, comprehension, and fluency–comprehension groups. For the fluency group that is still working on improving ORF, a gain of 20–30 wcpm is desired in order for students to attain the spring benchmark of 100 wcpm.

PLANNING FOR IMPLEMENTATION LOGISTICS

Finally, logistics for organizing the Tier 2 interventions are planned, using the appropriate section of the DATR Follow-Up Form (Form 6.2, page 155). This discussion should follow the guidelines presented earlier for beginning-of-year meetings. At this point of the year, the team would have had experience with which logistical supports were helpful and need to be continued; which were helpful, but no longer needed; which were not helpful and can be discontinued; and which new supports should be identified and implemented in the next part of the school year. In our example (Figure 6.7, page 131), procedures outlined in the fall meeting continue to be pertinent and are repeated here.

Tier 3 Teaming

The team next turns its attention to plan evaluation, problem analysis, and plan development for those students who are most deficient and who have not made satisfactory progress during the time since the last meeting, using the final section of the DATR Follow-Up Form (Form 6.2) to guide the deliberations. The focus at this point is on each individual student. The DATR Follow-Up Form for students receiving Tier 3 interventions has been designed to accommodate two different scenarios: students who have received a drill-down assessment since the last formal meeting (Form 6.2, top half of page 156) and students who were assessed earlier and for whom the drill-down assessment results were annotated on a previous DATR Follow-Up Form (Form 6.2, bottom half of page 156). Each of these formats should be reproduced to accommodate all of the students being considered for Tier 3 supports.

PREPARATION AND REVIEW OF THE DATA

At this point, the team should have arranged for a drill-down assessment for any student considered for or currently receiving Tier 3 interventions. For a student who has very recently received this assessment, the results of this assessment should be transcribed to the DATR

Follow-Up Form (Form 6.2, top half of page 156). For students for whom the drill-down assessment results are recorded on a previous DATR Follow-Up Form, the team should access those results, but the focus should be on the student's ROI during the intervention. The ROI data should be displayed in the data set (as exemplified in Table 6.6). In addition, it has been long established that the review of graphed data is beneficial to instructional evaluation and planning (Fuchs & Fuchs, 1986), so the team should also prepare and review individual progress monitoring graphs for each student. Those data should be summarized in the "Student Progress since Last Assessment" section of the DATR Follow-Up Form (Form 6.2, page 156), by indicating the progress monitoring measure, the data (i.e., level and ROI), and a description of whether the preset goal was attained by the current date.

PLANNING FOR STUDENTS WHO ARE NEWLY IDENTIFIED FOR TIER 3 SUPPORTS

The procedures for goal setting, intervention planning, determination of the progress monitoring measure, and the intervener (i.e., intervention group) for students who are newly identified for Tier 3 supports follows the guideline presented earlier for beginning-of-year meetings. Annotations about these deliberations are made on the DATR Follow-Up Form (Form 6.2) using the top half of the form for these students. In our example (Figure 6.7, page 132), the team has conducted a drill-down assessment with Florence P, a student who has recently moved into the district, and has summarized the results and intervention plan in this section.

PLANNING FOR STUDENTS WHO HAVE BEEN RECEIVING TIER 3 SUPPORTS

For students who have been provided with intensive Tier 3 interventions during the preceding months, the team uses the collected progress monitoring data (i.e., the ROI and graphed display) to conduct a plan evaluation for each student, analyzing whether the intervention was effective in producing meaningful growth for the student. When reviewing graphed data, the team should determine whether the student met the preset goal, which may have been expressed in terms of a level to reach and/or adherence to a preset aim line (sometimes referred to as goal line), a graphed line that connects the initial data point with the preset goal. Readers unfamiliar with the use of graphed data should review texts, such as that by Hosp, Hosp, and Howell (2016) and other sources. As in other tier deliberations, the question as to whether the intervention was implemented with fidelity should be raised and evaluated, particularly for those students who are not making meaningful progress. The team's decision about the effectiveness of the intervention and whether it was implemented with fidelity is annotated in the corresponding section of the DATR Follow-Up Form (Form 6.2).

Next, the team engages in plan development for each student. First, the team resets the goal for the student for the next period of time, annotating the DATR Follow-Up Form accordingly. Depending on their evaluation of the effectiveness of the intervention, the team decides to continue, adapt, or implement a different intervention, with annotation made to the DATR Follow-Up Form in terms of the description, location, frequency, and intervener responsible. The type and frequency of progress monitoring is also determined and recorded. Planning for implementation, the team discerns whether any implementation logistics are needed to deliver customized interventions for the Tier 3 students discussed. Finally, the team should use this review to determine whether any students who have very deficient levels of attainment and poor ROI should be referred for full and individual evaluations to consider their eligibility for special education (cf. Kovaleski et al., 2013).

To complete our example (Figure 6.7, page 132), the team records their work with Bob S, who has made poor progress in spite of an evidence-based intervention delivered at an acceptable level of fidelity. In addition to continuing this intervention, the team now refers Bob for an individual evaluation, because his lack of progress is suggestive of evidence for a disability (e.g., SLD).

End-of-Year Meeting

The parameters for conducting other follow-up meetings, such as the meeting that occurs toward the end of the academic year (spring), follow the same guidelines as described for the follow-up meeting convened at midyear (winter). Of course, any plans made at this time will have only limited usefulness, as the end of the attendance year is perhaps a month or two away. For this reason, the team should not only construct a plan for this short time period, it should also convey its findings to the team at the next grade level. In the course of its year-long deliberations, the team has learned much about this particular group of students, and importantly, has attained significant insights in regard to strategies that are effective (or not), both in core instruction (Tier 1) and in group (Tier 2) and customized (Tier 3) interventions. This trove of critical information needs to be conveyed to the next group of teachers and other personnel who will work with these students. In our experience, this logical step is often not implemented in schools. We recommend a day at the end of the year that is dedicated to having teams from adjoining grades meet one another and formally and informally tell their stories about what has worked during the previous year. Plans can also be made to follow-up with these students in the following year to give them the best start possible.

KEY ISSUES

- The process for data-analysis teaming at the school and grade levels involves many steps that are summarized in the flowchart displayed in Figure 6.9.

- The data-analysis teaming process is greatly enhanced by using a preset group of forms to guide the process and memorialize the decisions made, such as those displayed in this chapter.

- The focus of data-analysis teaming at Tier 1 is the overall improvement of instruction for all students in the grade.

- The focus of data-analysis teaming at Tier 2 is the creation of small groups for the delivery of supplemental intervention.

- The focus of data-analysis teaming at Tier 3 is on customizing interventions for individual students.

- Throughout the data-analysis teaming process, data sources as described in Chapter 5 are used to guide the decision-making process.

- A key to the evaluation of strategies identified for use in the data-analysis teaming process is how students subsequently perform, as indicated by the results of benchmark-screening assessments (Tier 1) and progress monitoring (Tiers 2 and 3).

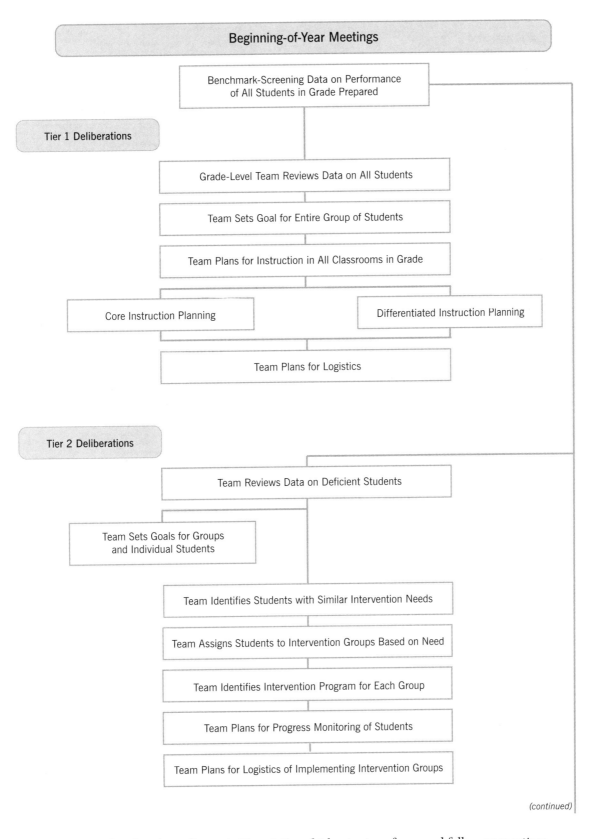

FIGURE 6.9. Flowchart of steps in Tiers 1, 2, and 3 beginning-of-year and follow-up meetings.

(continued)

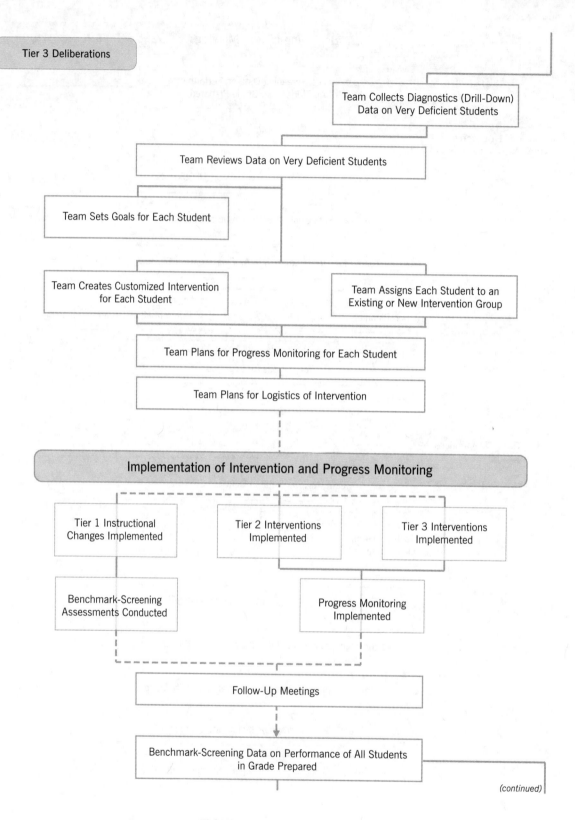

FIGURE 6.9. *(continued)*

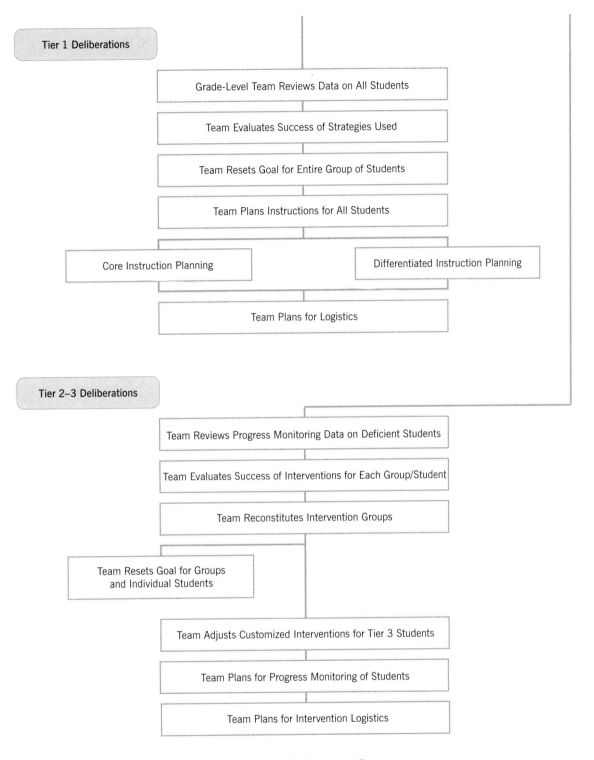

FIGURE 6.9. *(continued)*

Data-Analysis Team Recording (DATR) Form: Beginning-of-Year Meeting

Date: [   ]   Grade: [   ]

Meeting Attendees	Position

Meeting Attendees	Position

TIER 1

Critical Target Skill(s): Note number and percentage of students at designated level based on benchmark/standard assessment. Name of test(s): [   ]

Advanced	
Benchmark	
Strategic	
Intensive	

Goals: Note number and percentage of students who should display improvements on benchmark/standard assessment. Date of goal review: [   ]

(continued)

Strategies: Describe strategies identified for core instruction.

Logistics: Describe actions to be taken to support strategy implementation.

TIER 2

Students Identified for Tier 2 Interventions: Insert instructional focus of intervention groups and list students assigned to each group. Identify any student needing further assessment and indicate the type of assessment needed.

Group 1:		Group 2:		Group 3:	
Group 4:		Group 5:		Further Assessment	Name of Assessment

(continued)

Goals: Indicate goal for each group.   Date of goal review: [____]

Group 1:	
Group 2:	
Group 3:	
Group 4:	
Group 5:	

Strategies for Intervention Groups: Note strategy (or program) to be implemented with each group. Indicate the progress monitoring measure to be used and the frequency of monitoring.

Group	Strategy/Program	Progress Monitoring (PM)	PM Frequency
Group 1:			
Group 2:			
Group 3:			
Group 4:			
Group 5:			

Logistics: Describe actions to be taken to support strategy implementation.

Group	Frequency of Intervention (Days, Times)	Intervener	Other Logistics
Group 1:			
Group 2:			
Group 3:			
Group 4:			
Group 5:			
All:			

(continued)

TIER 3

Student Identified for Tier 3 (Customized Intervention):

Assessment Measures and Scores

Goal:	Date of Goal Review:
Intervention:	Location and Frequency:
Progress Monitoring Measure:	Frequency of Monitoring:
Intervener:	Progress Monitor:

Student Identified for Tier 3 (Customized Intervention):

Assessment Measure and Scores

Goal:	Date of Goal Review:
Intervention:	Location and Frequency:
Progress Monitoring Measure:	Frequency of Monitoring:
Intervener:	Progress Monitor:

(continued)

TO-DO LIST

Person Responsible	Task

FORM 6.2

Data-Analysis Team Recording Form (DATR): Follow-Up Meeting

Date: [   ]   Grade: [   ]

Meeting Attendees	Position

Meeting Attendees	Position

TIER 1

Critical Target Skill(s): Note number and percentage of students at designated level based on benchmark/standard assessment. Name of test(s):

Data since Last Assessment	
Advanced	
Benchmark	
Strategic	
Intensive	
Was overall goal met?	

Review of Strategies Used: Note the strategies for core instruction and differentiation planned in the last meeting. Rate their fidelity of use and their effectiveness in producing goal achievement.

Strategies	Fidelity	Success

(continued)

Reset Goals: Note number and percentage of students who should display improvements on benchmark/standard assessment. Date of next goal review:

Strategies: Describe strategies selected for core instruction and differentiation for the next time period. (Strategies may be maintained, revised, or replaced.)

Logistics: Describe actions to be taken to support strategy implementation.

TIER 2

Student Progress since Last Assessment: Note the progress made by each student in each group as indicated by midyear benchmark and rate of improvement (ROI) assessments.

Group 1:		
Student	Goal Attained?	Progress

(continued)

Group 2:		
Student	Goal Attained?	Progress

Group 3:		
Student	Goal Attained?	Progress

Group 4:		
Student	Goal Attained?	Progress

(continued)

Group 5:		
Student	Goal Attained?	Progress

Review of Strategies Used: Note the strategies planned in the last meeting. Rate their fidelity of use and their effectiveness in producing goal achievement (e.g., percentage of students reaching their goal).

	Strategies	Fidelity	Success
Group 1:			
Group 2:			
Group 3:			
Group 4:			
Group 5:			

Students Identified for Tier 2 Interventions: Insert instructional focus of intervention groups and list students assigned to each group based on the most recent data. Identify any student needing further assessment and indicate the type of assessment needed.

Group 1:		Group 2:		Group 3:	
Group 4:		**Group 5:**		**Further Assessment**	**Name of Assessment**

(continued)

Strategies for Intervention Groups: Note strategy (or program) to be implemented with each group. (Strategies may be maintained, revised, or replaced.) Indicate the progress monitoring measure to be used and the frequency of monitoring.

Group	Strategy/Program	Progress Monitoring	PM Frequency
Group 1:			
Group 2:			
Group 3:			
Group 4:			
Group 5:			

Goals: Indicate goal for each group.   Date of goal review:

Group 1:	
Group 2:	
Group 3:	
Group 4:	
Group 5:	

Logistics: Describe actions to be taken to support strategy implementation.

Group	Frequency of Intervention (Days, Times)	Intervener	Other Logistics
Group 1:			
Group 2:			
Group 3:			
Group 4:			
Group 5:			
All:			

(continued)

TIER 3

Student Newly Identified for Tier 3 (Customized Intervention):

Assessment Measures and Scores

Goal:	Date of Goal Review:
Intervention:	Location and Frequency:
Progress Monitoring Measure:	Frequency of Monitoring:
Intervener:	Progress Monitor:

Student Previously Identified for Tier 3 (Customized Intervention):

Student Progress since Last Assessment: Note the progress made by the student as indicated by graphed data and rate of improvement (ROI).

Assessment Measure	Data	Goal Attained?

Was the intervention effective?	Was the intervention delivered with fidelity?
Reset Goal:	Date of Goal Review:
Intervention:	Location and Frequency:
Progress Monitoring Measure:	Frequency of Monitoring:
Intervener:	Progress Monitor:

CHAPTER 7

Implementing Data Teaming at the School and Grade Levels for Behavior and Social–Emotional Skills

ROADMAP

1. General considerations
2. The data-analysis teaming process for behavior and social–emotional skills
   a. Beginning-of-year meetings
      i. Tier 1 teaming
         - Preparation and review of the data
         - Goal setting
         - Identifying instructional strategies
         - Planning for the logistics of implementation
      ii. Tier 2 teaming
         - Preparation and review of the data
         - Identifying students for group interventions
         - Setting group goals
         - Identifying interventions and planning progress monitoring
         - Planning for Tier 2 implementation logistics
      iii. Tier 3 teaming
         - Preparation and review of the data
         - Setting goals for individual students
         - Customizing interventions and planning progress monitoring
      iv. Final steps
         - Formal follow-up meetings
         - End-of year meeting

157

In this chapter, the process of collecting and analyzing behavior and social–emotional data within an MTSS is described—however, the running example focuses on behavior data. The data-analysis teaming process within the academic context is well established as a best practice both in the literature and in practice as described in previous chapters (e.g., Chapter 6). The use of the data-analysis teaming process within the context of behavior management and social–emotional contexts is lagging behind and less utilized in schools today due in large part to the fact that there is not a readily "agreed upon general outcome measure" (Chafouleas, Volpe, Gresham, & Cook, 2010, p. 345). The strengths and limitations of the different GOMs are discussed in Chapter 5. The importance and utility of engaging in the systematic collection and analysis of these types of data is highlighted by the lower academic achievement and cost/burden on the juvenile justice system and welfare system found to be associated with significant behavior issues, as well as the significant amount of time spent in school responding to these concerns (National Research Council and Institute of Medicine, 2009). A meta-analysis involving 270,034 kindergarten through high school students demonstrated that significantly improved social and emotional skills, attitudes, and behaviors were correlated with an 11-percentile-point gain in achievement (Durlak, Weissberg, Dymnicki, Taylor, & Schellinger, 2011). Within the PBIS and SWPBIS literature, the structures for engaging in universal instruction and *tiered interventions* is laid out in detail (Bohanon et al., 2006)—however, the data collection elements, as well as guidance regarding the consequent use of those data, tend to be more vague (Albers, Glover, & Kratochwill, 2007; Walker, Cheney, Stage, Blum, & Horner, 2005).

In this chapter, the methods and type of behavioral data are discussed, as well as the process for examining those data and the provision of tiered support based on the data. The logistical considerations for the data-analysis team outlined in Chapter 5 apply to the process for behavior, including defined team roles and the scheduling of meetings. The potential sources of behavior and social–emotional data are discussed in terms of their strengths and limitations for use within the context of the school- and grade-level data-analysis teams. Specifically, the use of these data within the context of a data-analysis team to provide insight into school climate, to inform schoolwide positive behavior programming, as well as classroom-level management, and to identify groups of students who are at risk and in need of Tier 2 and 3 support are described in detail.

GENERAL CONSIDERATIONS

As a school district or school embarks on the path to engage in systematic MTSS for behavior there are a number of factors that need to be taken into consideration. Moving to a behavior management system that is focused on prevention and instruction is typically a massive paradigm shift. Traditionally, schools' approach to behavior focuses on the student as the problem rather than recognizing that there are a host of environmental factors that contribute to problematic behaviors. In doing so, critical opportunities for instruction and intervention are missed and it subtly communicates the message that the students need to be "fixed" and that the staff's ability to effect change is diminished. This mind-set causes a separation between instruction and behavior. Essentially, school staff abdicate their power in changing behavior. Rather than viewing appropriate behavior as something to be taught, it is viewed as a within-child flaw. In the MTSS model, the school must intentionally choose to provide proactive systematic behavioral instruction to all students.

Another flaw in the traditional approach to behavior in schools is that it is inherently reactive in nature. As a result, resources are inefficiently deployed to address problems on a case-by-case basis instead of addressing the root causes or function. Staff become "serial responders" with the goal of having the behavior stop in the short term rather than effecting long-term change. School staff become like a goldfish in a fishbowl—being surprised every time it sees the plastic castle. Similarly, the traditional approach treats behavior problems as if they are each novel, isolated events, which often can be demoralizing to staff. This reactive stance ultimately results in more staff and student time out of the instructional flow. However, once the paradigm is shifted to a proactive, data-oriented model, efficiency and effectiveness increases.

THE DATA-ANALYSIS TEAMING PROCESS FOR BEHAVIOR

The data-analysis teaming process for behavior functioning is parallel to the academic process that was described in Chapter 6. As was stated in prior chapters, the decision as to whether to separate out data teaming for academics from behavior functioning is a local decision. For the purposes of this chapter, the process is described solely for behavior concerns. The different assessment methods are discussed in Chapter 5.

Beginning-of-Year Meetings

One significant way in which the academic and behavior process diverge is in the scheduling of the initial meeting. Unlike academic screening, immediate data collection at the start of the academic year is not feasible and for a number of reasons would be fraught with inaccurate information. First, in terms of behavior screeners, as was mentioned previously, the raters need to have sufficient time to have a large enough sample of observations of the student to accurately rate student behaviors. If behavior screeners are completed too early, staff are forced to rate students on behaviors that have not been observed or to speculate based on a limited opportunity to interact with the student. As was stated previously, behavior screeners should not be completed until after a minimum of 4 weeks from the start of the school year. Hence, these initial meetings should be scheduled, at the earliest, for the beginning of October. The data to be discussed would include behavioral data from the previous year and current beginning-of-the-year behavior screeners, ODRs, and classroom-level data. These data are analyzed in terms of the entire grade (Tier 1), and then classrooms and students are identified for more intensive interventions, including groups (Tier 2) and individuals (Tier 3).

Tier 1 Teaming

In terms of the ODRs and classroom-level data, these data are collected from the beginning of the school year and provide some actionable data for individual students relatively early—however, in order to examine trends and to have a true depiction of the school climate, classroom climate, and individual student functioning, these data should be reviewed at the same interval as the behavior screeners, ideally after 4 weeks from the start of the school year. Throughout the rest of the academic year the typical winter and spring data collection/review intervals are appropriate. Any historical behavior data, such as previous ODRs, suspensions, classroom-level data, and behavior screeners, should be reviewed along with the current behavior data collection for the grade-level cohort.

PREPARATION AND REVIEW OF THE DATA

As mentioned in the previous chapter, a specific form should be used to assist data-analysis teams in analyzing and discussing students' behavioral performance. In order to effectively manage this process for behavior, the data-analysis team needs to document the concerns on the DATR Forms, which were introduced for academics in Chapter 6—here we introduce the Data-Analysis Team Recording for Behavior (DATR-B) Form (see Form 7.1 at the end of this chapter). The DATR-B Form is to be used as a tool for capturing the important information in this process (e.g., date, grade level, attendees and their positions). It is important to note that the DATR-B that is used for Tier 1 teaming does not allow for individual student names. In this regard, the form assists teams in remaining focused on grade-level concerns rather than getting distracted by individual issues.

Once the data (e.g., screeners, ODRs, and classroom-level data) are compiled, they are summarized and graphically depicted by the data manager into an easily understood format that is shared with data-analysis team members and/or projected for them to view. The team leader then prompts the team to examine the trends to identify any overall concern(s) for the grade level and to set goals for addressing the concern(s) prior to the midyear meeting.

In the behavior data-analysis teaming process, once the group accesses the behavior data, its task, as mentioned above, is to identify the primary behavior of concern. Typically, behaviors should be chosen based on the frequency of occurrence and/or the level of disruption that they cause to the instructional environment. Once a concern has been identified, it is critical that it be operationally defined. The operational definition specifies the criteria for observation of the behavior to all members. Put simply, everyone will know what the behavior looks like and sounds like when they adjourn from the meeting. For example, a data-analysis team reviews all of the data and determines that inappropriate hallway behavior is the overall concern for third grade, since the behavior screeners indicate elevated behavior concern among 43% of students (see Figure 7.1), with 68% of ODRs and classroom-level data being based on inappropriate behavior in the hallway (see Figure 7.2). The screener data indicate that a large portion of the grade level is engaging in problem behaviors and the ODR and classroom-level data indicate that the majority of those problem behaviors occur in the hallway. The data-analysis team examines the ODR and classroom-level data to determine that the target behavior is students being loud in the hallway.

GOAL SETTING

As discussed in Chapters 4 and 5, the next step is to set a goal for the reduction of the behavior of concern for each measure. As stated in previous chapters, goal setting is not an exact process—however, the emphasis needs to be on alterable factors. At times, behavior

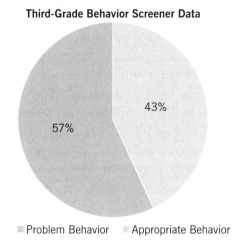

FIGURE 7.1. Sample behavior screener data.

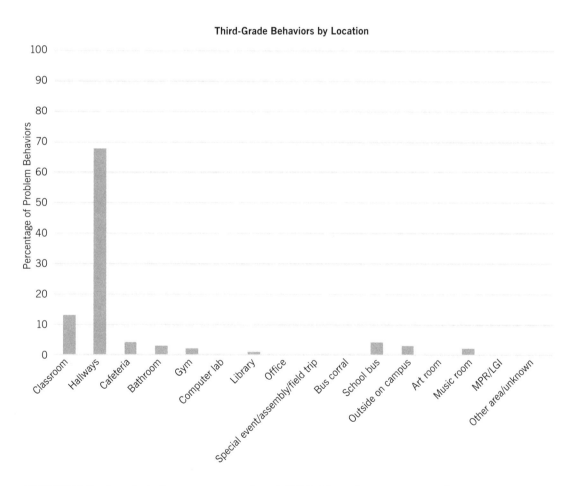

FIGURE 7.2. Sample behavior screener data. MPR/LGI, multipurpose room/large group instruction room.

problems, in particular, influence the decision making. For example, a behavior that is a significant safety concern would likely have a more stringent goal set in order to reduce the likelihood of harm more quickly. In our example, being loud in the hallway is not a safety concern—it is just extremely disruptive to the educational process for students. Unlike the academic process that allows for goal setting that is based on typical and ambitious growth rates, no such information exists for behavior. Therefore, teams set the goal based on what they deem to be reasonable and attainable for their setting. The team determined that hallway behavior problems will be reduced to 20% of all behavior concerns and will represent no more than 10% of the third-grade population by the next data-analysis team meeting, which would coincide with the midyear benchmark.

IDENTIFYING INSTRUCTIONAL STRATEGIES

The next step on the DATR-B is for the data-analysis team to identify the instructional strategies to address the goals that have been set. As mentioned in Chapter 2, when addressing a systems-level issue, we examine the discrepancy between what is occurring and what is expected. As with the academic process, the selection of an intervention is not the product of brainstorming, but rather choosing the most appropriate intervention based on the presenting need from the pool of research-based intervention approaches. As interveners, we want to leverage the highest-impact strategies to address/teach the behaviors that we want to see our students engage in.

As with the academic section, once an adequate list of options is created, the team is led through a series of questions that are designed to facilitate the selection of one or two strategies that are research based *and* that are also deemed by the teachers to be practical and readily assumed into their daily instructional routines. The suggested prompts are the same as they were for the discussion of academic intervention ideas in Chapter 6:

"Let's rate these ideas."
"Which ones have a good research base?"
"Of those, which ones are most practical?"
"What materials do we have available?"
"What materials do we need?"
"Based on what we see on the display, what's our choice for the best strategy(ies)?"

Many of the resources noted in Chapter 4 are also helpful in exploring interventions for behavior. The What Works Clearinghouse (*ies.ed.gov/ncee/wwc/topic.aspx?sid=15*) may serve as a starting point for teams to explore larger intervention approaches. It has reviews of character-education programs and interventions, as does the Collaborative for Academic, Social, and Emotional Learning (CASEL; *www.casel.org*). Again, the goal is to select the most effective intervention, which may not be a packaged program, but rather instruction based on sound behavior principles. The Evidence Based Intervention Network (*ebi.missouri.edu/?page_id=227*) is one resource for interventions that can be utilized at the individual and group levels. There are also resources and reviews of interventions available at the National Center on Intensive Intervention at American Institutes for Research (*https://intensiveintervention.org/chart/behavioral-intervention-chart*).

In our example (Figure 7.3), the team decided to generate a series of lessons that teach the expected hallway behaviors that are specific to this school setting with a clear objective, an activator (a technique to activate students' prior knowledge and engage them in the learning), and the provision of examples and nonexamples along with practice of the examples with an embedded formative assessment. The approaches that are decided upon are documented on the DATR-B Form (see Figure 7.3).

PLANNING FOR LOGISTICS

The team must determine the needed materials, steps, schedule, division of labor, and so on needed to realistically implement the chosen strategies. Simply asking teachers to "go forth and implement" is not likely to meet with success. In our example (Figure 7.3), the first step is to provide all of the teachers with the lesson plans and all supporting materials, as well as for the principal to create a weeklong schedule to accommodate the time needed to implement the lessons first thing in the morning. This would potentially require a modified schedule.

The team has determined that the school psychologist and school counselor will work together to generate the lessons based on feedback from the teachers regarding the mutually agreed-upon expected behaviors. The lessons are provided to the teachers and reviewed with them prior to implementation. The principal, school psychologist, and school counselor observe the implementation of the lessons as a fidelity check and provide supportive feedback for the teachers, as well as getting feedback on any revisions.

Tier 2 Teaming

The next phase of data-analysis teaming involves analyzing the available screening data and other data for individual students who are manifesting similar needs and should be sorted into supplemental-level groups (Tier 2). This process should be conducted after the Tier 1 discussions have concluded. It is helpful to have additional data available to the team for review for individual students that help to clarify the nature and extent of the behavior concerns. Additionally, those data are then used to group students of similar need so as to use resources to the greatest effect.

PREPARATION AND REVIEW OF THE DATA

The data needed to make a decision regarding Tier 2 support include the previously collected grade-level data. The data manager would provide reports with this type of identification by disaggregating the data based on classroom and specific students. These data permit grouping of students by similar need so as to leverage the most robust intervention. In addition to identifying the individual students, we can also identify "classrooms of concern." At times, a particular classroom may have a critical mass of students engaging in the problematic behavior, which then allows for group instruction tailored to a particular classroom to take place, as well as a review of existing management procedures to determine their effectiveness. More specific individual assessments may be necessary—however, that discussion is reserved for Tier 3. In the present behavior example (Figure 7.3), the spe-

Date:	October 5, 20XX		Grade:	3

Meeting Attendees	Position
Camilla Pascual	Principal
James Kaat	Teacher
Victoria Powers	Teacher
Rachel Rollins	Teacher
Erline Battey	Teacher

Meeting Attendees	Position
Cesar Tovar	School Psychologist
Allison Mincher	School Counselor

TIER 1

Target Behavior(s): Note the number and percentage of students and the frequency and intensity.

Frequency	ODRs and classroom-level data indicate that 68% of problems reported are students being loud in the hallway.
Intensity	Out of the entire third grade 43% of the students have been reported to engage in loud behavior in the hallway.

Goals: Percent decrease in numbers of identified target behavior/increase in positive behavior.

Frequency	Hallway ODRs and classroom level will be reduced to 20%.
Intensity	10% of third grade will engage in unexpected hallway behaviors.

Strategies: Describe strategies for each target behavior in observable terms.

All students will be taught mini-lessons on expected hallway behavior.

All students will practice newly taught skills in the classroom and then hallway.

Teachers will review hallway expectations with all students prior to exiting classrooms and will post the expectations by the door.

Logistics: Describe actions to be taken to support implementation.

Mr. Tovar and Ms. Mincher will generate mini-lessons covering expected hallway behaviors and provide digital examples.

Teachers will teach mini-lessons (15 minutes) on expected hallway behavior each morning for 1 week beginning on 10/12/20XX.

Ms. Pascual, Mr. Tovar, and Ms. Mincher will conduct fidelity checks of the lessons.

FIGURE 7.3. Sample completed Data-Analysis Team Recording Form for Behavior (DATR-B): Tier 1.

cific students engaging in the problematic behaviors can be identified based on the ODRs, behavior screenings, and the classroom-level data.

IDENTIFYING STUDENTS FOR GROUP INTERVENTIONS

The team begins the problem identification process by analyzing the existing data displayed. The DATR-B Form (see Figure 7.4) has been prepared for five intervention groups with space to list student names, additional assessments, goals, and intervention procedures.

The first task is to determine what type of need each student is presenting. The students are generally sorted into groups of similar need by grade level. It is possible, even likely, to have students exhibiting similar needs, but who are in different grades. Careful thought must be given to the appropriateness of mixing grade levels when dealing with behavior concerns. In the present example, the team reviewed the ODR, behavior screener, and classroom-level data, noting that two types of issues in the hallway occurred with greater frequency. It is possible that as the Tier 1 interventions are implemented, other behavioral issues may emerge that could influence the Tier 2 groupings—however, for the purposes of this example, we continue with the issue identified at Tier 1. The two biggest hallway concerns were students being noisy (i.e., calling out) in the hallway and students running in the hallway. Once those problems were identified, the students were sorted into two groups based on the nature of the hallway concern they presented and the chronic nature of this presentation. The first group was calling out and generally being loud in the hallways and the second group was running in the hallways.

SETTING GROUP GOALS

Similar to the goal setting in Tier 1, the goal setting should be ambitious and should be tied to the school expectations, as existing benchmarks do not exist. If your school has set the threshold of allowed noise very low, then your goal should reflect that threshold. In some schools, the hallway noise expectation, even during transitions, is that there is no talking—if that is the case, then the goal for the Tier 2 group that is being noisy in the hallway is set at being quiet in the hallway 100% of the time. However, in the present example, the threshold allows for some incidental noise and is set at being quiet in the hallway 95% of the time. The second group's goal is a bit easier in that it is essentially a safety goal. For the students who are running in the hallway, the goal is set at walking in the hallway 100% of the time. Safety goals, as a rule, are set at 100%; otherwise, one is ostensibly endorsing some degree of unsafe behaviors. The classic example is that one would not set a goal of crossing the street safely 90% of the time, because the implication is that it is fine to be hit by a car one out of 10 times.

IDENTIFYING INTERVENTIONS AND PLANNING PROGRESS MONITORING

Depending on the nature of the behavior concern presenting, there may be an option for a commercially available product or procedure that is manualized and can be consistently and effectively delivered. In that case, there are a wide variety of options, but to narrow the field a bit, the National Center on Intensive Intervention at American Institutes for

TIER 2

Students Identified for Tier 2 Interventions: Insert instructional focus of intervention groups and list students assigned to each group. Identify any student needing further assessment and indicate the type of assessment needed.

Group 1: Calling out in hallways		Group 2: Running		Group 3:	
Angie Dave Denise Zoe Tom Nathaniel		Susan Pam Mark Tim Nate Tara	Beth Maggie		

Group 4:		Group 5:		Further Assessment	Name of Assessment

Goals: Indicate goal for each group.   **Date of goal review:** In 4 weeks

Group 1: Calling out in hallways	Students will walk quietly in the hallway 95% of the time.
Group 2: Running	Students currently walk quietly 52% of the time and will walk in the hallway quietly 100% of the time.

Strategies for Intervention Groups: Note strategy (or program) to be implemented with each group. Indicate progress monitoring measure to be used and the frequency of monitoring.

Group	Strategy/Program	Progress Monitoring (PM)	PM Frequency
Group 1: Calling out in hallways	Students will be taught why they should be quiet in the hallway and will practice walking in the hallway quietly.	Hallway direct behavior rating scale	Daily
Group 2: Running	Students will use a behavior academy approach of repeatedly practicing the desired behavior.	Hallway direct behavior rating scale	Daily

Logistics: Describe actions to be taken to support strategy implementation.

Group	Frequency of Intervention (Days, Times)	Intervener	Other Logistics
Group 1: Calling out in hallways	20 minutes daily during designated intervals for 5 consecutive days.	Ms. Mincher	For 15 minutes daily during designated intervals for 5 consecutive days.
Group 2: Running	15 minutes daily during designated intervals for 5 consecutive days.	Mr. Tovar	Teachers will monitor progress using the rubric.

FIGURE 7.4. Sample completed Data-Analysis Team Recording Form for Behavior (DATR-B): Tier 2.

Research offers reviews that would assist in making the best decision for either a group or individual intervention, as well as the most appropriate method of progress monitoring (see *www.intensiveintervention.org/chart/behavioral-intervention-chart*).

However, there are many times with behavior concerns in which there is not a readily available tool to implement. This is when having good data is critical in narrowing the target of the intervention and then using those data as a starting point for developing the intervention approach and developing a tool to assist with progress monitoring. In the current example, both groups are pretaught the behavioral expectations; CHAMPS (Sprick & Baldwin, 2009) is used as a method of teaching and reminding the students of the specific hallway expectations. In addition, the noisy-hallway group is taught why it is important to be quiet in the hallways, including the potential negative impact on other students' learning. The running-hallway group is taught the expected behavior and then engages in repeated practice sessions of the desired behavior of walking in the hallway.

Finally, a DBR scale describing the desired behaviors is developed and provided to the classroom teachers to use in addition to ODR data to monitor progress toward the specific desired behaviors.

PLANNING FOR TIER 2 IMPLEMENTATION LOGISTICS

The formation of groups often requires considerable planning. The first issue to be tackled is finding time in the schedule for the intervention to be delivered. Unlike academic Tier 2 groups that often have an interval already planned for in the schedule, Tier 2 for behavior requires a consideration of the most effective time, frequency, and overall duration to deliver the intervention based on what the student will be missing in the schedule and how long (per session) the intervention will take. In general, most interventions will likely last no more than 30 minutes and should have a target number of weeks or sessions planned out.

The next issue is the "who" question—that is, who is going to be designated to deliver the intervention? The team makes this determination based on the skill required to deliver the intervention. At times it may be appropriate to have the teacher deliver the intervention, particularly if the chosen Tier 2 support is a classwide intervention. For other types of interventions, it may be more appropriate to have the school psychologist or school counselor deliver it.

Tier 3 Teaming

The team next moves to plan evaluation, problem analysis, and plan development for those students who are most deficient and who have not made satisfactory progress during the time since the last meeting. The team will need to drill down to the individual student as well. In the behavior example (see Figure 7.5), this includes utilizing a multigated series of individually administered rating scales that become increasingly narrow in their focus and can be used by the team in addition to the ODR and classroom-level data to assess specific behaviors that are being manifested by certain students. This process enables the team to triangulate those data and focus on the specific behavior of concern. The team should also give consideration to conducting an FBA and/or a functional analysis at this point. As discussed in Chapter 5, different states have regulations indicating when it is appropriate

Student Identified for Tier 3 (Customized Intervention):   Beth

Assessment Measures and Scores
Behavior screener — 1/5 indicating high levels of problem behaviors
ODRs — 15 referrals for hallway behaviors
Classroom-level data — 27 classroom incidents
Hallway rubric — 2/5

Goal: Beth will reduce the number of ODRs to less than five and reduce the number of classroom incidents to less than five and improve her performance on both rubrics to a 4 or better.	**Date of Goal Review:** 1/15/20XX
Intervention: Beth will be taught, monitored, and reinforced for appropriate hallway behavior.	**Location and Frequency:** Classroom and hallway; daily 15 minutes
Progress Monitoring Measure: Hallway direct behavior rating scale and brief behavior rating scale	**Frequency of Monitoring:** Daily
Intervener: Ms. Mincher	**Progress Monitor:** Mrs. Powers

Person Responsible	Task
Ms. Mincher	Coordinate with Mrs. Powers on the scheduling of the intervention. Check progress on 10/25/20XX.
Mrs. Powers	Collect PM data and report it to Ms. Mincher.

FIGURE 7.5. Sample completed Data-Analysis Team Recording Form for Behavior (DATR-B): Tier 3.

to secure parent permission for the FBA process. Regardless, the team should be thinking "functionally" throughout this process. The team would document the information on the DATR-B Tier 3 Form (Figure 7.5).

PREPARATION AND REVIEW OF THE DATA

As indicated above, at this point in the process, the team should have arranged for and completed any additional drill-down data collection, such as individual rating scales, an FBA, or functional analysis if deemed appropriate, and documented the results on the DATR-B Tier 3 section (Figure 7.5). The team should focus on the data collected as part of Tier 2 to determine the ROI. It is extremely beneficial for the team to graphically depict the data and prepare individual progress monitoring graphs for each student being considered for Tier 3. Additionally, it is important to document the student response to the intervention and whether the goal was attained.

SETTING GOALS FOR INDIVIDUAL STUDENTS

For any newly identified students for Tier 3, the procedures for goal setting, intervention planning, determination of the progress monitoring measure, and intervention grouping follow the guideline presented for beginning-of-year meetings. The decisions that are made are noted on the DATR-B Form (Form 7.1, Tier 3 section) using the top half of the form for these students. In our example (Figure 7.5), the team has conducted additional drill-down assessments with Beth, a student who has not responded to the Tier 2 interventions and has summarized the results and intervention plan in this section.

CUSTOMIZING INTERVENTIONS AND PLANNING PROGRESS MONITORING

This process is identical to that of academics. Teams graphically display the progress monitoring data for students who have been provided with intensive Tier 3 interventions during the preceding months and conduct a plan evaluation for each student, analyzing whether the intervention was effective in producing meaningful growth for the student. When reviewing graphed data, the team should determine whether the student met the preset goal, which may have been expressed in terms of a level to reach and/or adherence to a preset aim line (sometimes referred to as a goal line). As with each level of tiered intervention, the team must examine the question as to whether the intervention was implemented with fidelity, especially for those students who are not making meaningful progress, and document their findings.

Next, the team engages in plan development for each student. The team begins by resetting the goal for the student for the next period of time, annotating the DATR-B Form. Based on the team's evaluation of the effectiveness of the intervention, it determines whether to continue, alter, or change to a different intervention, which is then recorded on the DATR-B Form in terms of the description, location, frequency, and intervener responsible. The type and frequency of progress monitoring is also determined and recorded. As with the initial intervention development, the team must plan for the logistics that are needed to deliver customized interventions for the Tier 3 students discussed. Finally, the team should use this review to determine whether any students who have very deficient levels of attainment and poor ROI should be referred for full and individual evaluations to consider their eligibility for special education (cf. Kovaleski et al., 2013). Following the logic described in Kovaleski et al. (2013) for learning disabilities, a student who persistently fails to make meaningful behavior gains in response to a research-based individualized intervention should be referred for a comprehensive evaluation.

FINAL STEPS

As was the case with the academic meetings, the same process and procedures are used for conducting the midyear and end-of-year meeting. At this time of year, any intervention decisions/plans are inherently time limited—thus, the teams are responsible for two functions: creating the plan for the rest of the year and creating the plan for how the current year's data will be shared with next year's team and recommending the intervention to begin the new year. At this point, a significant amount of data has been collected on the students at Tiers 1–3 that needs to be shared with the next data team. It is also recommended that the data team reflect on and evaluate the effectiveness of its chosen plan and make appropriate recommendations for improvement to the next team. The data team can also use this reflection/evaluation to improve its implementation of intervention plans moving forward. Specific plans should be made for the formal or informal transfer of information and recommendations. Often data warehouses are useful as a tool to preserve this information over time, which is discussed in greater detail in Chapter 8.

KEY ISSUES

- The data-analysis teaming process is greatly enhanced by using a preset group of forms to guide the process and memorialize the decisions made, such as those displayed in this chapter.
- The focus of data-analysis teaming at Tier 1 is the overall improvement of instruction for all students in the grade.
- The focus of data-analysis teaming at Tier 2 is the creation of small groups for the delivery of supplemental intervention.
- The focus of data-analysis teaming at Tier 3 is on customizing interventions for individual students.
- Throughout the data-analysis teaming process, data sources, as described in Chapter 5, are used to guide the decision-making process.

Data-Analysis Team Recording Form for Behavior (DATR-B)

Date: [ ] Grade: [ ]

Meeting Attendees	Position

Meeting Attendees	Position

TIER 1

Target Behavior(s): Note the number and percentage of students and the frequency and intensity.

Goals: Percent decrease in numbers of identified target behavior/increase in positive behavior.

Strategies: Describe strategies for each target behavior in observable terms.

Logistics: Describe actions to be taken to support implementation.

(continued)

TIER 2

Students Identified for Tier 2 Interventions: Insert instructional focus of intervention groups and list students assigned to each group. Identify any student needing further assessment and indicate the type of assessment needed.

Group 1:	Group 2:	Group 3:	
Group 4:	Group 5:	Further Assessment	Name of Assessment

Goals: Indicate goal for each group.　　　　Date of goal review: _____

Group 1:	
Group 2:	
Group 3:	
Group 4:	
Group 5:	

Strategies for Intervention Groups: Note strategy (or program) to be implemented with each group. Indicate progress monitoring measure to be used and the frequency of monitoring.

Group	Strategy/Program	Progress Monitoring (PM)	PM Frequency
Group 1:			
Group 2:			
Group 3:			
Group 4:			
Group 5:			

(continued)

172

Logistics: Describe actions to be taken to support strategy implementation.

Group	Frequency of Intervention (Days, Times)	Intervener	Other Logistics
Group 1:			
Group 2:			
Group 3:			
Group 4:			
Group 5:			

TIER 3

Student Identified for Tier 3 (Customized Intervention):

Assessment Measures and Scores

Goal:	Date of Goal Review:
Intervention:	Location and Frequency:
Progress Monitoring Measure:	Frequency of Monitoring:
Intervener:	Progress Monitor:

(continued)

Student Identified for Tier 3 (Customized Intervention):

Assessment Measures and Scores

Goal:	Date of Goal Review:
Intervention:	Location and Frequency:
Progress Monitoring Measure:	Frequency of Monitoring:
Intervener:	Progress Monitor:

TO-DO LIST

Person Responsible	Task

BUILDING THE CAPACITY FOR A DATA-DRIVEN SCHOOL

Data Management Using Technology

Part III focuses on how to build the capacity for a data-driven school. This chapter addresses supporting a data-driven school through the use of technology to drive data management, and Chapter 9 is concerned with identifying and developing data leaders and sustaining a data-driven school by creating and maintaining connections across members of the school community. Effective data leaders, strong relationships between these leaders and the rest of the school community, and the use of technology tools to efficiently manage the data they are using to drive instruction are all essential components of successful data-driven schools.

One of the critical tools in a data leader's arsenal is technology. In this chapter, we discuss the impact technology is having on education as a whole, focus in on how technology can support the work of both systems-level problem-solving teams and individual data teams, and provide a roadmap for the many different technology tools found in education, as well as how they fit together. Technology is a fast-moving and ever-changing world, and as such, we take the risk of putting information to print that will quickly become outdated.

The focus of this chapter attempts to balance the need to help data leaders understand the current landscape of technology tools, while putting those tools in the broader, more timeless context of how technology in general can be a part of the systems-level problem-solving and individual data-teaming processes. Most importantly, data leaders should recognize that they, not the technology, are the essential catalyst for creating change and/or sustaining effective data practices in schools. Technology just happens to be an excellent tool to support this work.

THE EVOLUTION OF EDUCATION TECHNOLOGY

Technology has tremendous power to bring and already is bringing significant changes to education. Better tools to manage and analyze student data, tools that aid a teacher in delivering more effective and engaging instruction, software that simply delivers instructional content directly to the student, stronger parent communication, platforms for content collaboration . . . the list of different ways that technology is being used in education is seemingly never ending. The relevance of spelling tests in the age of autocorrect, the relative importance of factual knowledge in the age of Wikipedia, and the need to better engage students with instruction in the age of massive multiplayer video games are some examples of how technology is leading us to question the staid educational practices of yesteryear.

The realization of technology's impact on education has been further aided by the evolution of key infrastructure components that created fertile soil for this technology revolution. First, near universal access to high-speed Internet is one key component that has led to the ability for teachers to rely on tools that are entirely web based. While there is still some question as to whether Internet access is truly ubiquitous, and whether this lack of equity is deepening the digital divide (Krueger, 2015), the fact of the matter is that educators have jumped into instructional practices that have full reliance on continuous access to high-speed Internet. The universality of this kind of practice was unthinkable just 10 years ago.

The use of the Internet for "Web 2.0" interactive tools is another key component. Increasingly, the Internet has been used not only to deliver content down to the consumer but to allow individual users to interact with one another, share ideas, and share content. This transformative use of the Internet has enabled a wide range of applications to education, from teachers collaborating with other teachers to teachers working with students to students collaborating with one another, and so forth.

A further key component is the ability to rapidly develop and deploy software. At the dawn of technology in education, the major companies truly "owned" the landscape of software development and deployment. Districts needed to have extensive infrastructure in order to run software locally, and companies that wanted to build software to support education needed to spend significant overhead in order to get a product to market. Today, software that is directly relevant to solving problems in education can be built in a matter of weeks, and deployed to the cloud and made available to the world in a matter of minutes. That isn't to say all software only takes days to build, or that we should expect all of our problems to be resolved in a matter of weeks. But it does show how the software cycle has accelerated in its ability to identify a problem, develop a software tool to resolve that problem, implement that solution, evaluate the success of that solution, and iterate the software to continue to be more and more successful in meeting the needs of educators.

TECHNOLOGY FOR DATA

The opportunities are strong for technology to support both systems-level problem solving and individual-level data-analysis teaming. There are three key organizational practices that can guide the work of using technology to promote a data culture in schools. First, there is the management of the data itself. Managing the demands of ongoing organization, analysis, and communication of data in an exceedingly complex organization virtually compels anyone with an interest in data-driven decision making to use technology to support their efforts. Second, there is the ability to bring data together for analysis and communication. The extent of relevant data that are available and necessary to making informed decisions at the systems and the individual level is simply too great to not involve a broad range of technology tools. And third, there is the ability for technology to guide the behaviors of data leaders and data teams. Software can make sure that key steps are not missed in the best-practice processes outlined earlier in this book for governing the work of systems- and individual-level decision makers and teams. Technology leaders are recognizing the need for technology and data leadership to work together. In the Consortium for School Networking's (CoSN; 2016) *Framework for School System Technology Success,* "Data and Information Management" is listed as a primary implementation category. Each of these three key organizational practices, or ways that technology can support the establishment of a data-driven culture in schools, is described in this chapter.

But first, an important note about technology adoption. With all the excitement that new technologies can generate in schools, it is important to remember that software tools in and of themselves represent a *packaged intervention,* a term Toyama (2015) defines as a cookie-cutter solution that typically does not perform equally well across institutions. For example, packaged interventions typically show promise in pilot implementations where conditions are optimized, but often fail when implemented more broadly—this problem of generalization is already well-known to education, yet is overlooked with surprising frequency when considering whether to implement a promising technology tool.

Toyama (2015) further defines the necessary conditions within an organization, in order for a packaged intervention to be effective. Intention, discernment, and self-control (aka "heart, mind, and will," respectively) are the conditions that must already be present. In the case of data-driven decision making (and, more specifically, using technology for data-driven decision making), intention would be the belief in using data to make decisions; discernment would be the ability to use the technology effectively, as well as having a strong understanding of the data; and self-control would be the will to instill the use of data as a regular and consistent practice. The previous chapters of this book focus on intention and self-control (i.e., the practices that drive effective data teams and decision making at all levels of the organization); this chapter focuses specifically on discernment, with a goal of enhancing readers' skills and knowledge of the organizational practices that are critical for technology for data-driven decision making to be used effectively.

Data Management

If educators are going to use data to understand and inform decisions, a necessary condition is having at-the-ready access to the data in the first place. Asking educators to search for data is a significant barrier to creating a culture where the use of data is de rigueur. Certainly, there are an increasing number of education technology tools that, by nature, collect and report data on individual students, helping to break down this barrier. However, with so many education technology tools available, schools are often awash in data but lacking in coordination and a systematic approach to gathering and leveraging these data. The problem that needs to be solved is how these different tools can be coordinated to present the entire picture of data that are relevant to the issue at hand. That is where data management comes in.

Understanding Software

With software solutions providing a dizzying range of functionality, it can often be difficult to understand how these different products might fit together, which may be redundant with one another, and what value the data generated by each tool may present to the decision maker (i.e., the data team). From a functional perspective, there are some common components across the range of educational software that can help consumers to better understand conceptually how these products, and their data, all fit together. A visual guide that identifies these thematic components and how they are interrelated is presented in Figure 8.1. In this diagram, each key software component is presented as an oval, with arrows reflecting the connections among these systems. The column of ovals running along the left-hand side of the diagram is the "spine" of the implementation of education software. This series of components walks through the process of compiling instructional content, delivering it to students, tracking student formative performance, and communicating summative performance. This is essentially the core mission of schools: to deliver instruction and track student success.

As an example, let's take the following fourth-grade mathematics standard, in the area of data analysis, from the Minnesota state standards: "Collect, organize, display, and interpret data, including data collected over a period of time and data represented by fractions and decimals." Many software tools can come together to help understand how we address this important outcome. The *curriculum map* would help us to determine when this standard is introduced, how many times it is included in lessons, and when and how many times it is assessed. The *content management tool* would help to store lesson plans, activities, assessments, and any other relevant materials that may help in the instruction of this concept, while content collaboration tools would help an educator or team to add to and improve their library of content for addressing this particular concept. The *learning management tool* would aid in the delivery of content, including assessments of the concept, and student performance on those assessments would be tracked in the *grade book*. Any projects or other artifacts reflecting a student's mastery of this standard would be stored in their *eportfolio*, and the summative judgment of the student's mastery on this and other standards would be recorded in the *report card*. Further description of these and other important components of the overall software picture are provided below.

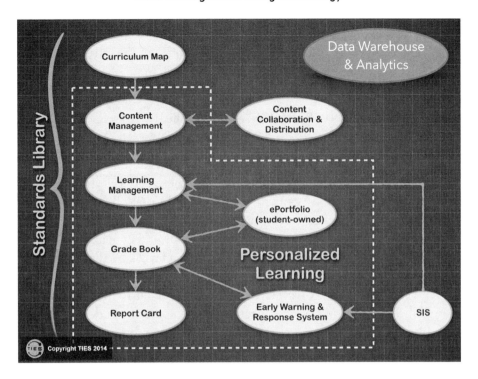

FIGURE 8.1. A visual diagram of education software. Reprinted with permission from Sourcewell Technology (f/k/a TIES), St. Paul, Minnesota.

CURRICULUM MAP

If the left-hand column of software components in this diagram is the spine, then the curricular content, and the map that outlines that content is the brain. Curriculum maps involve the process of collecting and maintaining a database of the operational curriculum in a school or district (Jacobs, 1997). Typically, these are calendar driven and define the scope and sequence of the actual curriculum delivered to students, rather than just the intended curriculum. Teachers have begun to wander further and further from relying solely on a single textbook from a single publisher, and instead are pulling together a wide range of resources and lesson plans to create a curriculum (Monahan, 2015). Similarly, more and more schools are focusing on a competency-based approach to tracking student learning by measuring student attainment of individual standards (specific skill mastery) of learning (Software and Information Industry Association, 2010). These trends make the use of a curriculum map even more essential to better understand any gaps between the scope of the curriculum actually delivered and the scope of expectations from state or district mandates, differences in scope across sections of the same course, and so forth.

In our experience, the curriculum map is overlooked with surprising frequency in schools implementing RTI/MTSS, especially after considering that the effectiveness of the core curriculum is one of the primary questions to be answered. The data stored in a curriculum map can be very informative in the process of problem analysis when it is determined that a school is experiencing a problem with effectiveness at Tier 1. Determining whether there are gaps between the skills being taught and the skill expectations of grade-level standards, whether the planned scope and sequence is being followed with fidelity, or whether the skills being taught are a mismatch with the capabilities of the current students are all questions that the data in a curriculum map can help to answer.

CONTENT MANAGEMENT, COLLABORATION, AND DISTRIBUTION

Content management refers to the ability to compile and store different curricular content. Materials such as lesson plans, activities, and assessments are examples of artifacts that may be stored in a content management system. While these materials themselves are often highly unstructured data, software can provide the ability to "tag" this content with a structured set of descriptors. These tags can be as broad as simply labeling the subject area being taught, or as narrow as the specific educational standards and benchmarks that are being taught or assessed by that particular material. Coding materials by their standards begins to provide a method for better tracking and understanding what skills are being instructed within the core curriculum, working hand in hand with the curriculum map. Content collaboration and distribution tools provide users with the ability to work together, online, to manage, modify, and share this content. This sharing can occur on a small scale, with teams in schools or districts, or on a large scale, using tools that support the open sharing of content worldwide (Achieve, 2013).

Content management, collaboration, and distribution tools perform distinct functions, but they are often provided in a single software system, sometimes along with curriculum-mapping functions (described above) and/or with learning management functions that are described below. Content management is distinguished from curriculum mapping in that the content management is the individualization of the curriculum map.

PERSONALIZED LEARNING

While the curriculum map represents the plan for *all* students, content management can begin to define the variations in that plan *across* students. For instance, the tool Newsela (*www.newsela.com*) provides the ability for students at different reading levels to each receive a personalized version of a common news article. This is an example of why the content management functionality exists within the dotted line that outlines the personalized learning ecosystem. The many technology tools inside this dotted line all represent functionality that can support delivery of, and track data on, the individual differences in both the learning environment/content experience and student performance. *Personalized learning* is currently a buzzword in education, with everyone understanding generally what it means, but a clear solution to the issue remains elusive (Johnson, Adams Becker, Estrada, & Freeman, 2015). Thus, while attempts at solutions are taking many different forms, at its core the concept of personalized learning is the idea that students each have a unique experience within their education, driven at least in part by the learners themselves (Schwartz, 2015). Technology provides the tools to support both delivering and tracking that personal experience for each student, as well as allowing the student in some cases to influence their own path of learning. For the data teams discussed in Chapters 5–7, tools that support this are essential to efficiently providing teaming and personalization for as many students as is feasible, given available resources.

LEARNING MANAGEMENT

Learning management systems (LMSs) have a wide range of definitions and a wide range of functions that they provide, but all with a common theme of being a delivery mechanism of content to students, including lesson materials, activities, and assessments (Ash, 2013). Some systems also provide content management capabilities, some provide a grade book, and some include early warning capabilities, but all have at a minimum the ability to deliver content to students. In order to more clearly define and delineate the different functions of the software ecosystem, these other capabilities are defined separately in the Figure 8.1 diagram. While a software system may call itself a "learning management system," it likely provides a broader range of functionality, and for our purposes we define learning management more narrowly as the management of the process of delivery of content to students.

GRADE BOOK

The grade book is a tool used to track individual student performance on tasks that are required as part of the course curriculum. While an entire book could be written on the grade book alone, for the purposes of building a data-driven school it should suffice to say that the grade book contains a wealth of important data on student performance. The grade book is also likely to contain a wealth of irrelevant data. Being able to understand student performance on the many assessments that are delivered on a day-to-day basis within the classroom can be an important tool in the problem-solving process, especially in problem analysis. But hurdles such as comparability of classroom assessments across classes (or even across students within classes), subjective and unstandardized grading practices, and grade calculations that are misaligned with state performance expectations are all issues that can prevent grade book data from adequately informing decision making. Software can be part of both the problem and the solution to these issues (Guskey, 2011). The data leader described in Chapter 9 certainly needs to understand and help address these potential problems, in order to leverage the grade book's data within the problem-solving process.

EPORTFOLIO

The concept of a student-owned electronic portfolio is a relatively new addition to education technology. An eportfolio provides students (and possibly teachers, for their own professional development) with a mechanism for managing electronically stored, self-produced artifacts that provide evidence of competency in a given skill area (Brown, 2016). Eportfolios vary both in the functionality of the tools and the ways they are implemented, but they typically involve some mechanism for feedback (i.e., from teachers or from peers), and are often "student owned," allowing the students to retain access to and grow their portfolios while they continue through their education. The data stored in eportfolios may be useful to the data-driven decision-making process, and are typically most useful when making decisions at the individual student level, due in large part to the unstructured nature of data in eportfolios. However, they may be one of the few sources of data that are truly personalized, in the sense that the student has a high degree of ownership over the ways in which the student's portfolio is used to demonstrate learning.

REPORT CARD

While the grade book is a tool for storing formative data on student performance within the course, the report card is a tool for storing and communicating summative data on that performance. Report cards typically either assign grades to total performance, or communicate status toward mastery of individual learning targets that are addressed within the given course. Report card performance is typically stored within a student information system (SIS), and made available to a variety of stakeholders within that system, including teachers, parents, and the students themselves. Since report cards are a summary of, and thus a reflection of, the data stored in a grade book, they are subject to the same possibilities and concerns for the data leader as described above in the "Grade Book" section.

STUDENT INFORMATION SYSTEM

The SIS is an example of enterprise-level software that assists the school or district in running the entire "enterprise" that is the "business" of education. As a result, the SIS often focuses on the tasks associated with management, such as student enrollment tracking and reporting, course roster management and scheduling, and attendance tracking and reporting. However, the SIS is a system that is likely "touched" by almost every stakeholder in the organization, including teachers; administrators; nurses; related service staff, such as school psychologists and counselors; clerical staff; students; and parents. Because of its impact across the organization, the SIS has evolved to become a tool that supports more than just the simple management of students, with many SISs developing critical features for progressive instructional and data leadership, such as strong, integrated grade book and report card features; behavior management and referral systems; and communication and alerting features to support teaming among staff, parents, and students, to name a few (Calhoun, 2015).

However, the capabilities of the SIS as a data leadership tool varies widely from product to product, and in many cases, it requires the integration of outside software systems to provide many of the other components in the Figure 8.1 diagram, such as learning management, grade book, and early warning and response. Because of this, the individual functions that may or may not be provided by an SIS are separated in this diagram, with the assumption that an SIS minimally provides a source of data to track student enrollment, course roster, behavior (unfortunately, still referred to as "discipline" in many systems), attendance, and transcript (final grade and course completion) information. This information can then feed the LMS with course roster information, allowing teachers to more easily maintain rosters of students when delivering content, and can also feed the early warning system (described below) with needed data on attendance, behavior, and transcript information. All of these are essential data elements for decision making, and building an effective data-driven school will certainly require the involvement of an SIS.

EARLY WARNING AND RESPONSE SYSTEM

An early warning and response system is a mechanism for tracking the wide range of relevant data generated by this diverse set of technology tools, assigning meaning to those data in a systematic way, and providing the necessary alerts and mechanisms for tracking the response of the system to those alerts. An effective early warning and response system provides a tool both for data management and for instilling a culture of data-based decision making. By providing a consistent method for alerting educators when data reach levels that indicate the need for a response, as well as reporting that indicates when alerts have yet to be responded to, the software creates a climate that encourages responsiveness (Frazelle & Nagel, 2015). This can greatly assist and standardize the process by which data teams choose to focus on particular students. An example of an early warning and response system is provided in Figure 8.2, demonstrating a view of an individual student.

STANDARDS LIBRARY

Note that the series of components along the left-hand column of the Figure 8.1 diagram are all connected via a standards library. As schools move more rapidly toward competency-based approaches to tracking student learning (e.g., standards-based grading), it becomes increasingly important to establish a well-defined library of skills (e.g., standards, benchmarks, learning targets) that collectively approximate the entirety of the content area to be learned. One of the advantages of a standards library is that it provides a method for linking the data across these disparate software systems.

DATA WAREHOUSE AND ANALYTICS

Data warehouse and analytics software are represented in the diagram as a separate oval standing on its own, but this is only due to the limitations in the possibilities for visually representing this particular tool. In reality, the data warehouse and related analytics represent an all-encompassing tool that brings together all of the data across these disparate software systems, as well as from other systems not mentioned (e.g., financial, human resources, transportation, community education), which may also include relevant data for decision

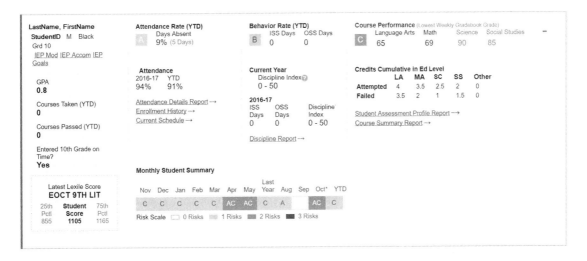

FIGURE 8.2. View of an individual student within an early warning and response system. Reprinted with permission from James Appleton.

making. Connecting these disparate sources of data, creating methods for understanding how these data sources may be interrelated, analyzing the impact of changes in the education system, and communicating the results to key decision makers are all functions of the data warehouse. As such, data warehouses tend to provide tremendous value within systems-level decision making. Data warehouse software is an essential and complex component of building a data-driven school, and as such warrants additional explanation and discussion, provided in a separate section later in this chapter.

DATA MANAGEMENT PLANS

Hopefully, the previous section provided the reader with a helpful overview of the ecosystem of technology functionality and software tools for supporting educators, with a focus on the data generated by these systems. This "thousand-foot" view can help discern what software tools need to be coordinated when building a complete data picture at both the individual and systems levels. The comprehensiveness of this "picture" is an essential component for creating a data-based culture, and school district technology teams are increasingly focused on ways to coordinate existing tools and add new tools, in order to complete this picture.

We argue that before schools start buying more software, however, they should first undertake building an essential and often-overlooked component of the data-driven school: a data management plan. Data management plans are essential for mapping out what is becoming an increasingly complex web of data sources (and their related management systems) in schools. Built with the end goal in mind, the effective data management plan ensures that each step is carefully planned and accounted for along the process from systems-level problem solving to individual data teaming, from the initial action or event that needs to be collected to the presentation of results. A well thought-out plan can become a guiding document for individuals' roles and responsibilities, creating lasting change in the organization that lives on beyond the inevitable staff turnover and transition that exists in any school.

Armed with the framework of educational software systems and components provided above, educators can begin to plan their data management. Since it is likely that most schools have some technology systems already in place, the process can start by examining what practices are already occurring. This process should ask critical questions about the ways in which your organization uses information, such as

"Which of the above components are we using and which aren't we?"

"Where are there gaps in our available data?"

"Are there potential sources of key data that we don't have available to us when we make decisions?"

"What steps are needed to ensure all relevant data are available to decision makers at the time of the decision?"

Building a data management plan can get fairly complex fairly quickly, but the process is best approached by starting with a minimum set of critical data-based decisions that need to be supported by technology, and then building the plan around these decisions. In this way, the plan has immediate relevance before getting bogged down in complexity, and can simply grow to accommodate more and more needs, as it establishes its utility and success to support those initial needs for which it was originally designed.

Because the education cycle tends to be calendar driven, one tool that can be very useful in building an initial data management plan is a simple spreadsheet, arranged as a timeline. With time on the *x*-axis, in columns, rows can be stacked for the various data elements that are critical to decision making. The decisions themselves, and the key times that they occur, then represent the intersection of the rows and columns. For example, if teachers meet in grade-level teams to review data and make decisions about instructional placement and intervention needs in October, then the column for October should include this activity, in each of the rows that represents a data element that is needed for these meetings. One can quickly see how this activity ties into the data-analysis teaming process described in Chapters 6 and 7.

This straightforward approach then provides a mechanism to plan from—if a certain set of test scores need to be available in a data warehouse by this meeting, then someone needs to be responsible for making sure data are transferred to that warehouse on time, so that the necessary reports are available to the necessary users. An example data management spreadsheet is included in this book's online supplement (see the box at the end of the table of contents), from a specific school district that we worked with (with identifying information removed) to help readers consider how they might go about developing their own data management plan for their school or district needs.

INTEROPERABILITY

Disconnected efforts in a school (or in technology) are like a grocery store where the aisles aren't connected and you have to check out and pay each time you leave an aisle. Consumers would quickly tire of an environment that was set up this way, with an end result that most would likely purchase fewer products, either strategically grabbing one or two items from a given aisle, or worse yet, simply always going only to the produce aisle (since it typically is the first aisle in the store) and then heading to their car after their first time checking out. Having our critical data stored in multiple software systems, each requiring its own unique log-in information and having its own unique user experience, creates a similar conundrum.

Interoperability refers to the ability for disparate software systems to work in a coordinated fashion (EdNET Insight, 2013). This often includes three key areas: sharing of data, single sign on, and coordinated access management. Single sign on is the ability to enter your log-in credentials only once and easily access functionality across a multitude of systems. Access management means that when you are "handed off" from one software system to another, the range of students and the range of software features you have access to are consistently implemented across systems. While these are both important facets of interoperability, the most relevant aspect of interoperability to this chapter is data sharing.

Data sharing is the means by which key data are provided from one software system to another. Since different software systems provide different functions, often one system is designated as the "source of truth" for the data. For example, the SIS is typically the "source of truth" for which students are enrolled in a given school, their demographic characteristics, and what classes they are enrolled in. An LMS needs these data in order to be useful—teachers would not be able to "see" their students and deliver necessary content to them if the LMS did not include course roster information. So, it is important that the SIS share these critical data with the LMS.

As the variety of disparate online systems grows, and as our reliance on them for day-to-day activities grows, so grows the need for advances in interoperability of data. Perhaps it was once sufficient for a teacher to simply hand enter their student rosters in a software system, but now that feels like a time-consuming barrier to the software's utility. Technology tools are available that allow data to undergo an extract–transform–load (ETL) process, in which the data are taken out of one system (extract), formatted to "fit" the destination system (transform), and placed into that destination system (load), all automatically and with little to no human intervention once initial setup is completed.

While this certainly enhances the experience for the end user of the destination system over and above manual entry, ETL processes can still be error prone (requiring constant tinkering as each software system is updated), are often done only on a nightly basis (meaning data in systems may be out of sync), and must be set up for every single pair of systems that intend to share data. The Schools Interoperability Framework (SIF) provides a universal standard for the sharing of education data that is specifically designed to overcome these issues (SIF Association, 2015). By standardizing both the formatting of the data to be exchanged, as well as standardizing the infrastructure by which these data are communicated, SIF creates a common language for any two educational software systems to exchange data seamlessly and in real time.

This "hub-and-spoke" approach to data sharing means that when an SIS communicates data according to SIF standards, it is immediately available to the LMS, the transportation system, the library system, and the multitude of other software that may rely on having ready access to these "source of truth" data. What this means for students, of course, is that they can now check out a book, log in to their LMS, and so on, all at the moment they are enrolled in the SIS. What this means for the data-driven educator is that systems can exchange data with one another, simplifying the process of getting all of your data in one place. In addition, systems can more easily exchange data across districts, meaning that students might not only be able to check out a book on their first day but their teacher might be able to make informed instructional decisions on that first day as well. More and more, state departments of education or other consortia of local education agencies are instituting SIF-based initiatives to better promote data interoperability both within and across schools.

BRINGING YOUR DATA TOGETHER

Once you have a strong data management plan in place, supported by a solid understanding of the different technology components in place in your system, as well as the functions those components are designed to provide, along with a strong interoperability solution to ensure data are being shared across systems, you are finally ready to leverage your data to institute a culture of decision making in the education system. As you can see, the notion that a single technology solution can instantly make you "data driven" is a fallacy that is often foisted on educators by overexcited software vendors. This isn't to say that these products don't have value; it's just that the developers of these products often lose sight of the fact that their solution isn't a panacea.

An analogy from recent political events is the Arab Spring that began in 2011—many were calling the events that caused repressive governments to be overthrown in Tunisia and Egypt the "Facebook Revolution." But Facebook was no more responsible for these revolutions than bubble sheet scanning technology was responsible for the spread of standardized testing in schools. These technologies act as "amplifiers" (Toyama, 2015), but they can amplify the seeds of change in both positive and negative directions. By having a thorough understanding of the scope of education software, implementing a thoughtful data management plan, and ensuring interoperability across systems, the technology infrastructure and knowledge is in place to ensure that "discernment" is in place—a necessary condition for the effectiveness of technology to drive positive change (Toyama, 2015).

Being data driven involves an understanding of the three necessary elements to using data: organizing and accessing, analyzing, and communicating results. When a system has the ability to gather data across a variety of sources, technology has taken care of the organizing and accessing of data, as was discussed earlier in this chapter. We now focus on analysis and communication of data, exploring tools ranging from simple spreadsheet software, such as Microsoft Excel, to advanced data warehouse and business intelligence tools.

Data Warehouse/Business Intelligence Tools

The data warehouse, and corresponding business intelligence platforms that provide visualizations of the data, remains the gold standard for achieving the goal of having all of your data in one place (Beyer & Edjlali, 2015). Data warehouses are essentially databases designed specifically for the purpose of storing and aggregating vast arrays of data from disparate sources, across time, and are architected in ways that support rapid retrieval of these data. In education, especially with the proliferation of single-function software systems (see below for a description of single-function software), there is a need for a tool to "pull it all together," and this need is growing across organizations both large and small. Well-designed data warehouse solutions perform this function exceptionally well.

The term *business intelligence* is included in the title of this section because it is, in fact, a distinct tool set, different from the data warehouse itself. While most users colloquially refer to the entire package as a "data warehouse," in fact, the data warehouse is strictly the database ("back-end" system), while the business intelligence tool is the product that provides the user access to visualizations of the data in the warehouse, as well as self-service tools for exploring the information ("front-end" system). For simplicity, we refer to both tools as the "data warehouse."

Data warehouses serve a number of key functions related to data, including summarizing and reporting, tailoring access to different users, exploring relationships across data types, and providing context. Take an example of a school district looking at their districtwide behavior data. Data may be *summarized* by school, allowing for fast and easily accessed comparisons of behavior patterns across schools, in order to understand where there may be differences. Access to these reports may be *tailored* for district leaders, who likely have broader and deeper access to the entire district, versus school leaders, who may only see summary-level data for schools other than their own. When drilling down into the data, in addition to looking at comparisons across population groups, a warehouse may allow for *exploring relationships* across data—for example, comparing credit attainment for students who have and haven't been suspended. And, in order to make sure leaders have a common understanding of the data, behavior rate data may be compared to a universal criterion, providing important *context* to data that might otherwise just appear as numbers. Each of these functions is described in further detail below.

Summarizing Data

One of the most salient functions of a data warehouse is its ability to provide a single-stop location to access summary-level information across a variety of data sources. This saves time for users who no longer need to log in to multiple software systems to get a complete picture of the relevant data. A single log-in provides access to reports ranging from student performance metrics, enrollment information, data on staff—including key operational data, such as leave and staff:student ratios—to organization-level financial information for budgetary authorities. Both day-to-day operational decision-making needs and historical trend data for longer-term decision making can be provided in summary form. Stronger tools also provide conveniences, such as scheduling reports to be delivered via e-mail.

Tailored Views

Another strength of a data warehouse solution is its ability to drive consistency across the organization, through the use of tailored views. By eliminating the need to log in to multiple systems to gain a complete picture of the relevant data, the organization also eliminates the need to deal with training on both access and interpretation of data that will invariably be presented in unique ways across systems. Typically, the organization implementing a data warehouse has more control over the ways that reports are presented, both in form and function, than with single-function "off-the-shelf" software. When supported by expertise around appropriate ways to summarize and interpret data, this ensures that users are viewing data in similar ways across the organization, driving consistency and accuracy of decision making across levels of the organization, across similar users throughout the organization, and across time.

Tailoring not only occurs in the organization-specific ways that data are to be presented but also in ways that are specific to the role of the user in the organization. For example, school board members can be provided access to the data warehouse to support their governance role, giving them fast, anytime, and anywhere access to high-level information across many facets of the organization. This helps keep board members informed about the organization's progress in meeting the goals of its strategic plan, for example, and may be tied directly to agreed-upon metrics from a balanced scorecard or similar governance tool. Likewise, a school principal may have access to these same key governance metrics, but the data would likely be summarized at the level of their particular school. Additionally, the principal's access would likely support a deeper level of "slicing and dicing" the data, including drill downs to examine particular groups of students or individual students in greater depth, to support their management (rather than governance) role.

The use of tailored views serves not only to provide control over what data users are accessing when making decisions but also to provide convenience. Many tools include the ability to construct "data dashboards" that give users quick access to the key performance data they need to view quickly. Data consumers shouldn't need to wade through mountains of irrelevant data to get at the answer to their question. The analogy to an automobile's dashboard is worth diving into more deeply—just as you shouldn't have to pull the car off the road to see how fast you are going and how much gas you have left in the tank, you should not need to close your office door in order to view the data on your dashboard. However, if a warning indicator goes off on your car's dashboard, then you likely will need to pull over and take the car to the shop for a detailed diagnosis. In data-driven decision-making parlance, this is when it is time to explore analytic reports that dive more deeply into the data. But the use of a dashboard helps promote control over users' behavior with data, so they can choose when to engage in these deeper explorations into the information, only when necessary, and also when convenient for them.

Exploring Relationships

By virtue of their ability to aggregate and draw connections between disparate sources of data, data warehouses promote the ability to explore connections between these data. Warehouses employ a data schema that predefines how these data sources should be connected (student behavior and student attendance data might be connected by a common student ID number, for instance), so that connections can be made and analyzed as soon as the data are imported into the warehouse. This is a key feature of the data warehouse, because it encourages decision makers to explore the complete context around a decision they may be faced with. A decision about what to do with an unsuccessful academic intervention program may be impacted by data on whether the program was delivered to the intended student demographic, what the attendance of students was within that program, whether it was adequately funded, and whether it was staffed with qualified personnel, as well as the student performance data that ultimately led to the designation that it was unsuccessful.

There are many examples in the literature of how exploring relationships across disparate data sources has improved educators' abilities to make informed decisions. One example is work by Heistad (1999) to create an advanced growth model that accounts for student population demographics and ties it to academic progress to identify schools and teachers that "beat the odds" by consistently seeing student gains that are greater than would be expected, after factoring in any relevant demographic predictors of the student populations they served. In another example, Appleton and Reschly (2015) were able to create a model of multiple factors that collectively predict student dropout in one large district, and implement a decision-making tool that brought this information to educators' attention through a warning system. In a third example, districts are increasingly exploring the academic return on investment of the financial programming decisions they are making (Hess & Osberg, 2010).

Providing Context to Data

Because data warehouses can aggregate data from a wide variety of sources, summarized at both global and granular levels, decision makers can be provided with key contextual information to support their interpretation of the data they are investigating. One especially crucial example of this context is the use of performance targets. Targets can apply to a range of data from academic to operational, and are generally derived through some meaningful determination of a benchmark for performance. Targets can also exist at the organization level (as in "60% of our students will demonstrate greater than 1 year's growth in 1 year's time"), as well as at the individual level (as in the comparison of an individual's growth in 1 year to the predefined metric of "a year's growth"). Targets provide important context for decision makers, and the method for establishing targets is critically important to the decision-making process.

While performance targets present a strongly criterion-referenced approach to data interpretation, normative data can also be a relevant and useful context for decision makers, and a data warehouse can support this process. In the earlier example of providing management-level information to a school principal summarizing information solely at their school, normative data can also be shared that allow the school-level data to be compared to other schools within the organization. Similarly, school- or even district-level data can be easily compared across regional consortia of districts that share information (Bollman, Silberglitt, & Gibbons, 2007), or public data repositories can be accessed for comparisons when such data-sharing agreements aren't available. Further exploration can ensure that comparisons are with "like" organizations, based on student demographics, rural/suburban/urban setting, organization size, and so forth.

Considerations

Data warehouses present a thorough technology and robust solution for supporting a data-driven school. However, there are some important considerations in implementation, and it would be useful for the data leader to heed these warnings before diving in. Data warehouses are typically not without considerable expense, in both the direct cost of the software and in the cost and expertise needed to implement a warehouse tool effectively. Warehouses can also require a lengthy runway to launch a tool across an organization, due to the training and communication needed to ensure successful implementation. Because warehouses by nature provide a greater number of options to users, both in functionality and in the types of data that can be accessed, there is often increased complexity and a need for careful attention to prevent this complexity from limiting the power of the solution.

In response to this, warehouse tools are increasingly providing more "out-of-the-box" solutions that can be implemented more quickly and with less local expertise, at the cost of some of the customization capability that can make a warehouse especially powerful. Another method to combat this issue is to organize a collaborative implementation across local education agencies, in which districts share in the cost both of the product and of the shared expertise needed for implementation (Silberglitt, 2010).

Single-Function Software

If the reason for the data warehouse is to pull all your relevant data together, one of the key reasons for this need is the rise of the use of what we call "single-function" software. Single-function software systems are software tools that were designed to resolve a single issue or provide a single source of data to a school. Tools such as the schoolwide information system (SWIS; *www.pbisapps.org*), AIMSweb (*www.aimsweb.com*), and NWEA (*www.nwea.org*)

are examples of single-function software tools. SWIS, for example, is a highly specialized software system designed to support the implementation of SWPBIS. The software itself focuses exclusively on the entry, tracking, and reporting of behavior data, allowing the organization developing the software to focus very deeply and specifically on ensuring best practices and maximizing the efficacy of SWPBIS in schools.

Single-function software is best implemented in organizations that are trying to solve an isolated need that is fairly specialized and may not be available in other, multifunction systems. They also work well when an organization wants a subset of users to have quick access to a specific area of information, often tied to a functional need. For example, a system that delivers assessments to students often also includes reporting on those specific assessments. It may only be a subset of staff that are actually engaged in the assessment delivery, as well as the interpretation of the highly specialized reports—while the rest of the staff can get the information they need for decision making from the more comprehensive, less specialized reports of a data warehouse. Single-function software is also especially useful when the institution wants to adopt the expertise of the software provider (i.e., reporting is complex and would be difficult to re-create in a data warehouse).

The advantage of single-function software is clear: highly specialized tools allow the developers of the software to remain focused on their area of expertise. However, it is important for the district to balance the number of different single-function tools implemented with the potential for confusion and frustration on the part of educators who need to then log in to multiple systems and learn to navigate a variety of user interfaces to see a complete picture of the data for a student or a system. In the example of SWIS, many SISs also include a module for tracking behavior data, and some have begun to evolve better, PBIS-friendly reporting. This creates the possibility of meeting the need, while reducing the overall number of systems and simplifying the data management plan.

Ultimately, it is a consideration of the district's and/or school's data and technology leaders to decide how best to balance this specificity with the concerns associated with too many unique software systems. Issues such as understanding the user experiences of different people with different roles in the organization, designing a sound and feasible data management plan, and, of course, cost, are all factors in this decision-making process.

Statistical Software

Statistical software is typically thought to be relegated to a single user's desktop, sitting in a windowless room in the district's central office for hours, only to emerge with an answer to a burning question facing the district (e.g., "Should we implement this curriculum?"; Is this program working?"). This image does remain a frequent staple of education settings across the country, and often yields a useful, actionable analysis of highly relevant information—the idea of research on one's own students is a powerful model that often is effective at driving change. The statistical software is typically a desktop version of a tool such as SPSS, SAS, STATA, or R, and in order to use it, the analyst must download all the relevant information onto their workstation, import it into the statistical software package in a "flat file" format, and run their analyses.

This approach can yield useful information for guiding decisions, and the notion of an impartial "data expert" behind the curtain can certainly help instill a culture of data-based decision making in schools. It evokes a sense of mystery and certitude that makes the final result hard to argue with, even if it goes against long-held opinions. In this way, leveraging statistical software to run data analytics in schools can be beneficial.

As an example, statistical software can be used in the process of setting performance targets on local assessments, based on their prediction to outcomes, such as performance on high-stakes state assessments (Silberglitt, 2008b). In this example, a logistic regression analysis is run on a complete set of student data, including both the local (predictive) assessment and the state (outcome) assessment, resulting in a "target" score on the local assessment, such that performance above target is predictive of success on the state assessment. These targets can then be applied to contextual data displays in tools such as the aforementioned data warehouse, allowing the analysis to have a much broader impact than just on the single user running that particular analysis. See Appendix 2 for a detailed discussion of this target-setting process.

This model requires a single, all-knowing analyst who in actuality is only as strong as both the depth of their skills with the technical side of the analysis, as well as the subject matter of the research question—a difficult combination to come by. Not to mention the inherent weaknesses of this approach from a technical perspective—it requires the work manually of connecting files filled with disparate sources of data (which can be error prone) in order to import them into the statistical software. Any analyses conducted will be limited to those data sources that were brought into the software, meaning that potentially relevant sources of information will be ignored. Even in the very simple and highly useful example above, of target setting, the methodology completely ignores all other potential sources of variance other than performance on the single predictive assessment.

A clear future direction in the development of statistical software is to take the software out of the single-workstation, single-user model, and instead embed the software directly into the overall data system (Butler Analytics, 2015). This is frequently paired with a data warehouse, providing a simplified data management plan and single, albeit complex, source of data for the statistical software to mine. Statistical software is now able to directly access all available online sources of data, rather than waiting for data to be imported, and, further, is able to proactively conduct analyses on the data based on some prespecified model or set of questions, rather than waiting for the analyst to tell the software which analysis technique to be leveraged. This is certainly not a panacea, and cannot solve every data analysis need in a school, but it represents a promising and useful trend in creating a data-driven culture. Both by being proactive and constantly examining trends in the data, and by including all available data and exploring connections that might otherwise be overlooked, the trend toward more automated data-mining approaches has significant promise for education. Infusing research into the process of guiding decisions, as well as identifying areas of concern, is an important part of a data-driven school. Tools to make that infusion more systematic are certainly worth exploring.

The ultimate goal of such tool sets is to reduce the need for advanced statistical understanding at the local level. Data teams could be informed by algorithmic calculations, and warning systems could be based on large-scale data, analyzed by data leaders at the district, consortia, state, or even national levels. The availability of such systems increasingly emphasizes the need for data leaders to be informed consumers of data and leaders in supporting their educator teams' understanding of how to use this information.

Spreadsheet Software

Spreadsheet software tools, while not the most technologically advanced or fanciest tool on the market, still have tremendous relevance and useful functionality in creating a data-driven school. What spreadsheet software tools ultimately provide the user, that may not be available in the myriad other tools described, is ultimate control over how and which data are analyzed, calculated, summarized, and presented, with a typically easy-to-use set of functions. There is a reason that, in many districts, regardless of the availability of high-powered data warehouse and analytics software, when it comes time to put together the school board presentation, the tool of choice is spreadsheet software. This complete control and simplicity gives users confidence that they can accurately and completely tell their "story" with the data.

Spreadsheet software includes several functions that can help mitigate the negative side of using this sort of tool—the amount of manual labor that is needed. For instance, cell calculations can help with repetitive tasks—if you have a standard presentation that you give regularly (e.g., annually) and it involves some specific calculations of numbers generated by other available reports, it can be helpful to store this set of calculations in a spreadsheet, so that these specific calculations can be automated rather than repeated each time the analysis is needed. Conditional formatting is another example of a useful function, through which you can establish color coding of data elements that will automatically be applied, depending on the values in a cell or range of cells. Pasting a table of data into a conditionally formatted spreadsheet can make data of concern immediately jump out. Pivot tables are another useful tool that allow a user to "slice and dice" a table of data and generate a set of parallel graphs from a data source. By simply modifying the parameters of the pivot table, one can quickly generate summaries of data across population groups, including graphs that can then easily be copied into reports or presentations.

Despite these features, spreadsheet software remains a tool to be used carefully—the more manual manipulation of data, the greater the likelihood that an error will be made. Additionally, a limitation of spreadsheet software is availability of the generated summary data. Similar to the issues with the model of statistical software, in which a single person sits in a windowless office, data created using spreadsheet software have no inherent mechanism for distribution. Graphs and charts that can help with decision making must be distributed using some other tool (creating a presentation, a report for a website, e-mailing files) in order to get the data in the hands of consumers. This can create delays in availability of the data, possibly rendering them less relevant (and "stale") by the time they reach their intended audience.

These caveats aside, two graphical templates using spreadsheet software are included in the online supplement to this book (see the box at the end of the table of contents), which may be useful to the data practitioner. The first, which is provided within the workbook "SOE template" is a template tool for producing a "Summary of Effectiveness" chart (Burns & Gibbons, 2011). This chart is a useful way to display data on student performance and change over time on a universal screening assessment. Many screening assessments are given using a fall/winter/spring schedule. By entering in data on the assessment type, the target scores for each assessment season, and the raw data from a group of students, the Summary of Effectiveness chart will automatically display the number and percentage of students at Tiers 1–3 at each season, as well as the numbers of students who move from one tier to another *across* seasons. This latter information can be invaluable for understanding the effectiveness of curriculum and interventions designed to support students at each tier, as described in Chapters 6 and 7.

The second template, which is discussed in Appendix 2 and provided within the workbook "LR Curves template," is a template tool for demonstrating the relationship between a predictive assessment and an outcome assessment. This tool allows you to enter the results of a logistic regression analysis, commonly used to predict a categorical outcome, such as whether performance will or won't meet grade-level expectations on a high-stakes assessment. Upon entering the beta values from this analysis, this template produces a table of probabilities, as well as a series of logistic response functions ("LR Curves"). This can be helpful in explaining the relationship between a predictive assessment and an outcome, as well as in determining target scores on the predictive assessment.

An additional benefit of the spreadsheet tools offered by Google is that they can be directly connected to data collection using Google Forms. Your own custom data entry form can easily be created and shared, and, if desired, made available only to individuals (staff or students) within your organization. Once data are entered, they are automatically stored in a Google Sheet, which allows for analysis there or possible uploading into a larger database of information. The customizability of this solution, as well as its ability to manage and connect the data collection process to the data-analysis process, makes it a very useful tool.

The specific features and functions of various software tools are constantly evolving so quickly that writing about them creates the risk of being outdated by the time the book goes to print. That said, there are some trends in spreadsheet software, specifically in Microsoft Excel, that are worth noting. The 2016 version of the Excel software represents a drive to include more of the "relational database" functionality that was typically limited to tools such as Microsoft Access or FileMaker Pro. Allowing for mapping of connections across databases reduces the difficulties of connecting data from disparate data sources. Excel is also beginning to offer collaboration tools, such as the ability to share queries with other users in your organization, which represents a drive to make Excel more of a true business intelligence software tool (Excel Team, 2015). This shift in functionality, combined with an increasing array of built-in charts and graphs, makes spreadsheet software, such as Excel, still worth paying attention to, as you build your overall strategy for data management and analysis in your school or district.

Presentation Software

The use of presentation software, such as Microsoft PowerPoint or Keynote, while it suffers from the same weaknesses of being a static, single-user view into data, remains an integral and useful part of utilizing data effectively in schools. One of the most significant reasons for this, despite the availability of dashboards and other tools that provide self-service access to the very same data, is that presentation software allows you to tell a story with your data. When communicating about data to an audience, creating a compelling narrative is even more important to the process than having interesting and dynamic visualizations (Stikeleather, 2013). In this way, the story becomes the focal point, and the data visualizations act as tools that simply help to tell it.

And, just as a story must have an introduction, rising action, climax, falling action, and resolution, we can leverage presentation software to guide our storytelling to include a similar structure. One of the best models for data storytelling is actually the problem-solving model itself, which allows us to introduce a problem, analyze it to provide interesting details to the audience, discuss the development of a plan to resolve the problem, present information on implementation, and then talk about the resolution (plan evaluation). This model is demonstrated in the included "Data Storytelling Template" PowerPoint presentation, which is available in the online supplement (see the box at the end of the table of contents) that readers can use to help structure their own data story. In this particular template, the presenter also attempts to bring the audience into the story by asking questions for the audience to consider and contribute to—in this way, presentation software can also help in "coaching" educators who may be more novice to the data analysis process. Regardless of your model, presentation software affords the ability to provide a richer, audience-specific presentation of the data, in ways that can be truly compelling and support a data-driven school.

Another use of presentation software is to help to standardize the data-review process of others. In the example described in Chapter 4, PowerPoint can assist data leaders in doing exactly that, by creating a "data book." The "data book" was distributed to building leaders across a consortium of districts on a periodic basis, and essentially guided the recipient through the data-analysis process in a linear fashion. This can be a unique way to take advantage of a key difference between data dashboards and self-service data-analysis software and presentation software—presentation software is by nature linear, and as such, can make sure that the viewer explores the data in a defined order, also without missing any charts or graphs.

Presentation software has evolved considerably since the early days of PowerPoint, and there are a range of options now available to design and deliver great presentations, many of which are cloud based. For instance, Prezi is an online presentation tool that allows a great deal more flexibility of presentation format than more traditional presentation software, while still allowing for a linear "path" through the content. Prezi also has a self-service capability, in that you can make a "Prezi" available online for others to view on their own. Canvas is yet another example of a tool that is even less structured, and can allow the designer to create stories that appear on a one-page "canvas." As a final example, Google has created a number of cloud-based tools to support data analysis and presentation, including the more familiar Google Slides, as well as tools for data analysis and visualization, such as Google Charts, Google Fusion Tables, and Google Refine.

Educators today have myriad tools available for "bringing it all together" to provide the most relevant and necessary data to educators at the time they need it to inform their decision making. Ranging from data warehouse tools that can connect everything under the sun to presentation software that provides a focused, guided walk through a data story, each tool has value to the process of creating a data-driven school.

Technology tools are both necessary for, and possess great potential for enhancing, the utilization of data to support educational decision making. With strong leadership, these tools can be leveraged in a coordinated fashion, centered around a data management plan, so that they become a part of the fabric of the daily work of educators. The *intention* to use data (and the belief in its benefits) must be there, leaving the data leader with the work of providing the organization with the *discernment* to select the right tools for the right purposes. With that discernment, technology then establishes itself as a tool to promote the *self-control* of the organization—to make the process of using data both a requirement and a routine.

KEY ISSUES

- As technology tools and infrastructure have evolved, technology is an increasingly critical part of educators' efforts to improve efficiency and communication, and accelerate problem solution.

- Data leaders can help avoid the common pitfall of believing the adoption of the technology tool will lead to problem solution, and instead work to ensure that intention, discernment, and self-control are in place prior to and during implementation.

- An understanding of the education technology landscape and various popular software solutions is essential to building an effective plan for data management.

- Building a data management plan can provide schools with a blueprint for their data, improving coordination across staff and interoperability across systems, and ensuring that decision makers will have the data they need, when they need it.

- There are a variety of software tools at the data leader's disposal for bringing data together and communicating it to stakeholders. Knowledge of the capabilities and limitations of these tools, as well as fluency with many of them, are important skills for data leaders.

CHAPTER 9

Developing Data Leaders

ROADMAP

1. Characteristics of successful data leaders
   a. Data and intervention literacy
   b. Belief in the value of systems-level data-driven decision making
   c. Leadership skills
   d. Relationships
      i. Staff–staff relationships
      ii. Staff–student relationships
2. Identifying and appointing data leaders
3. Keys to effective training of data leaders
4. Framework for assessing the context for data-driven leadership
5. Profiles of data leaders

This chapter begins by stressing the importance of identifying and developing potential data leaders. These future leaders may be drawn from a variety of different cohorts of school personnel, including, but not limited to, administrators, school psychologists, general education teachers, special education teachers, and other related services personnel.

CHARACTERISTICS OF SUCCESSFUL DATA LEADERS

Regardless of background, we believe that there are four key characteristics that any successful data leader must possess already or be able to develop. Scholars in a variety of different related areas, including data coaching, instructional coaching, and leadership, have suggested a wide range of qualities that they believe are essential (Hirsh & Killion, 2007; Love et al., 2008; Marzano, Waters, & McNulty, 2005). The four characteristics we highlight below stem from an attempt to identify patterns across this prior work and to refine the list to specifically target the skills and talents needed for what we believe to be the unique, emerging systems-level data leader role we describe in this book.

Data and Intervention Literacy

The first of these characteristics of successful systems-level data leaders is *data and intervention literacy*. While it is not essential, it is helpful for a potential data leader to come to the role with a strong understanding of the key elements of effective assessment and instruction. At the very least, the leaders must be interested in and able to develop these skills in themselves and in others. Dixon, Hyson, and Mahlke (2012) evaluated the data literacy of general and special education teachers within an educational cooperative. The study found that teachers did not demonstrate adequate data literacy in several key areas, including understanding the functions of assessment within a comprehensive assessment system (i.e., screening, diagnostic [drill down], progress monitoring, and outcomes data) and recognizing that GOMs used for progress monitoring do not need to measure all aspects of what was taught, even though they are markers of overall competence (e.g., R-CBMs directly measure ORF but are indicators of general reading ability). The results also suggested a need for more time and guidance for teachers in developing reliable and valid classroom formative assessments and for regular initial and ongoing training in MTSS, CBM, and progress monitoring, especially at the secondary level. Secondary teachers participating in the study appeared to need more evidence to convince them of the relevance of MTSS, CBM, and progress monitoring at the secondary level.

The results of this study confirm what we believe to be the most important initial assessment competencies for potential data leaders. First, data leaders need to be familiar with the four purposes of assessment. Second, they also need to possess a basic understanding of how to analyze the psychometric properties (e.g., reliability and validity) of assessments used within this comprehensive assessment system. Third, it is critical for data leaders to understand and be able to communicate to others the importance of these assessments being administered as intended, especially if high-stakes decisions are being made using the results. Finally, these leaders must be able to recognize what assessments serving each purpose can and cannot tell us as educators. It is particularly important to understand what they *cannot* tell us based on their purpose, psychometrics, and fidelity of administration, so as not to draw inappropriate conclusions.

A strong knowledge of and/or commitment to learning about the characteristics of effective instruction and intervention is also key. As part of a series of Minnesota Department of Education (MDE) MTSS grants the first author's (Hyson) education district received, four annual surveys were conducted with MTSS leaders within each of the five pilot districts participating in the grants. The surveys asked participants to self-report their awareness of different types and tiered levels of research-based intervention. As predicted, the results indicated that over the course of the 4 years of the grants, participants showed significant growth in their self-reported awareness of research-based interventions in the areas of early literacy, decoding for grades 1–3, and comprehension, all of which were specific focus areas of the grants. Interestingly, however, the number of Tier 2 and 3 intervention programs or methods/strategies they reported using to address student needs within their MTSS systems *declined* from year 1 to year 2. This was initially alarming to the education district's MTSS grant-implementation team, but when participants then reported a rebound and subsequent increase in Tier 2 and 3 intervention use in years 3 and 4, the team came to the conclusion that they may have not been clear in year 1, prior to more intensive involvement in the consultation associated with the MTSS grants, regarding exactly what Tier 2 and 3 interventions were. The participants may have thought they were engaging in more Tier 2 and 3 interventions in year 1 but then realized in year 2 that some of what they thought were Tier 2 and 3 interventions actually were not. We have also seen other schools that think they are intervening at Tier 1, and then after moving toward MTSS, realize that they actually are not adequately addressing Tier 1 and are instead engaging in extensive individual intervention, which is both unsustainable in the long term and does not fix core Tier 1 instruction.

Findings like those described above suggest to us that data leaders need to be at the forefront in ensuring that they and their colleagues are clear about the unique characteristics and purposes of different tiers of intervention within a data-driven school. They must also possess or develop at least a basic understanding of the level of research support for an intervention necessary for a team to be confident in using interventions for different purposes. Zirkel and Rose (2009) differentiated among four different levels of research support one might uncover for an intervention one is considering using. Readers should note that the definitions of these terms outlined here are not universal. Other sources may define them differently, but we find these definitions to be particularly helpful in outlining the different levels of research support an intervention might have.

1. *Scientifically based research.* Scientifically based research (SBR) support is the most rigorous standard and refers to experimental or quasi-experimental research support, preferably involving random assignment of participants to experimental and control conditions.
2. *Peer-reviewed research.* Peer-reviewed research (PRR) support overlaps to some extent with SBR but is not a subset of it. Many studies of this type published in academic journals are not experimental or quasi-experimental in design, but, regardless, they must undergo a blind review process by peers in the field.
3. *Research based.* Research-based support for an intervention indicates that the intervention was designed to be consistent with relevant research findings but has not yet garnered SBR or PRR support.
4. *Evidence based.* Evidence-based support refers to interventions that are linked to student performance data and/or have been evaluated locally to assess their effectiveness but are not yet clearly associated with research findings or supported by SBR or PRR evidence.

It is also essential for data leaders to not only recognize and support fidelity of assessment administration but fidelity of intervention implementation as well. As has been discussed throughout this book, if interventions are not implemented as intended, it is meaningless to discuss the needs of students not responding. Finally, data leaders must be able to understand what *assessments* can and cannot tell us and must also be aware of what *intervention* at each tier can and cannot tell us. It is once again equally, if not more, important to know what interventions *cannot* tell us based on their tier, level of research support, and degree of fidelity of implementation, so as not to draw inappropriate conclusions.

Belief in the Value of Systems-Level Data-Driven Decision Making

Knowledge is not enough, however. An effective data leader should also demonstrate and attempt to foster in others a *belief in the value of systems-level data-driven decision making* for changing instruction and improving student outcomes. This can be especially challenging when the data conflict with strong previously held beliefs. For example, despite a wealth of research demonstrating that vaccines do not cause autism, many individuals still remain convinced that they do. Similarly, while studies have consistently shown that ORF CBMs are highly—although admittedly not perfectly—correlated with overall reading competence, including comprehension, many educators still dispute this claim. At least some of this apparent resistance to data seems to stem from fear and ignorance (the latter in its nonpejorative sense, meaning a lack of adequate knowledge about a subject). To effectively address this resistance, data leaders must try to help create a culture within their data-driven schools in which all educators believe they are responsible for the success of all students and in which staff can overcome any fears they may have and feel comfortable making themselves vulnerable when discussing their data.

Another source of the resistance to data-driven decision making is a general mistrust of published research. Some school practitioners are appropriately skeptical about the parade of new educational fads that pervade non-research-based educational publications and in-service workshops. Indeed, the field of education is plagued by an antiscientific mind-set (Ellis, 2005) that stems from seeing instructional fads adopted, fail, and be abandoned. What is needed here is an understanding of the difference between published information based on untested theories and that based on empirical research. Data leaders need to be cognizant of this distinction, embrace information supported by research, and categorically avoid or repudiate non-research-based initiatives that pose as the newest educational trends. Communicating this distinction to school practitioners is an especially important task of the data leader.

We also agree with Love and colleagues (2008) that this belief and commitment to data-driven decision making must be particularly strong with respect to the issue of ensuring equity for all students. This should involve confronting a range of potential barriers to learning, including risk factors associated with minority status and poverty, as well as mental health issues and learning needs. Adelman and Taylor's (2005) learning supports model illustrates this particularly well (see Figure 9.1.)

For data leaders to effectively ensure equity, it is essential for them to engage in comprehensive problem analysis. The risk factors mentioned above (e.g., minority status, poverty, mental health, and learning needs) are rarely root causes themselves of the challenges individual students or groups of students face. They are instead markers of other underlying needs that more directly influence student outcomes. While data-driven practitioners would have a difficult time intervening to change these markers, if they are able to drill down and identify the root causes underneath them, those root causes are often more responsive to intervention. (See Chapter 3 for more discussion of tools and processes for doing this effectively.)

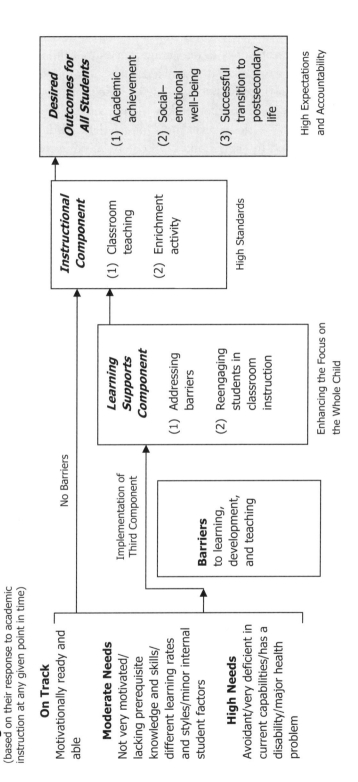

FIGURE 9.1. A learning supports component to address barriers and reengage students in classroom instruction. Reprinted with permission from Howard Adelman.

203

Leadership Skills

We believe effective data leaders must also possess or be able to develop strong *leadership skills*. This includes not only proficiency in managing procedures and routines but also the ability to communicate a clear vision and associated goals, and to facilitate collaboration among all members of the data-driven school to achieve those goals. Successful data leaders must know and be able to ensure that others follow the processes described in Parts I and II of this book associated with systems-level problem solving and data-analysis teaming, respectively. As we highlighted in Parts I and II, if one or more of these steps is skipped or inadequately followed, successful problem solving and data-analysis teaming becomes much more difficult. For example, an effective data leader must ensure that careful problem analysis occurs before an intervention is planned, since premature intervention planning can lead to an intervention that is not appropriately targeted at the true need of the individual student or group of students. If the intervention is then found to be ineffective, it will be difficult for the team to determine whether that was because the student did not respond and may need increased support, or whether the intervention was misidentified due to ineffective problem analysis.

Effective data leaders must also provide visionary and collaborative leadership in addition to providing direction in managing procedures and routines. If initiatives like systems-level data-driven decision making are to be sustained, it is critical for the school to have a vision for developing and maintaining a data-driven culture within the school. Effective data leaders are able to generate and communicate a vision for how this can be accomplished and outline specific goals and objectives for accomplishing it. No matter how well trained or visionary, however, we have stressed many times throughout this book that a data-driven school or district cannot be created by one data leader. It is critical that these leaders not be "lone nuts," as we described in Chapter 1. They must be able to involve other school staff in decisions and create a climate within which it is safe and encouraged for staff to share student performance data and collaborate in using it to improve student outcomes. Relationships at all levels of the school community are essential, including, in particular, staff–staff relationships and staff–student relationships.

Relationships

Recent research has highlighted the need for effective leaders to have both leadership skills and the ability to foster supportive *relationships* within the school (Goleman, 2011; Svobodny, 2013). As mentioned previously, while it is helpful for potential data leaders to possess these certain skills prior to taking on the role, training in the essential roles and responsibilities of data leaders can also be effective in developing these skills in future leaders. The following story provides one example of the importance of these skills.

> *Introduction of the PLC School Reform Model at an Elementary School*
>
> The principal at a Midwest suburban elementary school participated with other principals in the school district in a book study of DuFour and Eaker's (1998) *Professional Learning Communities at Work*. Following that book study, the principal invited a select group of staff to accompany him on a site visit to Adlai E. Stevenson

High School in Lincolnshire, Illinois, the high school where DuFour himself was principal and had first implemented PLCs. As mentioned in Chapter 1, among those chosen to go on this trip was a veteran fifth-grade teacher with over 20 years of experience who was not only well connected to and well respected by other staff within the school but also initially somewhat skeptical of the PLC initiative based on her past experience.

At the beginning of the next year, the principal then proposed a series of book studies with staff at the elementary school, similar to the one he had participated in with other school district principals. The school psychologist participated in the first of these book studies and then led subsequent book studies with other staff. The book studies were conducted during school hours, with substitute teachers or parent volunteers contracted to cover participating teachers' classrooms. It is also important to note that the focus of the discussions was not on trying to convince participants to support the PLC model but on helping them better understand the model and then reflect on whether they thought it could be successful in their school.

During a faculty meeting at the conclusion of that school year, the staff voted on whether they were willing to commit to pursuing a PLC school reform initiative. As recommended by PLC experts, the principal stated that the initiative would not go forward without 90% of staff voting in favor of it. The school achieved 95% approval.

Among the keys to the success of the process this school followed to introduce PLCs, we believe, was the commitment to fostering trusting staff–staff relationships. The principal garnered trust with and among his staff in a number of important ways: (1) by inviting potential skeptics like the veteran fifth-grade teacher on the initial field trip to Stevenson High School, (2) by scheduling book study sessions during school hours and thus communicating to staff that this activity was not just an add-on to be done before or after school if time allowed, but was equally as valuable as student contact time, (3) by focusing book study discussions not on trying to persuade participants of a predetermined viewpoint but on allowing them to learn and reflect on the material and come to their own conclusions, and (4) by committing to following the will of the staff in requiring that at least 90% of them agree to pursue the initiative before the school committed to moving forward.

Staff–Staff Relationships

Staff–staff relationships like those described above are especially important in creating a data-driven school, since staff within a school like this need to feel comfortable making themselves vulnerable in sharing data from their own classrooms with other staff and administrators. In traditional schools, teachers can often be "islands," closing the doors to their classrooms and working alone to try to help their students meet learning standards. The success of their students is dependent solely on these individual teachers—for better or for worse. They are not expected to share their data with anyone else but also are not provided with the time and resources to get support from anyone else—with the possible exception of the principal and special education and other student support services staff for at-risk students.

In contrast, within data-driven schools with established PLCs, staff participate in regular grade-level or content-area team meetings and are expected to share and discuss their data with other staff on the team. In these schools, all staff are responsible for the learning of all students, regardless of which classroom teacher(s) the student happens to have. As a result, teachers are less likely to feel alone and more likely to get the time and resources they need to help all of the students meet the learning standards. At the same time, to get the most benefit from a data-driven school, teachers in these schools need to be willing to expose their results and instructional practices to the scrutiny of others, a potentially threatening exercise.

This can seem especially threatening within the current context of increased school and teacher accountability. Of course, teachers need to be held accountable and shoulder some responsibility themselves for their own classrooms. Staff–staff relationships within a successful data-driven school, however, must be founded on the shared belief that ultimately the staff and administrators are all working together to help all students grow toward proficiency. For staff to buy into the focused collaboration that is essential to effective systems-level data-driven decision making, they must be convinced that they can trust that their administrator is first and foremost committed to helping them—and their students—be successful.

Administrators who are able to demonstrate the leadership necessary to develop these types of relationships with and among their staff have been found to exhibit higher levels of emotional–social intelligence, including increased self-awareness, self-management, social awareness, and relationship management (Goleman, 2011; Svobodny, 2013). Svobodny found that of the 21 McREL balanced leadership responsibilities (Waters & Cameron, 2007) the "relationships" responsibility—which measures the administrator's awareness of the personal aspects of teachers and staff—was most highly correlated with principals' emotional–social intelligence.

As mentioned in the PLC story shared above, making time within the school day to provide training and support to staff so that they can regularly collaborate with one another to improve student achievement is essential to an effective data-driven school. The time must ideally be within the school day so as to communicate to staff that collaboration is a key component of their core job and not an add-on. Teams should be cautioned, however, that time for collaboration without a specific agenda or goal can contribute to collaborative efforts concentrating too much on day-to-day classroom logistics and "problem admiration" rather than on student learning.

Teams may think that they know how to run productive meetings, but this is often not the case. Staff–staff collaborative relationships can be significantly strengthened if data leaders are able to provide teams with additional guidance on how to set appropriate group norms and goals and how to effectively facilitate team discussions. Chapters 5–7 discuss these characteristics of successful data teams in much more detail. Finally, staff must be shown and provided with ongoing coaching in how to access student achievement results using technology tools if they are to have the data they need to engage in successful staff–staff collaboration. It is important to acknowledge as well that even those adequately trained initially in these areas can easily drift from their training without regular refresher trainings or an accountability system to help them maintain the skills and knowledge they have gained.

As mentioned earlier, while administrators should attempt to establish staff–staff relationships that emphasize a collaborative approach to improving outcomes for all students, they—or at least someone in the data-driven school—must still hold staff accountable for generating products from their collaboration. This accountability is essential to sustaining the momentum necessary for true change to occur. DuFour and Eaker (1998) and we have seen firsthand that collaboration by invitation without accountability is rarely productive and successful. This is admittedly a delicate balance.

The accountability should not be about personnel evaluation but instead should be about sustaining the alignment of the collaborative work being done with the school's data-driven vision, mission, and goals. In the PLC story shared earlier, this was accomplished in a couple of different key ways. First, the principal required PLC grade-level teams to submit meeting minutes to him after each meeting, which he reviewed and on which he provided feedback. Second, he asked teams to submit summary products to demonstrate their progress on their primary annual tasks. For example, the primary task for grade-level teams during the first year was to review the state standards and identify the essential learning objectives that they believed students at their grade level needed to meet before the end of each year. Another accountability measure, as a result, was for teams to submit a list of those objectives to the principal by the end of the year. The next year, the primary task was to design and submit to the administrator common grade-level assessments to measure student progress with respect to the identified objectives. A wealth of research has demonstrated that providing staff with the opportunities and resources they need to collaborate in this way to improve student achievement is one of the best predictors of increases in student achievement, regardless of the demographic characteristics of the school (Schmoker, 2006).

Staff–Student Relationships

A wealth of research has also demonstrated the association between staff–student relationships and student achievement and engagement. Research at the secondary level has identified a connection between a student and at least one caring adult in the school community as one of the strongest predictors of students staying in school and not dropping out (Sinclair, Christenson, Lehr, & Anderson, 2003). A common staff development activity highlights the importance of these connections. The name of each child in the school is written on an index card and the cards are all taped to the walls of the room where the staff is meeting. Each staff member is then given a set of adhesive dots and directed to stick a dot to the index card of each student in the school with whom the staff member feels a personal connection on some level beyond just having them in class. After all participants are done placing their dots, the staff members step back and look at the cards. A large number of cards often do not have a single dot on them. To help these students to establish a connection with at least one adult in the school, each staff member is then assigned to check in (say hello and make some sort of non-class-related contact) with one student without a dot at least once a week for the rest of the school year.

The quality of these connections is important as well. Effective teacher–student interactions have been linked to increased student achievement and engagement across age levels (Hamre & Pianta, 2006). These outcomes of increased student achievement and engagement are particularly important at this time since teacher-evaluation models across the country are increasingly focused on holding teachers accountable for growth in these areas. Despite this well-established association between teacher-student interactions and student achievement and engagement, schools and districts have yet to focus sufficient attention on measuring and providing staff with coaching to help them improve staff–student relationships. Although using research-based instruction and interventions and implementing them with fidelity are critically important in data-driven schools, teachers must also be able to deliver instruction and manage student behavior within the context of a trusting, supportive staff–student relationship. Students are much more likely to respond to instruction and interventions delivered within this context. We believe that the converse is true as well: students whose teachers consistently deliver instruction or interventions that demonstrate that the teacher can identify and respond to the student's needs are more likely to form positive, trusting teacher–student relationships.

The quality of these staff–student relationships can be assessed both indirectly through survey measures or directly through external observations. Indirect survey measures include both teacher report measures (e.g., Student–Teacher Relationship Scale [STRS]; Pianta, 2001) and student report measures (e.g., the Teacher–Student Relationship Scale of the Student Engagement Instrument [SEI]; Appleton, Christenson, Kim, & Reschly, 2006). Direct external observation measures include both those based primarily on frequency counts (e.g., Randy Sprick's Basic Five and Classroom Management STOIC Checklist; Sprick, Knight, Reinke, Skyles, & Barnes, 2010) and those that call on observers to make global ratings of the quality of teacher–student interactions across multiple domains and dimensions (e.g., the Classroom Assessment Scoring System [CLASS]; Pianta, La Paro, & Hamre, 2008).

Experts agree that indirect survey measures of student and teacher perspectives regarding their teacher–student relationships, while valuable, may not be consistent with each other or with direct external observation measures, are not sufficient on their own, and may even lead to misidentification of students experiencing low-quality teacher–student relationships (Hamre & Pianta, 2006; Hughes, 2011; Wu, Hughes, & Kwok, 2010). Further study in this area should therefore continue to build the literature on the link between teacher–student relationships and student academic growth, and be sure to include observational measures of these relationships. Hamre and Pianta (2006) contend that studies that include observational measures provide essential information that can help in designing interventions for teachers looking to improve their interactions with students.

As mentioned above, the CLASS (Pianta et al., 2008) is an example of a direct external observation measure in which trained researchers micro-analyze discrete teacher and student behaviors within this relationship dyad, potentially allowing them to identify critical global characteristics of these associations and their connection to student engagement and student growth. The CLASS assesses three specific global characteristics (referred to as "domains") of teacher–student interactions: emotional support, classroom organization, and instructional support. Each of these domains consists of three to four "dimensions" that are independently rated by the observer on a scale of 1–7. For example, the instructional support domain encompasses the concept development, quality of feedback, and language modeling dimensions. Ratings of each dimension are determined by analyzing the behavioral indicators that the CLASS manual lists for that dimension (e.g., for quality of feedback, behavioral indicators include scaffolding, feedback loops, prompting thought processes, providing information, and encouragement and affirmation). Finally, the CLASS manual includes detailed descriptions and examples from classrooms that would be rated low, medium, and high on each behavioral indicator. Observers are required to complete four to six 20-minute observations over the course of 1–2 days prior to arriving at their ratings for any observation period.

Despite their limitations, the student and teacher indirect survey rating scales of staff–student relationship quality mentioned above have the potential advantage of providing users with a more nuanced window into the student's or teacher's perspective on their relationships with each other. Reporters may also therefore feel more ownership of and buy-in regarding the results. Finally, these tools are easy to give and require little time and training to administer and score. Observational tools like the CLASS have their potential advantages as well, however. They could be considered more objective by some, since they provide an outside observer's perspective on the staff–student relationship. Assuming observers complete the training necessary to learn and become certified to use the tools, these tools are also likely to produce results that could be considered to be more valid global indicators of the quality of teacher–student interactions. Yet it is important to acknowledge that, at least for the CLASS, this training is time and resource intensive.

Measuring staff–student interactions is only the beginning, however. The data we gather from tools like the ones described above are truly useful only if they can be used to target staff needs and help them improve the quality of their interactions. The CLASS provides two specific training and coaching models to assist with this aim: feedback strategies, a model for how to appropriately share results of observations with participating teachers, and instructional support strategies, a model for providing monthly coaching to teachers to help them improve upon their interactions within a dimension they collaboratively identify with the coach. Head Start requires the use of the CLASS and these feedback and coaching models for several years now as part of their classroom evaluations, with promising results (Improving Head Start for School Readiness Act, 2007). Preliminary findings from research suggest that the model's success may also be able to be extended to the early elementary level as well (Hyson, 2017).

IDENTIFYING AND APPOINTING DATA LEADERS

Based on our experience serving as and working with data leaders in schools, we have several key pieces of advice for employers looking to create or fill already-created data leader positions in data-driven schools. First, our experience has been that there is an increased likelihood of data leaders being effective if the position created is a unique, separate position. Ideally, we recommend that it be a full-time position, given the varied roles that data leaders can and do play. We recognize, however, that some schools may not have the resources to be able to support a full-time position. If that is the case, we would advocate for a part-time position with clearly defined hours and responsibilities. When the position is conceptualized as simply an added set of tasks assigned to an already-full-time employee, we have rarely seen that data leader be able to successfully complete those tasks and fulfill the data leader role as intended. Beyond the assigned hours and responsibilities, we also recommend that employers consider the way in which the position is described and promoted to others within the data-driven school, being sure to clearly communicate the decision-making authority granted to the data leader and the relation between their responsibilities and the mission, vision, and goals of the school (Love et al., 2008).

Since the responsibilities of most data leaders will likely include analyzing and summarizing the results of state accountability tests, which are typically administered in the spring, we advise employers to employ data leaders under contracts that include summer hours. This allows the data leader to be able to review the accountability test results when they become available (typically during the summer) and prepare to present, and facilitate discussions of, those accountability test results and other relevant data at the beginning-of-year professional development meetings. To help data-driven schools get the most out of the hours allocated to data leaders, we also recommend that employers consider providing data leaders with access to paraprofessional or other office support staff assistance to help with tasks, such as test proctoring or data entry. Requiring data leaders themselves to fulfill these roles leaves them less time to engage in other roles more consistent with their knowledge and skills, including data analysis and consultation.

Speaking of professional development, sufficient funding and release time should be allocated to data leaders so that they may attend face-to-face, and participate virtually in, trainings like the ones described in the next section of this chapter. As noted below, these trainings should not only ensure that data leaders are well versed in the content critical to their responsibilities but also in the skills necessary to use and train others to use that content knowledge in the service of a data-driven school. In our experience, the most successful data leaders demonstrate strengths in both data analytical and technological skills and in systems consultation skills. One set of skills without the other is rarely sufficient. As alluded to earlier, however, data leaders need not enter their positions experts in either or both sets of skills. What they must bring with them, however, is a commitment to take risks, make mistakes, and continuously learn (Love et al., 2008).

KEYS TO EFFECTIVE TRAINING OF DATA LEADERS

The content of effective trainings for data leaders should be aligned with the four characteristics discussed earlier in this chapter (i.e., data and intervention literacy, belief in the value of systems-level data-driven decision making, leadership skills, and relationships), as well as with the focus of each of the three parts of this book (i.e., systems-level problem solving, data-analysis team facilitation, and using technology for data management).

With respect to data and intervention literacy, effective trainings for data leaders should ensure that participants can understand, interpret, and use assessment data addressing each of the four functions within a comprehensive assessment system to drive instruction. This is, of course, necessary before data leaders can be expected to train others to do the same. Speaking of which, data leaders should also be trained in how to identify research-based interventions and train others to implement them with fidelity and monitor their effectiveness. Finally, with respect to leadership skills and relationships, data-driven schools should provide data leaders with training in how to lead change effectively by establishing a clear vision and commitment to change and facilitating staff–staff relationships through providing time within the school day and the resources for staff to engage in focused collaboration. Given the importance of staff–student relationships to student outcomes, data leaders must be well versed regarding how to gather data on these relationships and use those data to inform instruction and intervention.

In addition, we recommend that training for data leaders be aligned with the focus of the three parts of this book (i.e., systems-level problem solving, data-analysis team facilitation, and using technology for data management). Data-driven schools should ensure that data leaders are well versed in the five steps of the systems-level problem-solving model discussed in Part I (i.e., problem identification, problem analysis, plan development, plan implementation, and plan evaluation) and how to use data serving the appropriate functions to help facilitate discussions regarding each step. These discussions most often occur within data-analysis teams, so data leaders need training in the key characteristics of these teams and how they can most effectively be facilitated, by the data leader or by someone else. Finally, as outlined in Chapter 8, technology tools are essential to efficient and effective data management using the problem-solving model within data-analysis teams. Data leaders, therefore, need to be able to receive training in how to access, organize, analyze, and use data from these technology tools, since they will likely be seen by other staff within their schools as support resources for staff use of the tools.

Not only must data-driven schools consider the content data leaders need to be trained in but they should also consider the most efficient and effective methods for providing that training. Our experience suggests that one of the keys to effective training of potential data leaders is regular collaborative meetings of key cohorts of potential data leaders. At the state level, this could include groups similar to the Minnesota RTI Community of Practice data coaching and problem-solving subgroup. The IDEA Partnership defines communities of practice as "groups of people that agree to interact regularly to solve a persistent problem or improve practice in an area that is important to them. . . . . CoPs are a way of working that invite the groups that have a stake in an issue to be a part of the problem solving" (Creating Community, n.d.). In the case of the Minnesota RTI Community of Practice, the participants were MTSS implementers and stakeholders who were collaborating to build effective sustained implementation of MTSS at the local, district, regional, and state levels. The functions of the community were to:

1. Develop a shared repertoire of resources, experiences, stories, tools, and ways of addressing implementation challenges;
2. Apply collective knowledge to improve practice, inform policy decisions, and develop technical guidance community members can use, scale-up, and integrate with other evidence-based practices and systems of support; and
3. Provide positive examples for districts at earlier stages of implementation to observe.

Out of this overall community emerged several subgroups focused on specific elements of MTSS implementation, one of which was data coaching and problem solving.

We have also helped facilitate regular meetings of cohorts of potential data leaders, including school principals, testing and assessment leaders, and school psychologists. Every June, at the annual retreat for principals of the school districts within the educational cooperative, the first author (Hyson) led half-day to full-day workshops addressing a range of data leadership topics, including accessing, interpreting, and effectively collaborating to use data to drive instruction. A draft of the data book PowerPoint mentioned in Chapter 4—a sample copy of which is available in the online supplement (see the box at the end of the table of contents)—was also typically introduced at this retreat and feedback sought from the principals to improve its usefulness for them in their roles as data leaders.

In designing the PowerPoint, data leaders should keep in mind four keys to effective systems-level data presentations:

1. *Include key guiding questions and systems-level goals to guide interpretation of data included in the PowerPoint.* As discussed in Chapter 4, four key guiding questions should be included to facilitate consumers' use of the systems-level problem-solving process in interpreting and using their data to drive instruction. A slide could be inserted into the PowerPoint reviewing the four functions of assessment data within a comprehensive assessment system that we discussed in Part I and referred back to throughout this book, along with a copy of the Identifying Gaps in Your Comprehensive Assessment System activity (Appendix 1). Finally, as the reader can see in the sample data book PowerPoint, data leaders could choose to draw a line on some of the graphs to highlight the 80% proficiency target associated with MTSS and provide users with a clear visual to guide them in identifying gaps between what was expected and what was occurring within their schools as part of problem identification.

2. *Highlight connections among assessment, intervention, problem solving, and system organization.* As discussed in Chapter 4, the fourth key guiding question addressed the connection between assessment and intervention. To facilitate this connection, the sample data book PowerPoint includes links to clearinghouses of research-based interventions and online research-based intervention websites, as well as critical questions to ask in interpreting data and identifying appropriate interventions (see Chapter 4 for discussion about these critical questions). As we highlighted in Part II of this book, effective data-analysis teaming is essential to helping schools connect assessment and intervention, and interpret and use data to drive changes in instruction. To address that need, we recommend that data leaders include recommendations for best practice in data-analysis teaming within the data book PowerPoint, as well as links to recorded webinars on such topics. Recorded webinars, in general, are a tool we have found very helpful in more efficiently training and making refresher training resources available to potential data leaders, especially in school districts/cooperatives with a large number of buildings.

3. *Ensure the data book is user-friendly for data leaders to create and for consumers to understand and use.* Based on our consultations with administrators in schools, we recommend creating the data book in PowerPoint format so it can be easily presented (by district- or school-level data leaders) to staff, school boards, or the community. Hyperlinks can be included within the table of contents for the PowerPoint so that users can easily locate the section addressing a specific question, since the tool is designed to most often be presented in parts rather than all at once.

4. *Build the capacity of consumers to access and interpret the data themselves in the future.* The ultimate goal of the data book PowerPoint is to move away from an expert consultation model in which the district-level data leader is the only one who can access the graphs within and produce the PowerPoint toward a more collaborative consultation model in which users can access the graphs themselves. As a result, the data book PowerPoint template was made to primarily include data displays that consumers of the PowerPoint

would have access to themselves through their online data systems. Links to directions and recorded webinars were added here as well, showing users how they could access the data themselves. Finally, we caution users not to interpret the data within the PowerPoint for consumers, but instead to provide them with the previously discussed key guiding questions so that they can engage in the systems-level problem-solving process themselves.

We also have, on a monthly or semimonthly basis, facilitated meetings among testing and assessment leaders and among school psychologists within the districts we have served. One of the primary purposes of these meetings has been to serve as train-the-trainer opportunities, ensuring that these local data leaders are sufficiently proficient themselves to be able to teach others within their districts how to access, interpret, and collaborate to use data to drive instruction. This has been especially essential given the large and diverse range of schools that state education agencies, educational cooperatives, and large districts often attempt to serve. An expert model in which the data leader is the only one who could provide support to staff in each of the schools is not sustainable.

Book and article studies have also been found to be beneficial in nurturing future data leaders. For example, as part of a data academy for principals and other district data leaders, participants read and discussed a series of articles about different key components of systems-level data-driven decision making. The previously mentioned data coaching and problem-solving subgroup of the Minnesota RTI Community of Practice also conducted a book study on *The Data Coach's Guide to Improving Learning for All Students* (Love et al., 2008). The Community of Practice was able to purchase copies of the book with state MTSS grant money. The books were then shared among participants in the subgroup. Participants completed a jigsaw approach to reading the book, dividing up chapters and generating, sharing, and posting written summaries of the ones they read with the rest of the group. Finally, the first author's (Hyson) educational cooperative used some of its MTSS grant money to purchase copies of Schmoker's (2006) *Results Now* for principals in each school district that was a part of the cooperative. The book study was introduced and jump-started at the annual retreat described earlier. Principals were then asked to read a section of the book for each subsequent monthly meeting. The sections were briefly discussed at each of the meetings.

Below are a few of the lessons we learned from conducting book studies like these:

1. Make time for the group to meet within the school day.
2. Groups of 5–10 staff members seem to work best.
3. Try to involve a cross-section of school staff in each group.
4. Take time to foster a supportive, fun group atmosphere.
5. Provide participants with discussion questions to guide their reading and to prompt them to apply book concepts to their everyday work with their students.
6. Take time at the end of the book study to plan for follow-up activities (Hyson, 2005).

From these and other experiences, we have learned that to train future data leaders, it is most beneficial to provide them with data first and discuss its usefulness before asking them to access it themselves. If potential data leaders are to persist through technical challenges that may arise when they attempt to access data using technology tools, they must be convinced that the data they are attempting to access will be useful to them. If they are convinced that this is the case, they will be much more likely to persist when confronted with problems logging in or accessing reports with the desired data. In other words, even though the ultimate goal of data leaders should be to "teach others to fish" (or in this case, access data themselves), they should not jump into this too quickly. Before others can learn how to fish themselves, they must be given some fish and shown that the fish are worth the effort of fishing.

FRAMEWORK FOR ASSESSING THE CONTEXT FOR DATA-DRIVEN LEADERSHIP

We feel that a missing component of previous data leadership self-assessments is a framework not only for assessing the individual data leader's skills and talents but also for assessing the degree to which the school in which the data leader works is set up to allow the data leader to demonstrate those skills and talents. The National Association of School Psychologists' (2010) *Model for Comprehensive and Integrated School Psychological Services* includes six "organizational principles" designed to highlight the components that need to be in place within a school or district if a school psychologist is to have a genuine opportunity to play a comprehensive role.

Since one aspect of this comprehensive role for school psychologists—or other educators for that matter—is systems-level data leadership, we believe that these organizational principles could pertain to helping all future data leaders, not just school psychologists, evaluate the context for their activities as well. They include:

1. Organization of service delivery.
   - Services are provided based on a needs assessment and regularly evaluated for effectiveness.
   - Funding sources do not drive provision of services.
   - Services are integrated with services of other school and community providers to provide a range of services.
   - Services include consultative services.
2. Climate.
   - Systems promote cooperative and collaborative staff relationships.
   - Data leaders are encouraged to professionally advocate for services in the best interests of students and families.
   - Systems maximize job satisfaction of data leaders and promote balance between data leaders' professional and personal lives.
3. Physical, personnel, and fiscal support systems.
   - Systems ensure recruitment and retention of data leaders adequate to meet the needs of the system.
   - Sources of funding are maximized to ensure adequate support for services.
   - Data leaders have adequate technology and clerical support, and an adequate physical work environment.
   - Data leaders have adequate access to continuing professional development.

4. Professional communication.
   - Data leaders have opportunities to communicate with one another about professional issues.
   - Data leaders have access to technology necessary to perform their jobs and maintain confidential communications with others.
   - The system's policy on student records is consistent with state and federal rules and laws, and protects the confidentiality of students and families.
5. Supervision and mentoring.
   - Data leaders' supervisors have adequate training in systems-level data-driven decision making themselves.
   - Data leaders are allowed time for supervision and mentoring within the district or outside the district in small or rural systems.
6. Professional development and recognition systems.
   - Data leaders have adequate access to continuing professional development.
   - Supervision provides adequate feedback to data leaders about their developing skills (adapted from National Association of School Psychologists, 2010).

If data leaders find that the organizational principles necessary for them to have the best chance of being successful in their role are not yet present, it is important that they not accept that as an ongoing reality. We think the work of data leaders is in the best interests of children and families, and so we believe it is the responsibility of data leaders to advocate for any needed changes in the system in which they are working. If that advocacy is to be successful, it must include, however, collaboration with other key data leaders within the data leader's organization. Change is most likely to occur if data leaders truly strive to understand any perceived barriers their fellow data leaders see to supporting their work and collaboratively problem solve to address those barriers.

PROFILES OF DATA LEADERS

We conclude this chapter with a couple of real-life profiles of data leaders to provide the reader with a picture of what they might look like and to highlight the variety of backgrounds and expertise these data leaders bring to the role, as well as potential challenges based on their role in the school.

Alex was an grade 8 math teacher. Due to his math background, Alex already had a strong understanding of and belief in the importance of data for decision making. In fact, he was the teacher at the grade 7–12 high school where he worked who most frequently and intensively used a computer-based, diagnostic formative assessment measure to track student progress with respect to state math standards, identify individual and classroomwide needs, and adjust instruction. Alex was asked by his principal to attend monthly regional testing and assessment leader meetings. Because of his role as a classroom teacher, he was able to make direct connections among the topics discussed in these meetings, state learning standards, and classroom instruction in ways other participant data leaders from different backgrounds did not. His position as a classroom teacher (along with the lack of resources for him to be provided with regular release time), however, also made it more difficult for him to continue to attend the meetings regularly, since they often conflicted with his class schedule.

Levi was a school psychologist. His background and training not only contributed to a similarly strong understanding of and belief in the importance of data for decision making, but it also provided him with systems consultation skills that Alex did not necessarily have. This allowed Levi to take on a leadership role in facilitating regular data team meetings in his school, helping general and special education teachers and administrators to access, interpret, and use summative, screening, progress monitoring, and diagnostic data to identify individual student and group-level needs. Because of the training school psychologists receive in scientifically research-based intervention, Levi was then able to assist the team in identifying and evaluating the appropriateness of Tier 2 and 3 interventions to address these identified needs. It was critical for Levi to build the capacity of other team members, since, like many school psychologists, he was only at this building for 2 days per week and therefore was not able to form the collaborative relationships or directly implement interventions in the same way that a general education teacher data leader might be able to.

KEY ISSUES

- Data-driven schools should identify data leaders who already possess data and intervention literacy and/or demonstrate the potential to develop these characteristics.
- Effective data leaders should not only develop a knowledge base in the areas of data and intervention literacy but should also be able to ask the right questions and seek out the right resources, as well as believe in the value of systems-level data-driven decision making for changing instruction and improving student outcomes.
- This belief and commitment must be particularly strong with respect to confronting potential barriers to student learning.
- Data leaders must foster staff–staff relationships founded on the belief that administrators and staff are working together to help all staff and students be successful.
- They must advocate for time during the school day to provide staff with training and support so that they can engage in focused collaboration to improve student achievement.
- Staff teams should be accountable for regularly producing products based on their focused collaboration.
- The quality of staff–student relationships should be assessed and plans made to improve them as needed in order to increase the likelihood that interventions will result in growth in student engagement and achievement.
- To ensure the development of these skills within their data leaders, administrators who support data-driven schools should promote ongoing collaborative training opportunities, including such opportunities as Communities of Practice, train-the-trainer sessions with cohorts of potential data leaders, and book and article studies.
- Data leaders must also assess and advocate to improve the context within which they are working. Even if a data leader has developed the skills and talents necessary to be effective, their school must also be set up to provide the leader with the opportunity to demonstrate them.

Identifying Gaps in Your Comprehensive Assessment System

1. In each quadrant of the table below, write the names of the assessment tools your school *administers* to address that purpose within a comprehensive assessment system. *Note:* The same assessment tool may be listed in more than one quadrant if it is used for multiple purposes.

2. Circle the assessment tools in each quadrant, the results of which your school *uses* to make instructional decisions.

Outcomes Related	Screening
Progress Monitoring	**Diagnosis**

Case Example

Setting Your Own Target Scores

If you are reading this section, we assume that you have a unique interest not only in interpreting the data but in generating the very statistical analyses that create a framework for those data to be interpreted. The methodology for setting target scores provides such a framework and enables the district or school to conduct the powerful analyses described in Chapter 2, using data that are uniquely focused on the population represented by your district or school.

Logistic regression provides the most promising statistical analysis tool for establishing the target scores needed for backward planning (Silberglitt, 2008b). Logistic regression allows the analyst to use one or more quantitative or categorical variables to predict a single categorical outcome (Neter, Kutner, Nachtsheim, & Wasserman, 1996). Let's take the example of linking Measures of Academic Progress—Math (MAP-M) to performance on the state-mandated math assessment. In this example, the outcome is divided into two categories: successful or not successful in meeting the grade-level standard on the state test. The logistic regression process then establishes the minimum score on the MAP-M so that a student is highly likely to end up being successful on the outcome. The logistic regression process can be divided into three steps: (1) establishing the slope and intercept of the logistic response function (which characterizes the relationship between performance on the predictive variable and probability of success), (2) applying that function to determine the target score(s), and (3) reviewing the diagnostic accuracy of those score(s).

In the MAP-M example, we might look at the scores on the grade 3 spring benchmark assessment. We would pull together a spreadsheet of these scores, with an additional column demonstrating performance on the state test (categorized simply as 0 for "did not meet standards: and 1 for "met standards"). We then run the logistic regression in a statistical software package to determine the values of β_0 and β_1 in the logistic response function. These values, known as "beta values," determine the intercept and slope of the logistic response function—the steeper the slope, the stronger the predictive relationship. We then repeat this process for each benchmark period and grade level of MAP-M data. So, we would have a set of beta weights describing the relationship between the grade 2 fall MAP-M and the grade 3 state test, the grade 2 spring MAP-M and the grade 3 state test, the grade 3 fall MAP-M and the grade 3 state test, and so on.

Next, we can enter the beta values into the Excel template provided in the book's online supplement (see the box at the end of the table of contents). Follow the instructions on the Logistic Regression Model Excel template. This produces a graph of the logistic response function for each benchmark period. From this graph, we can then apply a consistent standard for establishing target scores at each benchmark period, based on the probability of success on the outcome. The graph below shows a labeled series of logistic response functions covering MAP-M benchmark testing across grades 2–8, linked to the grades 3–8 Minnesota Comprehensive Assessments (MCA), the statewide assessments of mathematics.

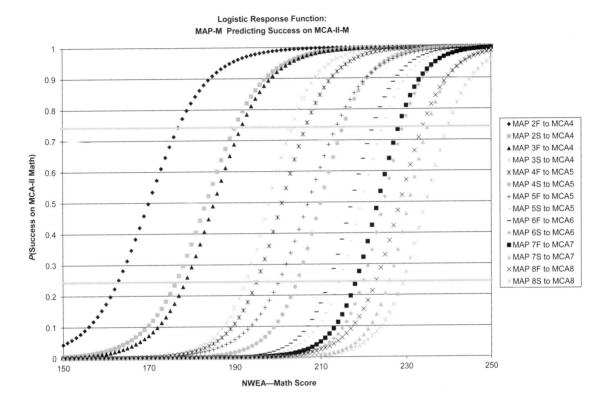

The horizontal lines at .75 and .25 on the *y*-axis represent *P*(Success) of 75% and 25%, respectively, which are then used to determine the Tier 1 (75% predicted success on the MCA-II) and 2 (25% predicted success on the MCA-II) target scores. The point on the *x*-axis at which these lines intersect the logistic response function for that benchmark period represents the target score for that benchmark. Having two consistent target scores (one for Tier 1 and one for Tier 2) across benchmark periods provides a mechanism for differentiating which students may need varying levels of intensity of support—students below the Tier 2 target need the most intense level of support, students between Tiers 1 and 2 need moderate levels of intensity of support, and students above the Tier 1 target require the least intensive support (i.e., core instruction).

Once these target scores have been determined, we can go back to our data set to run some basic diagnostic accuracy statistics on the target scores. The two key statistics are the positive predictive power (PPP) and the negative predictive power (NPP). The logistic regression gives us the likelihood of success at each specific score. In the example above, students scoring exactly at the Tier 1 target would have a 75% probability of success. However, NPP and PPP give us likelihood of success or failure, respectively, for the entire group of students above or below target. Typically, using the 75/25 rule for establishing Tier 1 and 2 targets yields the following probabilities: 90% probability of success for the group of students at or above the Tier 1 target, 50% probability of success for the group between the Tier 1 and 2 targets, and 10% probability of success for the group below the Tier 2 target.

However, these probabilities can vary depending on the relationship between the predictive variable and the outcome. For example, in a Minnesota study of the relationship between the MAP and the MCA in both math and reading, the probabilities of success for the group below the Tier 2 target tended to be higher in grade 2 (Silberglitt, 2008b). This is likely because there is a greater amount of time between the predictive assessment and the outcome (the MCA does not begin until spring of grade 3), and thus the correlation is not as strong. It may also reflect that interventions were happening for these students between the time of the grade 2 MAP assessment and the time of the grade 3 MCA. The outlook for students below target in grade 2 fall may not be as dire as for students below target in grade 3 spring, as there is virtually no time between the grade 3 spring MAP assessment and the MCA in which to intervene. Because of these variations, it is important to assess the diagnostic accuracy of the targets after they are developed.

APPENDIX 3

Data Activity

STEP 1: GENERATING DATA QUESTIONS

In your groups, review the Venn diagram on the next page from Victoria Bernhardt (which appeared as Figure 3.2 in Chapter 3). This diagram is intended to provide a context for asking critical questions of your data. Consider the four domains of data presented in this diagram as you generate critical data questions about your school or district. While not every critical question does so, many of the more valuable questions cut across two or more of these domains. For example, rather than asking, "How much are students in my school improving in math?" (Student Learning), you might ask, "How much are students in my school with low versus high attendance improving in math?" (Demographics and Student Learning), or "How much are students who participate in the supplemental math program improving in math, and how is this improvement different across students with low versus high attendance, as well as students who have positive versus negative attitudes toward their placement in this program?" (Perceptions, School Processes, Demographics, and Student Learning).

After reviewing the diagram, develop a list of questions that are critical to your school or district. For each question, be sure to note which of the four domains are included in the question. Try to develop as comprehensive a list as possible. Questions such as "What is the demographic makeup of my school?" are often overlooked during this exercise. Note that not every question cuts across multiple domains, and not every question includes Student Learning.

At this point in the exercise, do *not* be concerned with whether or not the data to answer these questions are readily accessible. The goal of this activity is to brainstorm a list of data-based questions that are important to better understanding your school or district. Write down as many questions as you can. It may be helpful to write these questions on sticky notes or index cards, with one question per card. We will organize these questions later in the exercise.

STEP 2: ORGANIZING DATA QUESTIONS AND IDENTIFYING GAPS IN AVAILABLE DATA

The goal of this part of the activity is to take the list generated in Step 1 and organize it by domain of data and priority level, consider any duplication or overlap, and identify which questions naturally group together (e.g., "Attendance by ethnicity" and "Attendance by limited English proficiency [LEP] status" would be similar and grouped next to each other on the list).

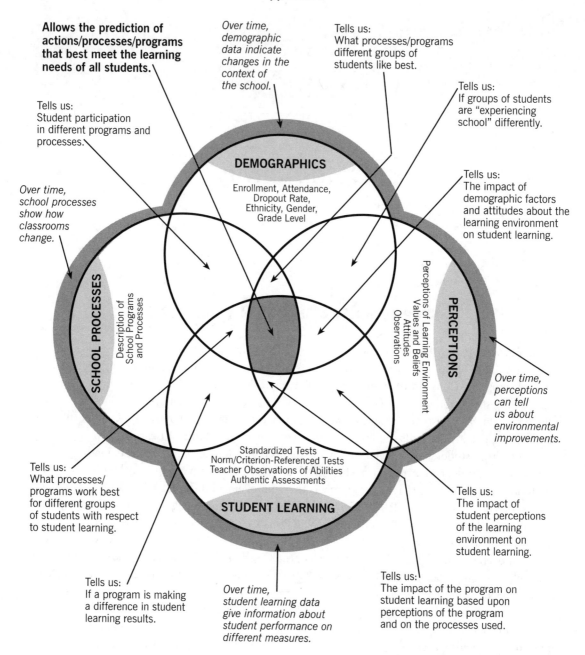

Allows the prediction of actions/processes/programs that best meet the learning needs of all students.

Over time, demographic data indicate changes in the context of the school.

Tells us:
What processes/programs different groups of students like best.

Tells us:
Student participation in different programs and processes.

Tells us:
If groups of students are "experiencing school" differently.

Over time, school processes show how classrooms change.

Tells us:
The impact of demographic factors and attitudes about the learning environment on student learning.

DEMOGRAPHICS

Enrollment, Attendance, Dropout Rate, Ethnicity, Gender, Grade Level

SCHOOL PROCESSES

Description of School Programs and Processes

Perceptions of Learning Environment Values and Beliefs Attitudes Observations

PERCEPTIONS

Over time, perceptions can tell us about environmental improvements.

Standardized Tests
Norm/Criterion-Referenced Tests
Teacher Observations of Abilities
Authentic Assessments

STUDENT LEARNING

Tells us:
What processes/ programs work best for different groups of students with respect to student learning.

Tells us:
The impact of student perceptions of the learning environment on student learning.

Tells us:
If a program is making a difference in student learning results.

Over time, student learning data give information about student performance on different measures.

Tells us:
The impact of the program on student learning based upon perceptions of the program and on the processes used.

Multiple measures model. Reprinted with permission from Bernhardt (1998).

Take the list of questions from Step 1 and enter them into the chart on page 225. Write in the question, and circle the question's priority level, as well as which domains the question applies to (circle all domains that apply).

Attempt to group like questions together. If you wrote your questions down on sticky notes or index cards, you can begin to physically sort them into groups. It may be helpful to copy the chart several times, entering all questions from a given group onto a common page.

Once you are finished grouping questions and entering them into the chart, go back through the list and identify the Data Tools/Gaps for each question. List any tools you currently have at your disposal (e.g., surveys, assessments, software where data are stored) that can help you to gather the information necessary to answer the question. Also, list any gaps in your current data collection—for example, data elements that are not currently being gathered but need to be, in order to answer the question. (See the completed example on page 224.)

STEP 3: BUILDING A DATA MANAGEMENT PLAN

Many of the questions generated in this exercise need to be answered at specific times during the school year (e.g., at data retreats, team meetings). Ensuring that all needed data are available at these critical data-based decision-making events helps to ensure that the events are effective. A data management plan is a helpful way to organize this process. The plan should be developed with the end in mind, so start with the events where data are needed, and work your way backward through the steps necessary to make sure the data are available. Consider the following questions:

- What key events occur in our district and which require availability of data (e.g., parent–teacher conferences, grade-level team meetings, data retreats, board presentations, grant applications)?
- List each event, along with the date, the participants, the data that are needed, and the tools to be used to access these data.

Based on this list, work backward to determine how the data will get there. Consider the following:

- When are the data gathered (e.g., testing windows for assessment data)?
- How are the data gathered (e.g., stored in software), who is responsible for this process, and how much time does the person need?
- What training may be needed for participants prior to the event?
- Are any special reports needed? If so, who will develop them, and how much time does the person need?

Example of a Completed Data Question Organizer

School/District: _____   Team Members: _____

Question	Priority			Domain(s)				Data Tools/Gaps
	High	Med	Low	SL	SP	D	P	
1. Is all-day, everyday kindergarten more effective than half-day kindergarten in terms of academic achievement?	**High**	Med	Low	**SL**	**SP**	D	P	Tools: Literacy and math assessments primary Gaps: Finding comparable schools with half-day kindergarten
2. How do targeted services students (K–8) compare to nonserviced students of similar demographics and preservice levels of achievement?	High	**Med**	Low	**SL**	**SP**	**D**	**P**	Tools: MCA, Literacy and math assessments, SIS
3. What are the components of targeted services that are effective?	High	**Med**	Low	**SL**	**SP**	D	P	Gaps: Need to gather individual teacher content
4. What are the differences in achievement for students enrolled in targeted services vs. nothing?	High	Med	**Low**	SL	**SP**	D	P	Gaps: Need targeted services participation loaded into SIS
5. Which variables affect our racial population groups' levels of achievement?	**High**	Med	Low	SL	SP	D	**P**	Gaps: Need student perception data
6. How does school climate impact student learning?	**High**	Med	Low	SL	SP	D	**P**	Gaps: Need student perception data
7. Do the types of electives a student takes affect test scores?	**High**	Med	Low	**SL**	**SP**	**D**	**P**	Tools: SIS, Literacy and math assessments, MCA
8. How can we track students who withdraw or drop out?	High	**Med**	Low	**SL**	**SP**	D	**P**	Gaps: Need access to student data beyond our rights to collect it
9. How does attendance impact performance for ELL students?	**High**	Med	Low	**SL**	**SP**	**D**	**P**	Tools: SIS, Literacy and math assessments, MCA
10. Do students with IEPs related to math and reading experience increased achievement?	**High**	Med	Low	**SL**	**SP**	**D**	**P**	Gaps: Gather IEP content
11. Which students, who were below grade level in reading and math, are closing the gap with their peers?	High	**Med**	Low	SL	**SP**	**D**	P	Tools: SIS, Literacy and math assessments, MCA
12. Are intervention classes resulting in improved performance in regular language arts and math classes?	**High**	Med	Low	**SL**	**SP**	D	P	Tools: SIS, Literacy and math assessments, MCA
13. Are intervention classes resulting in improved MCA proficiency?	**High**	Med	Low	**SL**	**SP**	D	P	Tools: SIS, Literacy and math assessments, MCA
14. Is parent perception of remedial class placement impacting student enrollment?	High	Med	Low	SL	SP	**D**	**P**	Tools: SIS Gaps: Parent perception data

SL, Student Learning; SP, School Processes; D, Demographics; P, Perceptions; MCA, Minnesota Comprehensive Assessments; SIS, Student Information System.

Data Question Organizer

School/District: _____ Team Members: _____ Page: _____

Question	Priority			Domain(s)				Data Tools/Gaps
	High	Med	Low	SL	SP	D	P	
	High	Med	Low	SL	SP	D	P	
	High	Med	Low	SL	SP	D	P	
	High	Med	Low	SL	SP	D	P	
	High	Med	Low	SL	SP	D	P	
	High	Med	Low	SL	SP	D	P	
	High	Med	Low	SL	SP	D	P	
	High	Med	Low	SL	SP	D	P	
	High	Med	Low	SL	SP	D	P	
	High	Med	Low	SL	SP	D	P	
	High	Med	Low	SL	SP	D	P	
	High	Med	Low	SL	SP	D	P	
	High	Med	Low	SL	SP	D	P	
	High	Med	Low	SL	SP	D	P	

SL, Student Learning; SP, School Processes; D, Demographics; P, Perceptions.

References

Achieve. (2013). State support for open educational resources: Key findings from Achieve's OER Institute. Retrieved from *www.achieve.org*.

Adelman, H., & Taylor, L. (2005). Mental health in urban schools. Retrieved from *www.niusileadscape.org/docs/FINAL_PRODUCTS/LearningCarousel/MentalHealthinUrbanSchools.pdf*.

Adelman, H., & Taylor, L. (2012, November). *Four systemic concerns that will shape the futures of school psychology*. Webinar presented as part of the 2012 Conference on the Future of School Psychology, Bloomington, IN.

Albers, C. A., Glover, T. A., & Kratochwill, T. R. (2007). Where are we, and where do we go now?: Universal screening for enhanced educational and mental health outcomes. *Journal of School Psychology, 45*(2), 257–263.

Alexander, K. L., Entwisle, D. R., & Horsey, C. S. (1997). From first grade forward: Early foundations of high school dropout. *Sociology of Education, 70*(2), 87–107.

Allensworth, E., & Easton, J. Q. (2007). *What matters for staying on-track and graduating in Chicago Public High Schools: A close look at course grades, failures, and attendance in the freshman year*. Chicago: Consortium on Chicago School Research at the University of Chicago. Retrieved from *http://ccsr.uchicago.edu/publications/07%20What%20Matters%20Final.pdf*.

Altrichter, H., Feldman, A., Posch, P., & Somekh, B. (2008). *Teachers investigate their work: An introduction to action research across the professions* (2nd ed.). New York: Routledge.

Annie E. Casey Foundation. (2007). *Early warning!: Why reading by the end of third grade matters*. Baltimore: Author. Retrieved from *www.aecf.org/~/media/Pubs/Initiatives/KIDS%20COUNT/123/2010KCSpecReport/Special%20Report%20Executive%20Summary.pdf*.

Appleton, J. J. (2012). Systems consultation on student engagement: Developing the assessment-to-intervention link with the Student Engagement Instrument. In S. Christenson, A. Reschly, & C. Wiley (Eds.), *Handbook of research on student engagement* (pp. 725–741). New York: Springer Press.

Appleton, J. J., Christenson, S. L., & Furlong, M. J. (2008). Student engagement with school: Critical conceptual and methodological issues of the construct. *Psychology in the Schools, 45*(5), 369–386.

Appleton, J. J., Christenson, S. L., Kim, D., & Reschly, A. (2006). Measuring cognitive and psychological engagement: Validation of the Student Engagement Instrument. *Journal of School Psychology, 44*(5), 427–445.

Appleton, J., & Reschly, A. (2015, October 7). The Student Engagement Instrument (SEI): Systems level measurement and intervention [PowerPoint slides]. Retrieved from *http://checkandconnect.umn.edu/conf/2015/docs/Appleton.pdf*.

Ash, K. (2013, June 11). How to choose the right learning management system. Retrieved from *www.edweek.org/dd/articles/2013/06/12/03lms-evaluation.h06.html*.

Balfanz, R., Legters, N., West, T. C., & Weber, L. M. (2007). Are NCLB's measure, incentives and improvement strategies the right ones for the nation's low-performing high schools? *American Educational Research Journal, 44*(3), 559–593.

Batsche, G., Elliott, J., Graden, J. L., Grimes, J., Kovaleski, J. F., Prasse, D., . . . Tilly, W. D. (2005). *Response to intervention: Policy considerations and implementation.* Alexandria, VA: National Association of State Directors of Special Education.

Batsche, G. M., & Knoff, H. M. (1995). Best practices in linking assessment to intervention. In A. Thomas & J. Grimes (Eds.), *Best practices in school psychology III* (pp. 569–586). Bethesda, MD: National Association of School Psychologists.

Beaver, J. (2006). *Developmental Reading Assessment: Grades 4–8* (2nd ed.). Parsippany, NJ: Pearson.

Bergan, J. R. (1977). *Behavioral consultation.* Columbus, OH: Merrill.

Bernhardt, V. L. (1998, March). *Multiple measures.* Invited Monograph No. 4, California Association for Supervision and Curriculum Development (CASCD).

Beyer, M., & Edjlali, R. (2015, February 12). Magic quadrant for data warehouse and data management solutions for analytics. Retrieved from *www.gartner.com/doc/2983817/magic-quadrant-data-warehouse-data*.

Bohanon, H., Fenning, P., Carney, K. L., Minnis-Kim, M. J., Anderson-Harriss, S., Mortoz, K. B., . . . Pigott, T. D. (2006). Schoolwide application of positive behavior support in an urban high school: A case study. *Journal of Positive Behavior Interventions, 8*(3), 131–145.

Bollman, K., Silberglitt, B., & Gibbons, K. (2007). The St. Croix River Education District model: Incorporating systems-level organization and a multi-tiered problem-solving process for intervention delivery. In S. Jimerson, M. Burns, & A. VanDerHeyden (Eds.), *Handbook of response to intervention: The science and practice of assessment and intervention* (pp. 319–330). New York: Springer.

Brown, M. (2016, January 22). Using technology: Electronic portfolios in the K–12 classroom. Retrieved from *www.educationworld.com*.

Brown-Chidsey, R., & Bickford, R. (2015). *Practical handbook of multi-tiered systems of support: Building academic and behavioral success in schools.* New York: Guilford Press.

Brown-Chidsey, R., & Steege, M. W. (2010). *Response to Intervention: Principles and strategies for effective practice* (2nd ed.). New York: Guilford Press.

Burns, M. K. (2016). Effect of cognitive processing assessments and interventions on academic outcomes: Can 200 studies be wrong? *Communique, 44*(5), 27–29.

Burns, M. K., & Gibbons, K. A. (2011). *Implementing response-to-intervention in elementary and secondary schools: Procedures to assure scientific-based practices.* New York: Routledge.

Burns, M. K., & Gibbons, K. (2012). *Implementing response-to-intervention in elementary and secondary schools: Procedures to assure scientific-based practices* (2nd ed.). New York: Routledge.

Burns, M., VanDerHeyden, A., & Boice, C. (2008). Best practices in implementing individual interventions. In A. Thomas & J. Grimes (Eds.), *Best practices in school psychology* (5th ed.). Bethesda, MD: National Association of School Psychologists.

Burns, M. K., VanDerHeyden, A. M., & Zaslofsky, A. F. (2014). Best practices in delivering intensive academic interventions with skill-by-treatment interaction. In P. L. Harrison & A. Thomas

(Eds.), *Best practices in school psychology VI: Student-level services* (pp. 129–142). Bethesda, MD: National Association of School Psychologists.

Butler Analytics. (2015, June 17). Business intelligence software vendors. Retrieved from *www.butleranalytics.com.*

Calhoun, K. (2015, July 24). Market guide for K–12 student information systems. Retrieved from *www.gartner.com.*

Chafouleas, S. M., Volpe, R. J., Gresham, F. M., & Cook, C. R. (2010). School-based behavioral assessment within problem-solving models: Current status and future directions. *School Psychology Review, 39*(3), 343–349.

Christ, T. J., Zopluoglu, C., Long, J. D., & Monaghen, B. D. (2012). Curriculum-based measurement of oral reading: Quality of progress monitoring outcomes. *Exceptional Children, 78*(3), 356–373.

Christ, T. J., Zopluoglu, C., Monaghen, B. D., & Van Norman, E. R. (2013). Curriculum-based measurement of oral reading: Multi-study evaluation of schedule, duration, and dataset quality on progress monitoring outcomes. *Journal of School Psychology, 51*(1), 19–57.

Christenson, S. L., Reschly, A., Appleton, J. J., Berman, S., Spanjers, D., & Varro, P. (2008). Best practices in fostering student engagement. In A. Thomas & J. Grimes (Eds.), *Best practices in school psychology V* (pp. 1099–1120). Bethesda, MD: National Association of School Psychologists.

Consortium on Reading Excellence. (2008). *CORE multiple measures for kindergarten through twelfth grade* (2nd ed.). Novato, CA: Arena Press.

Consortium on School Networking. (2016, July). Framework for school system technology success. Retrieved from *www.cosn.org/schoolsuccess.*

Covey, S. R. (1992). *The 7 habits of highly effective people: Restoring the character ethic.* New York: Simon & Schuster.

Creating Community. (n.d.). Retrieved from *www.ideapartnership.org/creating-community.html.*

Daley, E., Witt, J., Martens, B., & Dool, E. (1997). A model for conducting a functional analysis of academic performance problems. *School Psychology Review, 26*(4), 554–574.

Daly, E. J., Wright, J. A., Kelly, S. Q., & Martens, B. K. (1997). Measures of early academic skills: Reliability and validity with a first grade sample. *School Psychology Quarterly, 12*(3), 268–280.

Davenport, T. H., & Patil, D. J. (2012, October). Data scientist: The sexiest job of the 21st century. Retrieved from *https://hbr.org/archive-toc/BR1210.*

Deno, S. L. (1985). Curriculum-based measurement: The emerging alternative. *Exceptional Children, 52*(3), 219–232.

Deno, S., & Mirkin, P. (1977). *Data-based program modification.* Minneapolis, MN: Leadership Training Institute for Special Education.

Dixon, R., Hyson, D. M., & Mahlke, A. (2012, February). *Assessment literacy and RTI: Advancing teacher development.* Paper presented at the annual meeting of the National Association of School Psychologists, Philadelphia, PA.

Dowdy, E., Ritchey, K., & Kamphaus, R. W. (2010). School-based screening: A population-based approach to inform and monitor children's mental health needs. *School Mental Health, 2*(4), 166–176.

DuFour, R., DuFour, R., Eaker, R., & Many, T. (2006). *Learning by doing.* Bloomington, IN: Solution Tree.

DuFour, R., & Eaker, R. (1998). *Professional learning communities at work.* Bloomington, IN: National Educational Service.

Durlak, J. A., Weissberg, R. P., Dymnicki, A. B., Taylor, R. D., & Schellinger, K. B. (2011). The impact of enhancing students' social and emotional learning: A meta-analysis of school based universal interventions. *Child Development, 82*(1), 405–432.

EdNET Insight. (2013, October). Interoperability: Definitions, expectations, and implications. Retrieved from *www.sifassociation.org.*

Elbaum, B., Vaughn, S., Hughes, M. T., & Moody, S. W. (2000). How effective are one-to-one tutoring programs in reading for elementary students at-risk for reading failure?: A meta-analysis of the intervention research. *Journal of Educational Psychology, 92*(4), 605–619.

Elliott, S. N., & Gresham, F. M. (2008). *Social Skills Improvement System Performance Screening Guide.* San Antonio, TX: Pearson.

Ellis, A. (2005). *Research on educational innovations* (4th ed.). Larchmont, NY: Eye on Education.

Every Student Succeeds Act of 2015, Public Law No. 114-195 §114 Stat. 1177 (2015).

Excel Team. (2015, September 18). New ways to get the Excel business analytics features you need [Web blog post]. Retrieved from *https://blogs.office.com/2015/09/18/new-ways-to-get-the-excel-business-analytics-features-you-need.*

Family Education Rights and Privacy Act, 20 U.S.C. § 1232g; 34 CFR Part 99 (1974).

FastBridge Learning. (2015). Computer-adaptive tests. Retrieved from *www.fastbridge.org.*

Finn, J. D. (1989). Withdrawing from school. *Review of Educational Research, 59*(2), 117–142.

Floyd, R. G., Hojnoski, R., & Key, J. (2006). Preliminary evidence of the technical adequacy of the preschool numeracy indicators. *School Psychology Review, 35*(4), 627–644.

Frazelle, S., & Nagel, A. (2015). *A practitioner's guide to implementing early warning systems* (REL 2015-056). Washington, DC: U.S. Department of Education, Institute of Education Sciences, National Center for Education Evaluation and Regional Assistance, Regional Educational Laboratory Northwest. Retrieved from *http://ies.ed.gov/ncee/edlabs.*

Fredricks, J. A., Blumenfeld, P. C., & Paris, A. H. (2004). School engagement: Potential of the concept, state of the evidence. *Review of Educational Research, 74*(1), 59–109.

Fuchs, D., Fuchs, L. S., & Compton, D. L. (2012). Smart RTI: A next-generation approach to multi-level prevention. *Council for Exceptional Children, 78*(3), 263–279.

Fuchs, L. S., & Fuchs, D. (1986). Effects of systematic formative evaluation: A meta-analysis. *Exceptional Children, 53*(3), 199–208.

Gibbons, K. A., & Silberglitt, B. (2008). Best practices in evaluating psychoeducational services based on student outcome data. In A. Thomas & J. Grimes (Eds.), *Best practices in school psychology V* (pp. 2103–2116). Bethesda, MD: National Association of School Psychologists.

Gladwell, M. (2000). *The tipping point.* New York: Back Bay Books.

Goleman, D. (2011). *Leadership: The power of emotional intelligence.* Northampton, MA: More Than Sound.

Goodwin, S. (1996). Data rich, information poor (DRIP) syndrome: Is there a treatment? *Radiology Management, 18*(3), 45–49.

Guskey, T. (2011, April). *Standards-based grading workshop.* Presentation at the TIES Technology Consortium, St. Paul, MN.

Hagermoser Sanetti, L. M., & Kratochwill, T. R. (2009). Toward developing a science of treatment integrity: Introduction to the special series. *School Psychology Review, 38*(4), 445–459.

Hamre, B. K., & Pianta, R. C. (2006). Student–teacher relationships. In G. G. Bear & K. M. Minke (Eds.), *Children's needs III: Development, prevention and intervention* (pp. 59–71). Bethesda, MD: National Association of School Psychologists.

Hasbrouck, J., & Tindal, G. A. (2006). Oral reading fluency norms: An assessment tool for reading teachers. *The Reading Teacher, 59*(7), 636–644.

Hasbrouck, J., & Tindal, G. (2017). An update to compiled ORF norms (Tech. Rep. No. 1702). Eugene: Behavioral Research and Teaching, University of Oregon.

Heistad, D. (1999, April). *Teachers who beat the odds: Value-added reading instruction in Minneapolis 2nd grade classrooms.* Paper presented at the American Educational Research Association Conference, Montreal, Canada.

Hess, F. M., & Osberg, E. (2010). *Stretching the school dollar: How schools and districts can save money while serving students best.* Cambridge, MA: Harvard Education Press.

Hirsh, S., & Killion, J. (2007). *The learning educator: A new era for professional learning.* Oxford, OH: National Staff Development Council.

Horner, R. H., Albin, R. W., Todd, A. W., Newton, J. S., & Sprague, J. R. (2011). Designing and implementing individualized positive behavior support. In M. E. Snell & F. Brown (Eds.), *Instruction of students with severe disabilities* (7th ed., pp. 257–303). Upper Saddle River, NJ: Pearson Education.

Hosp, J. L., Hosp, M. K., Howell, K. W., & Allison, R. (2014). *The ABCs of curriculum-based evaluation: A practical guide to effective decision making.* New York: Guilford Press.

Hosp, M. K., Hosp, J. L., & Howell, K. W. (2007). *The ABCs of CBM: A practical guide to curriculum-based measurement.* New York: Guilford Press.

Hosp, M. K., Hosp, J. L., & Howell, K. W. (2016). *The ABCs of CBM: A practical guide to curriculum-based measurement* (2nd ed.). New York: Guilford Press.

Howe, K. B., Scierka, B. J., Gibbons, K. A., & Silberglitt, B. (2003). A school-wide organization system for raising reading achievement using general outcome measures and evidence based instruction: One education district's experience. *Assessment for Effective Intervention, 28*(3–4), 59–71.

Hughes, J. N. (2011). Longitudinal effects of teacher and student perceptions of teacher–student relationship qualities on academic adjustment. *Elementary School Journal, 112*(1), 38–60.

Hyson, D. (2005). Conducting a staff book study: The story of one experience. *School Psychology Minnesota, 37*(1), 16–17.

Hyson, D. (2006). RTI in practice: An interview with Ben Silberglitt, outcomes manager in the St. Croix River Education District. *School Psychology Minnesota, 38*(1), 10–12.

Hyson, D. (2007a). RTI in practice II. An interview with Ann Casey, director of special education programs in Minneapolis Public Schools. *School Psychology Minnesota, 38*(2), 6–7.

Hyson, D. (2007b). RTI in practice III. An interview with Lynne Viker and Stacey Kosciolek, Mahtomedi Public Schools. *School Psychology Minnesota, 38*(3), 8–9.

Hyson, D. (2017, February). *Improving teacher–student interactions, engagement and achievement through observation and coaching.* Poster presented at the annual meeting of the National Association of School Psychologists, San Antonio, TX.

Hyson, D. M., Pederson, J., Richardson, R., McNamara, K., & Kovaleski, J. (2013, February). *The role of the school psychologist in RTI data-analysis teaming.* Symposium presented at the annual meeting of the National Association of School Psychologists, Seattle, WA.

Ihnot, C., & Ihnot, T. (2015). *Read naturally.* Saint Paul, MN: Read Naturally.

Improving Head Start for School Readiness Act of 2007, Public Law 110-134 (2007).

Individuals with Disabilities Education Improvement Act of 2004, Public Law 108-446 (2004).

Irvin, L. K., Horner, R. H., Ingram, K., Todd, A. W., Sugai, G., Sampson, N. K., & Boland, J. B. (2006). Using office discipline referral data for decision making about student behavior in elementary and middle schools: An empirical evaluation of validity. *Journal of Positive Behavior Interventions, 8*(1), 10–23.

Irvin, L. K., Tobin, T. J., Sprague, J. R., Sugai, G., & Vincent, C. G. (2004). Validity of office discipline referral measures as indices of school-wide behavioral status and effects of school-wide behavioral interventions. *Journal of Positive Behavior Interventions, 6*(3), 131–147.

Jacobs, H. H. (1997). *Mapping the big picture: Integrating curriculum and assessment K–12.* Alexandria, VA: Association for Supervision and Curriculum Development.

Johnson, L., Adams Becker, S., Estrada, V., & Freeman, A. (2015). *NMC Horizon Report: 2015 K–12 edition.* Austin, TX: New Media Consortium.

Joyce, B., & Showers, B. (2002). *Student achievement through staff development* (3rd ed.). Alexandria, VA: Association for Supervision and Curriculum Development.

Kamphaus, R. W., & Reynolds, C. R. (2015). *BASC-3 Behavior and Emotional Screening System (BASC-3 BESS).* San Antonio, TX: Pearson.

Kilgus, S. P., & von der Embse, N. P. (2015). *Social, Academic, and Emotional Behavior Risk Screener (SAEBRS).* Minneapolis, MN: FastBridge Learning.

Kingsbury, G., & Houser, R. (1997). Using data from a level testing system to change a school district. In J. O'Reilly (Ed.), *The Rasch tiger ten years later: Using IRT techniques to measure achievement in schools* (pp. 10–24). Chicago: National Association of Test Directors.

Knoff, H. M. (2002). Best practices in facilitating school reform, organizational change, and strategic planning. In A. Thomas & J. Grimes (Eds.), *Best practices in school psychology IV* (pp. 235–253). Bethesda, MD: National Association of School Psychologists.

Kovaleski, J. (2002). Best practices in operating pre-referral intervention teams. In A. Thomas & J. Grimes (Eds.), *Best practices in school psychology IV* (pp. 645–655). Bethesda, MD: National Association of School Psychologists.

Kovaleski, J. F., & Pedersen, J. A. (2014). Best practices in data-analysis teaming. In P. L. Harrison & A. Thomas (Eds.), *Best practices in school psychology VI: Data-based and collaborative decision making* (pp. 99–120). Bethesda, MD: National Association of School Psychologists.

Kovaleski, J. F., VanDerHeyden, A. M., & Shapiro, E. S. (2013). *The RTI approach to evaluating learning disabilities.* New York: Guilford Press.

Krueger, K. (2015). Digital equity and schools series. Retrieved from *www.cosn.org.*

Lane, K. L., Bocian, K. M., MacMillan, D. L., & Gresham, F. M. (2004). Treatment integrity: An essential—but often forgotten—component of school-based interventions. *Preventing School Failure, 48*(3), 36–43.

Love, N. B., Stiles, K. E., Mundry, S. E., & DiRanna, K. (2008). *The data coach's guide to improving learning for all students: Unleashing the power of collaborative inquiry.* Thousand Oaks, CA: Corwin Press.

Malecki, C. K. (2014). Best practices in written language assessment and intervention. In P. L. Harrison & A. Thomas (Eds.), *Best practices in school psychology VI: Data-based and collaborative decision making* (pp. 187–202). Bethesda, MD: National Association of School Psychologists.

Martella, R. C., Marchand-Martella, N. E., Woods, B., Thompson, S., Crockett, C. N., Northrup, E., . . . Ralston, N. C. (2010). Positive behavior support: Analysis of consistency between office discipline referrals and teacher recordings of disruptive classroom behaviors. *Behavioral Development Bulletin, 16*(1), 25–33.

Marzano, R. J., Waters, J. T., & McNulty, B. A. (2005). *School leadership that works: From research to results.* Alexandria, VA: Association for Supervision and Curriculum Development.

McConnell, S. R. (2000). Assessment in early intervention and early childhood special education: Building on the past to project into our future. *Topics in Early Childhood Special Education, 20*(1), 43–48.

McDougal, J. L., Bardos, A. N., & Meier, S. T. (2016). *Behavior Intervention Monitoring System (BIMAS-2).* Greeley, CO: Edumetrisis.

McIntosh, K., Campbell, A. L., Carter, D. R., & Zumbo, B. D. (2009). Concurrent validity of office discipline referrals and cut points used in positive behavior support. *Behavioral Disorders, 34*(2), 100–113.

McIntosh, K., Frank, J. L., & Spaulding, S. A. (2010). Establishing research-based trajectories of office discipline referrals for individual students. *School Psychology Review, 39*(3), 380–394.

Mellard, D., McKnight, M., & Jordan, J. (2010). RTI tier structures and instructional intensity. *Learning Disabilities Research and Practice, 25*(4), 217–225.

Miller, F. G., Cohen, D., Chafouleas, S. M., Riley-Tillman, T. C., Welsh, M. E., & Fabiano, G. A. (2015). A comparison of measures to screen for social, emotional, and behavioral risk. *School Psychology Quarterly, 30*(2), 184–196.

Miller, M. D., Linn, R. L., & Gronlund, N. E. (2013). *Measurement and assessment in teaching* (11th ed.). Boston: Pearson.

Minnesota Department of Education. (2011). Determining the eligibility of students with specific learning disabilities: A technical manual. Retrieved from *http://education.state.mn.us/MDE/EdExc/SpecEdClass/DisabCateg/SpecLearnDisab.*

Monahan, R. (2015, March 31). How common core is killing the textbook. Retrieved from *http://hechingerreport.org/how-common-core-is-killing-the-textbook.*

National Association of School Psychologists. (2010). Model for comprehensive and integrated school psychological services. Retrieved from *www.nasponline.org.*

National Association of School Psychologists. (2016). Building capacity for student success: Every Student Succeeds Act opportunities. Retrieved from *www.nasponline.org.*

National Center on Response to Intervention. (2012). *RTI implementer series: Module 2: Progress monitoring—training manual.* Washington, DC: U.S. Department of Education, Office of Special Education Programs, National Center on Response to Intervention.

National Institute of Child Health and Human Development. (2000). *Report of the National Reading Panel. Teaching children to read: An evidence-based assessment of the scientific research literature on reading and its implications for reading instruction: Reports of the subgroups* (NIH Publication No. 00-4754). Washington, DC: U.S. Government Printing Office.

National Research Council and Institute of Medicine. (2009). *Preventing mental, emotional, and behavioral disorders among young people: Progress and possibilities.* Washington, DC: National Academies Press.

National Student Clearinghouse. (2011). StudentTracker for high schools. Retrieved from *http://research.studentclearinghouse.org/studenttracker.html.*

Neter, J., Kutner, M. H., Nachtsheim, C. J., & Wasserman, W. (1996). *Applied linear statistical models.* (4th ed.). New York: WCB McGraw-Hill.

No Child Left Behind Act of 2001, Public Law 107-110 (2001).

Noell, G. H., Witt, J. C., Gilbertson, D. N., Ranier, D. D., & Freeland, J. T. (1997). Increasing teacher intervention implementation in general education settings through consultation and performance feedback. *School Psychology Quarterly, 12*(1), 77–88.

Noell, G. H., Witt, J. C., Slider, N. J., Connell, J. E., Gatti, S. L., Williams, K. L., . . . Duhon, G. J. (2005). Treatment implementation following behavioral consultation in schools: A comparison of three follow-up strategies. *School Psychology Review, 34*(1), 87–106.

O'Connor, R. E. (2014). *Teaching word recognition: Effective strategies for students with learning difficulties* (2nd ed.). New York: Guilford Press.

Pearson Education. (2011). Developmental Reading Assessment: K–8 technical manual. Retrieved from *http://assets.pearsonschool.com/asset_mgr/current/20139/DRA2_Technical_Manual_2012.pdf.*

Pianta, R. C. (2001). *Student–Teacher Relationship Scale: Professional manual.* Lutz, FL: Psychological Assessment Resources.

Pianta, R. C., La Paro, K. M., & Hamre, B. K. (2008). *Classroom Assessment Scoring System (CLASS) manual, K–3.* Baltimore: Brookes.

Renaissance Learning. (2015). *STAR Reading technical manual.* Wisconsin Rapids, WI: Author. Retrieved from *https://resources.renlearnrp.com/us/manuals/sr/srrptechnicalmanual.pdf.*

Reschly, A. L., Busch, T. W., Deno, S. L., & Long, J. (2009). Curriculum-based measurement oral reading as an indicator of reading achievement: A meta-analysis of the correlational evidence. *Journal of School Psychology, 47*(6), 427–469.

Reyna, V. F. (2004). Why scientific research?: The importance of evidence in changing educational practice. In P. McCardle & V. Chhabra (Eds.), *The voice of evidence in reading research* (pp. 47–58). Baltimore: Brookes.

Runge, T. J., Lillenstein, D. J., & Kovaleski, J. F. (2016). Response to intervention and accountability systems. In S. R. Jimerson, M. K. Burns, & A. M. VanDerHeyden (Eds.), *Handbook of response to intervention: The science and practice of multi-tiered systems of support* (2nd ed., pp. 103–120). New York: Springer.

Samuels, S. J. (1979). The method of repeated reading. *The Reading Teacher, 32*, 403–408.

Scantron Corporation. (2004). Examination of growth trajectories at the state level in reading and mathematics performance series test scores. Retrieved from *www.personal.psu.edu/dgm122/passkey/GrowthTrajectories-Top10Mat.pdf*.

Schmoker, M. (2006). *Results now: How we can achieve unprecedented improvements in teaching and learning.* Alexandria, VA: Association for Supervision and Curriculum Development.

Schoenbach, R., & Greenleaf, C. (2017). *Leading for literacy: A reading apprenticeship approach.* San Francisco: Jossey-Bass.

Schwartz, K. (2015). What do we really mean when we say "personalized learning"? Retrieved from *ww2.kqed.org/mindshift/2015/02/02/what-do-we-really-mean-when-we-say-personalized-learning*.

Shapiro, E. S., & Clemens, N. H. (2009). A conceptual model for evaluating system effects of response to intervention. *Assessment for Effective Intervention, 35*(1), 3–16.

Shapiro, E. S., & Guard, K. B. (2014). Best practices in setting progress monitoring goals for academic skill improvement. In P. L. Harrison & A. Thomas (Eds.), *Best practices in school psychology VI: Student-level services* (pp. 51–66). Bethesda, MD: National Association of School Psychologists.

Shinn, M. (2012). Curriculum-based measurement and general outcome measurement (GOM) and mastery monitoring [Webinar]. Retrieved from *www.aimsweb.com/mark-shinn*.

Shinn, M. (2013). Curriculum-based measurement (CBM): Suited for seamless contributions to SLD identification [Webinar]. Retrieved from *www.aimsweb.com/mark-shinn*.

Shinn, M. (2015, March). *Data-based decision making within a model of multi-tier systems of support/response to Intervention (RTI).* Workshop presented at the Wisconsin School Psychologists Association Spring Convention, Stevens Point, WI.

SIF Association. (2015, November 11). A guide to the SIF specification. Retrieved from *www.sifassociation.org*.

Silberglitt, B. (2008a). Best practices in using technology for data-based decision making. In A. Thomas & J. Grimes (Eds.), *Best practices in school psychology V* (pp. 1869–1884). Bethesda, MD: National Association of School Psychologists.

Silberglitt, B. (2008b). *Target scores on Northwest Evaluation Association assessments that predict success on the Minnesota Comprehensive Assessments-II: Results from a TIES-wide study.* Unpublished manuscript.

Silberglitt, B. (2010, October). *Building smarter schools by leveraging the wisdom of the crowd through an IBM Cognos community cloud.* Presentation at the IBM Business Analytics Forum, Las Vegas, NV.

Silberglitt, B., Burns, M. K., Madyun, N. H., & Lail, K. E. (2006). Relationship of reading fluency assessment data with state accountability test scores: A longitudinal comparison of grade levels. *Psychology in the Schools, 43*(5), 527–535.

Silberglitt, B., & Hintze, J. M. (2007). How much growth can we expect?: A conditional analysis of R-CBM growth rates by level of performance. *Exceptional Children, 74*(1), 71–84.

Silberglitt, B., & Hyson, D. M. (2014). Best practices in using technology for data-driven decision making. In P. Harrison & A. Thomas (Eds.), *Best practices in school psychology VI: Foundations* (pp. 489–502). Bethesda, MD: National Association of School Psychologists.

Silberglitt, B., Parker, D., & Muyskens, P. (2016). Assessment: Periodic assessment to monitor progress. In S. R. Jimerson, M. K. Burns, & A. M. VanDerHeyden (Eds.), *Handbook of response to intervention: The science and practice of multi-tiered systems of support* (2nd ed., pp. 271–292). New York: Springer.

Sinclair, M. F., Christenson, S. L., Lehr, C. A., & Anderson, A. R. (2003). Facilitating student engagement: Lessons learned from Check & Connect longitudinal studies. *The California School Psychologist, 8*(1), 29–41.

Six Sigma. (2015). Determine the root cause: 5 whys. Retrieved from *www.isixsigma.com/tools-templates/cause-effect/determine-root-cause-5-whys.*

Slavin, R. E., Lake, C., Davis, S., & Madden, N. A. (2011). Effective programs for struggling readers: A best evidence synthesis. *Educational Research Review, 6*(1), 1–26.

Slotnik, W. J., & Orland, M. (2010). Data rich but information poor. *Education Week, 29*(31). Retrieved from *www.edweek.org/ew/articles/2010/05/06/31slotnik.h29.html.*

Software & Information Industry Association. (2010, November). *Innovate to educate: System [re] design for personalized learning: A report from the 2010 symposium (in collaboration with ASCD and the Council of Chief State School Officers).* Washington, DC: Author (Mary Ann Wolf).

Sprick, R. S., & Baldwin, K. (2009). *Champs: A proactive and positive approach to classroom management.* Eugene, OR: Pacific Northwest.

Sprick, R., Knight, J., Reinke, W., Skyles, T. M., & Barnes, L. (2010). *Coaching classroom management: Strategies and tools for administrators and coaches.* Eugene, OR: Pacific Northwest.

Stage, S. A., & Jacobsen, M. D. (2001). Predicting student success on a state-mandated performance-based assessment using oral reading fluency. *School Psychology Review, 30*(3), 407–419.

Stikeleather, J. (2013, April 24). How to tell a story with data. *Harvard Business Review.* Retrieved from *https://hbr.org/2013/04/how-to-tell-a-story-with-data.*

Sugai, G., & Horner, R. (2002). The evolution of discipline practices: School-wide positive behavior supports. *Child and Family Behavior Therapy, 24*(1–2), 23–50.

Svobodny, J. A. (2013). *Connecting elementary principals' emotional–social intelligence and their use of balanced leadership responsibilities.* Unpublished doctoral dissertation, Hamline University, St. Paul, MN.

Tilly, W. D. (2008). The evolution of school psychology to science-based practice: Problem-solving and the three-tiered model. In A. Thomas & J. Grimes (Eds.), *Best practices in school psychology V* (pp. 17–36). Bethesda, MD: National Association of School Psychologists.

Torgesen, J. K. (2006). *A comprehensive K–3 reading assessment plan: Guidance for school leaders.* Portsmouth, NH: RMC Research Corporation, Center on Instruction.

Torgesen, J. K., Alexander, A. W., Wagner, R. K., Rashotte, C. A., Voeller, K. S., & Conway, T. (2001). Intensive remedial instruction for children with severe reading disabilities: Immediate and long-term outcomes from two instructional approaches. *Journal of Learning Disabilities, 34*(1), 33–58.

Toyama, K. (2015). *Geek heresy: Rescuing social change from the cult of technology.* New York: PublicAffairs.

United States Department of Education. (2010). U.S. Secretary of Education Duncan announces winners of competition to improve student assessments [Press release]. Retrieved from *www.*

ed.gov/news/press-releases/us-secretary-education-duncan-announces-winners-competition-improve-student-asse.

University of Connecticut. (2013). Direct Behavior Rating. Retrieved from *www.directbehaviorratings.com/cms.*

Vanderwood, M. L., & Nam, J. (2008). Best practices in assessing and improving English language learners' literacy performance. In A. Thomas & J. Grimes (Eds.), *Best practices in school psychology V* (pp. 1847–1858). Bethesda, MD: National Association of School Psychologists.

Vaughn, S., & Fuchs, L. S. (2003). Redefining learning disabilities as inadequate response to instruction: The promise and potential pitfalls. *Learning Disabilities Research and Practice, 18*(3), 137–146.

Von Secker, C. (2009). Closing the gap: Seven keys to college readiness for students of all races/ethnicities. Retrieved from *www.montgomeryschoolsmd.org/info/keys/documents/research.pdf.*

Walker, B., Cheney, D., Stage, S., Blum, C., & Horner, R. H. (2005). Schoolwide screening and positive behavior supports: Identifying and supporting students at risk for school failure. *Journal of Positive Behavior Interventions, 7*(4), 194–204.

Waters, T., & Cameron, G. (2007). *The balanced leadership framework: Connecting vision with action.* Denver, CO: McREL.

Wiggins, G., & McTighe, J. (2007). *Schooling by design: Mission, action, and achievement.* Alexandria, VA: Association for Supervision and Curriculum Development.

Wu, J., Hughes, J. N., & Kwok, O. (2010). Teacher–student relationship quality type in elementary grades: Effects on trajectories for achievement and engagement. *Journal of School Psychology, 48*(5), 357–387.

Zirkel, P., & Rose, T. (2009). Scientifically based research and peer-reviewed research under the IDEA: The legal definitions, applications, and implications. *Journal of Special Education Leadership, 22*(1), 36–50.

Index

Note. *f* or *t* following a page number indicates a figure or a table.